T0312211

DISALMANAC

DISALMANAC

A Book of Fact-Like Facts

Scott Bateman

A PERIGEE BOOK

A PERIGEE BOOK
Published by the Penguin Group
Penguin Group (USA)
375 Hudson Street, New York, New York 10014, USA

USA | Canada | UK | Ireland | Australia | New Zealand | India | South Africa | China

Penguin Books Ltd., Registered Offices: 80 Strand, London WC2R 0RL, England
For more information about the Penguin Group, visit penguin.com.

Library of Congress Cataloging-in-Publication Data

Bateman, Scott.
Disalmanac : a book of fact-like facts / Scott Bateman. —First edition.
pages   cm
ISBN 978-0-399-16311-1
1. American wit and humor.   I. Title.
PN6165.B38   2013
818'.602—dc23   2013014403

First edition: September 2013

Text design by Ellen Cipriano

While the author has made every effort to provide accurate telephone numbers, Internet addresses, and other contact information at the time of publication, neither the publisher nor the author assumes any responsibility for errors, or for changes that occur after publication. Further, the publisher does not have any control over and does not assume any responsibility for author or third-party websites or their content.

CONTENTS

HOW TO USE THIS BOOK

1. Using a saw, remove the top of your skull (or have a friend do it).

2. Reach in, grab your brain, and toss it out. Most major cities have brain recycling programs.

3. Place this book in your skull where your brain was.

4. Sew the top of your head back on.

5. Congratulations! You are now using this book the way it was meant to be used! Prepare to get a perfect score on your SAT, win *Jeopardy!* every day for the rest of your life, and become a medical doctor after less than three hours of med school!

PART ONE

The Days of the Damn Year

We have years pretty much every year, except leap years. Then, we just stay home and watch Game Show Network until it passes.

The Year in Review

Remember all that stuff that happened last year? No? Well, it's a good thing we here at Disalmanac wrote it all down for you. We recommend you memorize this entire list of news and events from last year, because most of it will be on the test.

JANUARY

1. The Bureau of Alcohol, Tobacco, Firearms, and Explosives reported that they, as always, had pretty much the greatest New Year's Eve party *ever*.

2. In the Middle East . . . look, it's just really complicated, OK?

3. Utah banned everything. Yes, that too.

4. The Dow was down over 200 points on fears that a poor person may have found a quarter on the sidewalk.

5. Biologists announced that they are close to understanding why birds are so angry with pigs.

6. Something happened in Ohio. J/K.

7. In Japanese elections, Mothra narrowly defeated Rodan to become the new prime minister.

▶ Fact-Like Fact

In the 1990s, Japan's economy crashed after Prime Minister Mecha-Godzilla blew out his timing belt.

8. Iowa held the first-in-the-nation caucus for the 2052 presidential election. The Democratic winner was Chelsea Clinton, while the GOP chose a now four-year-old grandson of Jeb Bush.

9. North Korea announced it had produced a nuclear device.

10. North Korea's "nuclear device" turned out to be an old 1970s microwave oven with some tin foil inside.

11. California legalized same-sex medical marijuana.

12. At WrestleMania in Detroit, a riot broke out when the crowd realized they'd wasted years of their lives on this fake-ass shit.

13. Scientists determined that the five people you meet in heaven are the J. Geils Band. Hope you like "Centerfold"; you'll be hearing it a *lot*.

14. Clint Eastwood announced that he's still pretty steamed at that empty chair.

15. New Hampshire held its first-in-the-nation presidential primary for the year 5896. The winner on the GOP side was a super-intelligent sea squid, while the Democrats chose a giant robo-ant from the planet Xyrtron 5000.

16. Haters announced they would continue to hate for the foreseeable future.

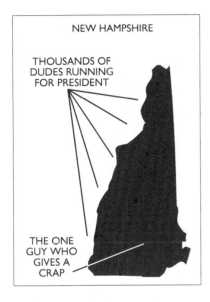

NEW HAMPSHIRE

THOUSANDS OF DUDES RUNNING FOR PRESIDENT

THE ONE GUY WHO GIVES A CRAP

17. Archaeologists discovered proof that there had once been life in Indiana.

18. The Federal Reserve cut rates. Or maybe they raised rates. Whatever. It had no effect on anything, anywhere.

19. Hey, the Iran guy got a new windbreaker!

20. House Republicans proposed a bill that invited House Democrats to eat their shorts.

21. A team of biologists discovered that during the 1980s, Duran Duran had only been as hungry as a badger.

22. The Supreme Court announced today that it had made a mistake in the 2000 case *Bush v. Gore*—they had meant to rule in favor of "Neither."

23. 41 percent of Americans said the country is on the wrong track, while 42 percent believe the nation is on the right track. Apparently, 83 percent of Americans think the nation is a train. Chugga chugga chooo-choo!

24. During his State of the Union speech, the President of the United States thanked Mr. Roboto for "doing the jobs that nobody wants to."

25. Controversy erupted when the Miss America pageant was won by the 1980s band Mr. Mister.

26. The Pentagon announced today that tanks are "cool and shit."

27. The unemployment rate fell from "everybody" to "everybody but Steve."

28. The U.S. Senate was cranky and but so was put down for its nap.

31. Brains, zombies announced.

FEBRUARY

1. The United States sent several battleships and an aircraft carrier to France, just to mess with them.
2. The Kansas legislature passed a law making masturbation illegal, even if it would save the life of the mother.
3. The Super Bowl Halftime Show featured some boring old band your dad used to listen to back in the 1700s or whatever.
4. The U.S. Army reinstituted its Don't Eat the Yellow Snow policy.

> **Fact-Like Fact**

The U.S. military's Don't Ask Don't Tell policy replaced their decades-old Don't You Forget About Me policy.

5. The FDA announced that cigarettes must not only carry the surgeon general's warning, but must come wrapped in a diseased lung.
6. Today was Groundhog Day. Punxsutawney Phil saw his shadow, which meant six more weeks of virgin sacrifices to Bondor, God of Darkness.
7. In a horrible freak accident, the *Huffington Post* nearly paid somebody for their work.
8. As part of a massive class-action suit, rapper Lil Wayne was found by a court of law to be, in fact, completely normal-sized.
9. The House GOP proposed a bill that would require the Democratic Party to rename itself "A Big Bunch of Poopy-Headed Poopy-Poops."
10. North Korea announced it had developed a "biological weapon."
11. Turns out, North Korea's "biological weapon" was a frog with a firecracker stuck up its butt.
12. During a blizzard in Cleveland, visibility was zero. "Good," said Clevelanders.
13. Administration officials announced they were going to administer the crap out of some stuff.
14. Lady Gaga wore some meat or a tire or a couple of midgets or

something. Who can keep track?

Lady Gaga, singing robot.

15. A survey showed that 91 percent of the population is 17 percent of the population.

16. At the Grammy Awards, John Mayer was awarded the Lifetime Douche-chievement Award.

17. Some shit went down in Pakistan or Yemen or some place. Dang.

18. The Dow was up 387 points today on reports that a poor person couldn't find that dollar he was sure was in his pocket.

19. The U.S. Senate passed a small spending bill so they could pick up some milk, a loaf of bread, and a thing of cereal on the way home.

20. New York City banned smoking in public places, but hey, piss anywhere you want!

21. Yahoo! announced that nobody has visited Yahoo.com since, like, 2002.

22. OMG, that one cat video on YouTube, right?

23. The unemployment rate rose back up to "everybody" after Steve got fired from Wendy's. Good one, Steve.

24. The Pentagon announced that its laser-guided missiles are "totally freaking awesome."

25. The robots took over Japan. Nobody was terribly surprised.

26. Iceland's most active volcano erupted, threatening Iceland's strategic ice reserves.

27. The nation's banks reported they don't know where your money is. They think it might have fallen behind the couch.

28. Nothing happened in Delaware. Just like every other damn day.

MARCH

1. The Minnesota State Legislature voted to define marriage as "between a passive-aggressive man and a passive-aggressive woman."
2. A major terrorist attack was foiled when Dane Cook canceled his upcoming tour.
3. In NBA action, people are still trying to figure out why the hell Oklahoma City even has a damn team.
4. The Vatican announced that, to go along with the Popemobile, engineers were building a really badass PopeJetSki.

▶ Fact-Like Fact

In the fourteenth century, the pope traveled from town to town in a giant, stained glass hamster ball.

5. The Texas Legislature approved the death penalty for lily-livered, rackin-frackin, no-good bush-whackin' varmints.
6. The FCC fined TV networks $3 million for saying "FCC" on the air, which apparently stands for something absolutely filthy.
7. Tone-Lōc announced he hasn't done the Wild Thing since at least 2004.
8. In Afghanistan, more shit went horribly awry.
9. Miners in West Virginia announced they were workin' in a coal mine, goin' down down, workin' in a coal mine, oooh! About to slip down.
10. The Federal Reserve lowered interest rates after consulting a Ouija board.
11. Henry Winkler was convicted of running a multimillion-dollar Fonzie scheme.
12. Teenaged girls in skimpy clothing began the Occupy Elm Street movement to protest the economic policies of Freddy Krueger.
13. North Korea said it conducted another nuclear test.
14. U.S. officials announced that by "nuclear test," North Korea

meant "tried to dry off the dog in the microwave."

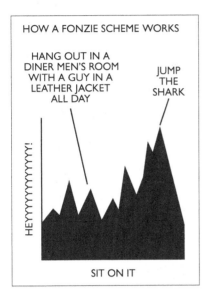

HOW A FONZIE SCHEME WORKS

HANG OUT IN A DINER MEN'S ROOM WITH A GUY IN A LEATHER JACKET ALL DAY

JUMP THE SHARK

HEYYYYYYYYYY!

SIT ON IT

15. The Senate was all, like, solar power? Tcha, as if.

16. Voters in Indiana rejected a law that would require them to stop dressing like it's 19-effing-87.

17. In Missouri, Grandma and Grandpa went to dinner at Applebee's around 4:30 and were in bed by 7 p.m.

18. NASA announced that although *Voyager 1* had left the solar system, it was still discovering a Starbucks on pretty much every damn block.

19. Anheuser-Busch introduced a new beer for Spring Break, Bud Stupid.

20. Experts predict that by 2019, Lady Gaga will run out of Madonna songs to rip off.

21. A landmark study found that over 90 percent of bosses can't do anything "like a boss."

22. The Pentagon announced today that the new F27 bomber was "sweeeeeeeet."

23. The government of Ireland passed out in its own vomit. Again.

24. The Czech Republic changed their national anthem to "You Better Czech Yourself Before You Wrzech Yourself."

25. In the March Madness NCAA basketball tournament, a surprising run into the Sweet Sixteen was made by Jewish Midget University.

26. The International Monetary Fund approved a 26 billion euro loan to Greece so they can get their shit together already, Jesus.

27. Several major banks announced a new mortgage plan where they just cut to the

chase and foreclose on your house before you even buy it.

30. The Dow was up over 300 points today based on news that bankers successfully stole candy from a baby.

31. House Democrats proposed a bill that asked House Republicans to stick the Washington Monument "where the sun don't shine."

APRIL

1. April was once again voted the cruelest month by *Months Monthly* magazine.

2. As always, *People* magazine's Sexiest Man Alive was some dude from some movie you didn't see.

3. The History Channel officially announced that yeah, they've pretty much given up on the whole history thing.

4. Members of Starship were arrested when it was discovered they built this city on shoddy welding and substandard girders.

5. Arab Spring continued, with Arab Weeding and Arab Fertilizing the Begonias.

6. Charles Manson had another parole hearing today, which, as always, lasted about 2.6 seconds.

7. The minimum wage in Arkansas was raised to half a roadkill possum that was done found on the dirt road back yonder.

 Random Bonus Fact!

MICHAEL IAN BLACK, COMEDIAN

Most people know that before they were Starship, they were Jefferson Starship. Before that they were Jefferson Airplane, and before that, Jefferson Biplane. If you go back a little farther, however, you find that they were Jefferson Bicycle, Jefferson Horseless Carriage, and before that, Jefferson Covered Wagon. Go back even farther, and we find they were Thomas Jefferson. What I am trying to say is that Thomas Jefferson is a vampire.

8. Psychologists announced that OCD is one of Jay-Z's 99 problems, because seriously—who the heck counts their problems?

9. A New Jersey judge found the entire state in contempt.

10. Scientists still cannot explain WTF, vis-à-vis *Fifty Shades of Grey*.

11. The United Nations announced that "Moldova" isn't a nation at all, but a kind of fish.

12. The 1970s rock band Foghat admitted that their "Slow Ride" is actually a very short, quick, and disappointing ride.

13. We don't know what happened on March 13. We were watching a *Sons of Anarchy* marathon.

14. The Federal Reserve lowered interest rates after consulting the entrails of a dead owl.

15. Massive flooding in Australia made it difficult to chunder up the ol' koala, or whatever it is they do down there.

16. In Wisconsin, cheese was named the state fruit.

17. Insane Clown Posse announced that they totally get magnets now.

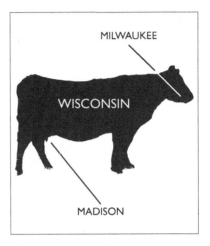

18. Microsoft announced its next version of Windows would have "70% more suck."

19. Someone somewhere remembered how Herman Cain ran for president that one time, and laughed and laughed and laughed.

20. Even after all this time, 4 Non Blondes still have no idea what's going on.

21. Israel asked the United States to ask Russia to ask Bulgaria if they like them.

22. Illinois instituted the death penalty for getting off an

escalator and just standing there in the way cluelessly.

23. Florida officials admitted today that yeah, Florida kinda sucks.

26. The World Bank announced it would raise its ATM fees to $5.5 billion per transaction.

27. Major banks announced a new mortgage program where they play Creed songs at you until you give them all your money.

28. The Dow was down 200 points today amid fears that a homeless orphan may have found part of a Big Mac in a Dumpster.

29. House Republicans proposed legislation that would require all House Democrats to "get a good running start and jump up their own butts."

30. House Republicans pledged allegiance to *Atlas Shrugged*.

MAY

1. A team of doctors at Johns Hopkins announced that "Johns" is a weird first name.

2. Hawaii's new long-form birth certificate will be a Post-it note with your name scrawled on it in crayon.

3. Vladimir Putin took off his shirt and then skinned a badger with his teeth.

4. The Federal Reserve lowered interest rates after consulting the ghost of Og, the caveman who invented money.

5. Justin Timberlake threatened to bring rickets back.

6. The people of Indianapolis were saddened to wake up, again, in Indianapolis.

7. Major League Baseball announced that up to 30 players could be implicated in a major junk-adjusting scandal.

8. The United Nations called for the immediate withdrawal of Texas from the United States.

9. A large meteor passed within 7,500 miles of the Earth; Liv Tyler and Ben Affleck did it, just in case.

10. The TSA announced its new security procedures would include whispering in your ear while cupping your general privates area ever so gently.

11. PETA denounced Yellowstone National Park, calling it "Bear Guantánamo."

12. Due to global warming, Vanilla Ice is now known as Vanilla Liquid.

13. "Shoooo-weeeee," announced Louisiana officials.

14. The Barenaked Ladies announced that they should probably get dressed pretty soon.

15. The Nepalese government asked the government of Gambia to the prom. The prom theme: Gangnam Style!

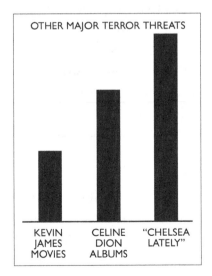

OTHER MAJOR TERROR THREATS

| KEVIN JAMES MOVIES | CELINE DION ALBUMS | "CHELSEA LATELY" |

16. An attempted terror attack was foiled when TBS was prevented from showing an Adam Sandler movie marathon.

17. The Dow dropped 513 points today on news that somewhere, there was still a poor person with a small amount of hope.

18. Afghanistan, still with the Taliban and the opium and who knows what else.

19. House Democrats proposed a bill that required all GOP House members to "consume large quantities of their own excrement and then promptly expire."

20. Google announced that all your base are belong to them.

26. A biography about the Notorious B.I.G. made the shocking claim that he hated it when you called him Big Poppa.

27. John Mellencamp announced that nearly 90 percent of his little pink houses were in foreclosure.

▶ Fact-Like Fact

Today, the protagonists of John Mellencamp's hit "Jack & Diane" are basically Sarah & Todd Palin.

28. Gas prices were expected to rise this summer, because, you know, oil companies are kind of evil.

29. The state of Rhode Island put itself up on eBay. So far? No bidders.

30. New Mexico announced it was whacked out on the shrooms again.

31. Officials in Arizona declared that life begins two weeks before conception, but ends when you move to Arizona.

JUNE

1. Indiana passed a right-to-work-it law. Drag queens nationwide celebrated.

2. The nation of Sudan held a free election, while the city of Chicago held a buy-one-get-one-free election.

3. Kanye West did some jackass thing. Obviously.

4. Vladimir Putin stripped down to his underwear, jumped into the Black Sea, and punched a shark in the nose repeatedly until it cried.

5. The Federal Reserve lowered interest rates after flipping a coin. Sadly, they lost the coin.

6. Delaware OK'ed no-sex marriage.

7. The USDA announced that basically, there's nothing you can eat that won't kill you somehow. So just have at that barrel of bacon and Cheetos.

8. Four suspected terrorists were charged with trying to blow up LaGuardia Airport by eating a whole bunch of tofu and then lighting their farts.

9. Somebody finally bought that German girl another luftballon so she'd have an even hundred.

10. Using the Hubble Space Telescope, astronomers discovered that Christopher Cross is now caught between the Crab Nebula and New York City.

11. The Red Cross airlifted over seven tons of Paxil to Adele.

12. Polls showed that 97 percent of Americans want to be Bob Dylan, but Mr. Jones wishes he was someone just a little more funky.

Mario. At his inauguration, he ran up some stairs and leapt at a flagpole.

13. For its next prime minister, Italy will choose between two plumbers named Mario and Luigi.
14. Man, like, Yemen—what the WTF?
15. In Massachusetts, a decidedly un-special election was held.
16. At Wimbledon, some people played tennis, which whoop-de-damn-do.
17. The European Union voted 16–2 that Americans are "fat-ass."

18. At least 30 are arrested at a misguided Occupy Wall Drug protest in South Dakota.
19. Doctors announced that the stomach is "that thing in your belly, where the food goes."
24. NASA looked up at the Moon wistfully and sadly sighed.
25. New York's Gay Pride Parade was overshadowed by the even more popular Gay Sloth and Gay Envy parades.
26. Spain's economy double dipped. Officials blame George Costanza.
27. The CEO of a major Wall Street firm received a bonus of $50 million for tripping an old woman and grabbing her purse.
28. Microbiologists announced, "Help, we're down here! We are ever so tiny!"
29. A study found that people with severe ADD have already stopped reading this sentence.
30. Wyoming announced they were bored. Bored bored bored. Does anyone want to come over and play video games?

JULY

1. Someone at the Los Alamos National Laboratory dropped something radioactive, and but so now giant ants.
2. Arkansas banned same-hairstyle marriages.
3. A 300,000-acre forest fire burned out of control in the Pacific Northwest. Smokey Bear claimed he was in Vegas at the time the fire started, but gasoline and old oily rags were found in the trunk of his car.
4. A heat wave hit the central United States. The entire state of Oklahoma melted.

▶ Fact-Like Fact

Oklahoma will now be used as a giant molten pool to drop evil Terminators into.

5. The United States announced that its new Middle East policy is "The enemy of my Yemeni is my frenemy."
6. Texas announced it would be totally OK with Megan Fox messing with Texas.

7. Ghana defeated the United States in soccer. According to FIFA rules, the entire United States, including Puerto Rico and Guam, now belongs to Ghana.
8. In a huge medical advance, Pfizer announced it had developed a new drug that will make it possible for a man and woman to hold hands while in the same bathtub, instead of separate ones.
9. George Lucas changed the ending of *Citizen Kane* so that "Rosebud" is Luke's father.
10. In Cairo today? No idea. That was crazy though, right? Dang.
11. Home foreclosures went down to zero as every American has now been thrown out of his or her home.
12. In a straw poll, Americans preferred the curly ones.
13. There was an uprising in Chad by a faction that wants to rename the country either Trevor or Jeremy.
14. For the third year in a row, Lance Armstrong won the Tour de Cheat.

15. Paleontologists announced that Gary Larson was right about how the dinosaurs went extinct, adding, "How the hell did they even get cigarettes?"

16. Glenn Beck's latest book was number one on the bestseller list, even though readers had to provide their own crayons.

Vladimir Putin, who plays the Nick Offerman role on Russia's *Parks and Recreation*.

17. Vladimir Putin stripped naked, slathered himself in bear grease, and wrestled a bull moose to the death.

18. Wendy's announced it still doesn't know where the beef is.

19. House Republicans proposed a new bill stating, "House Democrats are so ugly, they filmed that movie *Gorillas in the Mist* in their shower. Because, you know, gorillas are ugly, and showers are misty. Also, we haven't seen a movie since 1989 so this was the best reference we could come up with."

20. The Dow lost 387 points on reports that a poor person won $10 on a scratch-off lottery ticket.

21. At the annual G-8 meeting, world leaders acknowledged that the meeting was brought to you by the letter G and the number 8.

26. The United Nations was concerned that Angry Birds might be trying to develop a nuclear weapon.

27. Idaho announced that most of its potatoes? Not all that famous.

28. NASA wondered what the hell it was going to do with all this Tang.

29. John Mellencamp's hit "Pink Houses" was downgraded to "Little pink refrigerator boxes for you and me."
30. The National Weather Bureau announced there would never, ever be a Hurricane Souljah Boy Tell 'Em.
31. The federal government suddenly remembered that Delaware is a state, and that maybe someone should go check on it or something, see if everyone's OK and stuff.

AUGUST

1. Oasis's "Wonderwall" was downgraded to just "Wall."
2. Bank of America nearly collapsed when some guy got $20 at the ATM for beer.
3. Iowa announced it had a butt ton of corn.
4. Seriously: a butt ton.

> **Fact-Like Fact**

In the metric system, a butt ton is 2.77 deca-asses.

5. Congress raised the debt ceiling again, plus bought some nice debt drapes and a beautiful antique debt coffee table.
6. On Amity Island, officials announced they were going to need a bigger boat.
7. House Democrats proposed a new law stating that House Republicans are "so old, they were the waiters at the Last Supper. Which would make them, you know, really quite old."
8. Inspired by WikiLeaks, computer hackers started NoShitLeaks. Their first leak: that Snooki is a drunken orange idiot.
9. NoShitLeaks announces that Lady Gaga is "kinda weird."
10. A tornado struck Brooklyn. Tragically, six sucky indie bands formed as a result.
11. Archaeologists reported they found some old bones or whatever it is they do.
12. Suri Holmes-Cruise has proactively been named 2023's most annoying celebrity.
13. The Pentagon announced that Osama bin Laden is still dead. Awwwww yeah.

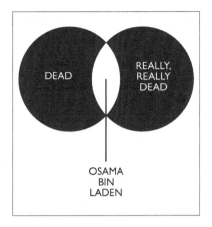

14. The video game Pong: Vice City Stories was released.

15. Armed militants took over Kashmir. Not the region of India, but the song by Led Zeppelin. The United States immediately cut off all diplomatic relations with the entire *Physical Graffiti* album.

16. Scientists developed a milkshake that could bring not just all the boys to the yard, but also several breeds of dog and species of bird.

17. Wildfires in Southern California raged all across Lindsay Lohan's general nether area.

18. Vladimir Putin bench-pressed Latvia.

19. On his radio show, Rush Limbaugh admitted he has never seen a real live naked lady.

20. The Canadian province of Manitoba was discovered to be missing. Officials aren't quite sure when it disappeared; nobody had heard anything from Manitoba since at least 1974.

21. The Occupy Walton Mountain movement hit a snag when someone pointed out that Walton Mountain was a fictional place on a TV show.

22. The Dow Jones was up on news that a poor person missed the bus and so was fired from one of his four jobs.

25. Montana banned same–eye color marriage.

26. Oh, man, that thing in Syria— man oh man.

27. Things aren't so great in Iraq, either.

28. Or: Pakistan.

29. And: that whole Kurdish deal.

30. Not to mention: Yemen.

31. Texas announced it had found a way to barbecue oxygen.

SEPTEMBER

1. Sarah Palin's latest book contained her newly invented words extelligence, fornify, and blorgle.
2. Alabama rejected same-sex marriage, but continued to recognize same-family marriage.
3. The Centers for Disease Control and Prevention announced, "Don't put that in your mouth, you don't know where it's been."
4. During a trip through Africa, the secretary of state took some time to do the things he never had.

▶ Fact-Like Fact

Then, the secretary of state immediately went to the land Down Under, where women glow and men plunder.

5. Florida was hit by Tropical Storm That One Guy with the Glasses Who Works in Accounting as the National Weather Bureau admitted it is running out of storm names.
6. On his TV show, Sean Hannity announced that he just says what his hair tells him.
7. The Dow Jones fell 512 points on news that a poor person was able to borrow $10 from his brother until payday.
8. Vladimir Putin beat his chest and did a Tarzan yell; thousands of jungle animals were then stampeding toward Moscow.
9. The USDA announced that the drought in the Midwest had decimated the Crunch Berry crop.
10. The State Department expressed confusion because "the State Department doesn't deal with states, but other countries. Shouldn't it be called the Nation Department? What is up with that?" Also, Jerry Seinfeld apparently is their spokesman now.
11. Ricky Martin announced that currently, he's living la vida Top Ramen.
12. The TSA announced that after a full-body search, TSA agents are now required to make you breakfast the next morning.

13. Japan moved to stimulate its economy by raising interest rates on horribly upsetting tentacle hentai.

14. NBA players went on strike for more ridiculous, ugly-ass shoes.

15. The musical based on the Green Day album *American Idiot* opened in Paris. In France, the play is simply called *Idiot*, since the original title is considered redundant.

THIS YEAR'S FEDERAL BUDGET

KEEPING THE HOUSE SPEAKER'S FACE ORANGE

EVERYTHING ELSE

16. The President's budget includes $4.7 billion for Slim Jims and Big Gulps.

17. Consumer confidence was declared so low, most people have to listen to several Tony Robbins tapes before buying a Diet Coke.

18. The state of Illinois announced it still had no idea why Sufjan Stevens recorded that album about it.

19. The Interior Department announced the nation's brush has grown at an alarming 45 percent per year since George W. Bush's presidency ended.

25. Some guy did some sports thing and everyone was all like "Holy crap!"

26. Facebook announced it was going to make you change all your damn preferences again, and then cackled evilly.

27. The United Nations voted to place sanctions on Slovenia for the spit wad incident during the General Assembly.

28. The Fed lowered interest rates because, you know, something to do.

29. House Republicans proposed a new constitutional amendment that would state that "House Democrats are so fat, they registered for their wedding at Arby's. No, we're not sure

whether or not Arby's has a wedding registry; all we're saying is that . . . Oh, forget it."

30. Turns out that, in fact, Rick Astley gave you up years ago.

OCTOBER

1. Kyrgyzstan reported that thousands more vowels had left the country.

2. Texas became the first state to execute a Death Row prisoner by "sticking a firecracker up his butt and seeing what happens."

3. Lobbyists for the oil industry got Congress to pass a new law requiring Americans to switch to an all-petroleum diet.

> **Fact-Like Fact**

The best part of an all-petroleum diet: all the Cheez Whiz you can eat!

4. The National Labor Relations Board disbanded, saying that having relations during labor is a bad idea for everybody involved.

5. In suburban Chicago, a fully gruntled postal worker gave everybody flowers and hugs.

Guy Fieri, who hosts a popular show on the Douche Channel.

6. The Centers for Disease Control and Prevention announced, "Put on a jacket! You'll catch your death of a cold out there!"

7. The President announced a plan to reduce the federal deficit by $400 billion over 10 years by putting a tip jar in the Oval Office.

8. MacArthur Genius Grants were announced today. For some reason, Michele Bachmann did not win one.

9. The Supreme Court heard oral arguments today. The word "oral," for the 40,000th time, made Clarence Thomas giggle.

10. The Nobel Prize in Literature was won by some guy or lady whose books you will never, ever read.

11. The Nobel Prize in Chemistry went to the guy who invented ranch dressing.

12. Eighty-five percent of Americans think Guy Fieri and the Smash Mouth dude are the same person, and that they are both lesbians.

13. In a landmark case, the Supreme Court ruled that putting Junior Mints on popcorn is "completely messed up."

14. FEMA announced that they would be providing disaster relief to themselves.

15. Hawaii legalized same-lei marriage.

16. NASA announced that ever since they stopped going to the Moon, they sometimes just stare at their Moon rocks and cry.

17. After a manhunt lasting nearly 25 years, the FBI announced it had finally found Waldo.

18. Experts are still shocked that this year's Nobel Prize in Medicine went to that Human Centipede dude.

19. Congress's approval rating is down to 14 percent, which is somewhere between stabbing yourself in the eye repeatedly and Nickelback.

20. The U.S. secretary of state arrived in Istanbul, not Constantinople. When asked why Constantinople got the works, he replied, "That's nobody's business but the Turks."

21. To keep Social Security solvent, Congress proposed raising the retirement age to 7,000.

22. The Dow fell 514 points when Wendy's put their chili back on the dollar menu.

23. At a press conference on Capitol Hill, House Democrats declared, "The House GOP is

so stupid that it takes them four hours to watch one episode of *60 Minutes.*"

24. Cheese. Delicious cheese. Mmmmmm, cheese.

28. The number one cause of death in the United States is now "total eclipse of the heart."

29. Eckhart Tolle announced he was pretty much never in the "now"; he was, in fact, in 1877 most of the time.

30. In Maine, someone said "lobstah," and it was adorable.

31. Seventy-nine percent of Americans are dressing up as the scariest thing they can think of for Halloween: namely, Madonna's pale, stringy arms.

NOVEMBER

1. This year's least popular Halloween candy was, as always, Reese's Feces.

2. To save money, the President will now fly coach on Air Force One.

3. The state of New York legalized same-weight marriage.

4. Voters in Ohio decided by a 57–43 percent margin to stay home tonight and play Halo.

5. Americans were urged to get flu shots, and then maybe some Jell-O shots.

6. That lady who's buying a stairway to Heaven became unsure about whether all that glitters is gold or not.

7. The mayor of Chicago officially apologized for every Chicago album since *Chicago VIII.*

❯ Fact-Like Fact

Also: "The Night Chicago Died."

8. The Tennessee state legislature announced, "Moonshine whiskey! Yeeeeeee hawwwwwww!"

9. McDonald's introduced the new McMcNugget, a breaded and deep-fried chicken McNugget.

10. The secretary of the treasury announced he'd been winging it for years now.

11. Tom of MySpace.com sat alone in front of a whiteboard

somewhere, wondering when it all went wrong.

12. The Centers for Disease Control and Prevention announced, "Eat your vegetables or you'll catch The Gout."

13. Ninety-six percent of Americans think those slide shows on news websites are bull-pockey.

14. Hillary Clinton announced that if you don't like her hair, tough shit.

15. For millions of Americans, suburban life continued to be a quiet, slow-motion nightmare of desperation, panic, and *Cheers* repeats.

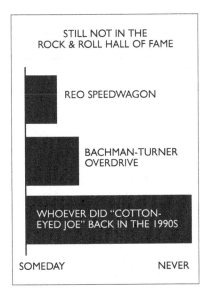

STILL NOT IN THE
ROCK & ROLL HALL OF FAME

REO SPEEDWAGON

BACHMAN-TURNER
OVERDRIVE

WHOEVER DID "COTTON-
EYED JOE" BACK IN THE 1990S

SOMEDAY   NEVER

16. Somehow, the Rock & Roll Hall of Fame failed to induct Loverboy.

17. In Germany, everybody drank beer or ate sausage and potato salad or whatever it is they do over there.

18. Seventy-five percent of Republicans continued to not see the hypocrisy of claiming to follow both Jesus and Ayn Rand.

19. Lisa Loeb's still wandering around that empty apartment, you guys.

20. There were accusations of fraud in Iraq's election, as the winner was "that guy from *Big Bang Theory*."

24. England updated its food pyramid by adding a third food group, "fried things," to its existing food groups "crumpets" and "knickers."

25. After a long investigation, the Swiss government announced it doesn't know how all the holes got in the cheese.

26. The members of Foreigner announced they still want to know what love is, and would be ever so happy if someone

could send them a book or a diagram or something.

27. Medical experts announced that 44 percent of migraines are caused by Skrillex.

28. Taylor Lautner announced he will star in the *Citizen Kane* reboot, in which Charles Foster Kane can fly, shoot lasers from his eyeballs, and is also a zombie.

29. The House GOP issued a proclamation today that stated, "House Democrats are so fat, their BMI is measured in hectares. Also: one hectare equals 10,000 square meters. Also: we are *not* condoning the metric system, which is still a Socialist plot of some sort, we think."

30. Wisconsin legalized same-cheese marriage.

DECEMBER

1. The Centers for Disease Control and Prevention announced, "Stop touching that! You'll go blind!"

2. A team of research scientists lost to the Baltimore Ravens, 87–3.

3. A Chinese factory was forced to recall millions of gallons of lead paint because it contained toys.

4. Kim Kardashian, something something something. What the hell ever.

5. Nevada banned same-species marriage.

6. Researchers have determined that MC Hammer is now exactly legit enough to quit.

7. In a new poll, 87 percent of Americans think Julian Assange looks like a James Bond villain.

▶ Fact-Like Fact

The other 13 percent think Julian Assange looks like an albino ferret.

8. The UN sent a seven-nation army in to stop Jack White.

9. The Dow gained 235 points today on reports that a lady was sure that all that glitters is gold and she's buying a stairway to Heaven.

10. People in the Midwest somewhere freaked out about

some Muslim guy just working, paying his taxes, and living his life like any other damn American.

11. The Koch Brothers bought the entire U.S. Congress for $1.7 billion. Kind of a bargain, really.

12. The Writers Guild of America went on strike, claiming, "semicolons are for suckers."

13. Due to the success of Somali pirates, the nation of Somalia announced plans to go ahead with Somali robots, Somali ninjas, and Somali zombies.

14. Credit card companies raised interest rates from 21 percent to "your left ball."

15. Gwen Stefani announced that her shit really was bananas. Doctors have been unable to determine why she is pooping delicious fruit.

16. Well, lightsabers still aren't a thing. Come on, science.

17. On Broadway, the musical version of Oedipus, *MILF: The Musical!* closed after one awful, awful performance.

18. Oklahoma announced that its shape was nearly as pornographic-looking as Florida's.

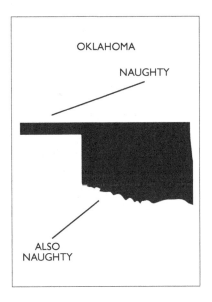

19. The USDA removed asparagus from the Food Pyramid, since "nobody eats that crap anyway."

25. The band that recorded "Grandma Got Run Over by a Reindeer" got run over by an 18-wheeler.

27. Hollywood executives announced an exclusive deal to ruin everything from your childhood.

28. Unemployment numbers would have been released today, but the entire

Department of Labor was laid off after getting bought out by Bain Capital.

29. House Democrats announced, "The House GOP is so short, they play handball on the curb, which they really shouldn't do because a car could run over them or something."

30. Big Brother was watching you. Just like every other day.

31. China issued the United States an eviction notice.

The Year in History

History. Culture. Politics. It seems like something happens every damn day. And it does. Cut it out, history, culture, and politics!

Here is a list of famous happenings throughout history, from January through December. We were going to do it alphabetically, but then April would have been first and, you know, screw April. Stupid month.

JANUARY

1. 1752: Betsy Ross was born: She was pretty much the Smurfette of the American Revolution.

2. 1968: Cuba Gooding Jr. was born. To this day, nobody has shown him the money.

3. 1892: J.R.R. Tolkien was born. He wrote about all the horrible things that will happen if you put a ring on it.

> **Fact-Like Fact**

Peter Jackson is turning one of Tolkien's grocery lists into a series of 16 movies.

4. 1896: Utah became a state. The most popular tourist attraction in Utah is the "You Are Now Leaving Utah" sign at the state line.

5. 1941: Animator Hayao Miyazaki was born. In real life, his neighbor Totoro was a toothless meth addict with a chain saw and a temper.

6. 1912: New Mexico became a state. It was like the old

Mexico, but with only half the calories!

7. 1782: The first American bank opened. Twenty years later, the government had to give them a bailout of over 1 billion beaver pelts.

8. 1942: Stephen Hawking was born. As the world's foremost theoretical physicist, he discovered why yo mamma so fat.

Thomas Paine. He wrote *Common Sense* and the erotic *Fifty Shades of Common Sense.*

9. 1788: Connecticut became a state. Connecticut's state motto is "Live Dull or Die."

10. 1776: Thomas Paine published *Common Sense.* Originally, it was a violent porn manga called *Happy Num Num Girls.* Lots of tentacles. *Very* upsetting.

11. AD 630: Muhammad conquered Mecca with an army of 10,000 men. Dude, Muhammad was *way* cooler than Jesus.

12. 1951: Rush Limbaugh was born. His political philosophy is summed up in the book *I Am So Whacked Out on Vicodin Right Now.*

13. Nothing has ever happened on this day. We recommend staying in bed.

14. 1978: The Sex Pistols broke up after Sid Vicious accidentally learned how to play bass.

15. 1967: The first Super Bowl was played. Football hadn't been invented yet, so the Packers beat the Chiefs at Candyland.

15. 1929: Martin Luther King Jr. was born. We honor his

inspiring legacy by not delivering the mail on a random Monday near-ish to his birthday.

16. 1547: Ivan the Terrible became czar of Russia. He was called "the Terrible" because he totally sucked at Ms. Pac-Man.

17. 1942: Boxer Muhammad Ali was born. He could float like a butterfly and sting like a bee (after the radioactive butterflies and bees bit him).

18. 2007: Justin Bieber's career took off when he starred in the viral video *Dramatic Chipmunk.*

19. 1807: General Robert E. Lee was born, the only souped-up Dodge Charger whose horn played "Dixie" to lead troops in the Civil War.

20. 1809: Edgar Allan Poe was born. The NFL's Ravens are named after a Poe story where a raven sacks the opposing quarterback five times.

21. 1997: Newt Gingrich was fined and reprimanded for being Newt Gingrich.

22. 1949: Steve Perry, the lead singer of Journey, was born. Few people know his dark secret: for a few brief moments in 1985, he actually stopped believin'.

23. 1737: John Hancock was born. He's that jerk with the big-ass signature.

24. 1941: Singer Neil Diamond was born. "No one heard at all, not even the chair"? Jesus, Neil Diamond has some asshole furniture.

25. 1919: The League of Nations was founded, but the next season the owners locked out the players in a labor dispute.

26. 1837: Michigan became a state. Sadly, this led directly to Kid Rock.

27. 1756: Wolfgang Amadeus Mozart was born. His life story was made into the popular 1980s movie *Buckaroo Banzai.*

27. 1984: Michael Jackson's head caught fire while filming a Pepsi ad, leading to Pepsi's catchy jingle "Help! My Hair! Aaaauuugghh!"

28. 1985: The song "We Are the World" was recorded. People could not wait to hear Kenny

Rogers *and* Latoya Jackson sing on the same record.

▶ Fact-Like Fact

Why Dan Aykroyd was on the record remains a complete mystery.

29. 1954: Oprah Winfrey was born. She now wanders the streets, randomly recommending books to people and giving them cars.
30. 1969: The Beatles played their famous Rooftop Concert in London. It was broken up by the police when Ringo threatened to sing.
31. 1919: Jackie Robinson was born. In baseball, he broke the color barrier and the sound barrier, surpassing Mach 2 in a game against the St. Louis Cardinals.

FEBRUARY

1. 1790: The Supreme Court first convened. It wasn't until 1995 that they wore anything beneath their robes.
1. 2004: We all kinda saw Janet Jackson's breast for, like, half a second or so, tops. Now, calm down, Slappy.
2. 1905: Ayn Rand was born. She called her philosophy "Objectivism" because "Being a Selfish Prick" wasn't nearly as catchy.
3. 1959: Buddy Holly and Ritchie Valens died in a plane crash, the worst musical disaster until Train's "Hey, Soul Sister."
4. 1789: George Washington was unanimously chosen to be our first president, and our first San Diego Chicken.
5. 1934: Hank Aaron was born. He would go on to hit 755 home runs without looking like the Stay Puft Marshmallow Man.
6. 1895: Babe Ruth was born. He hit 714 home runs while on several performance-suppressing substances.
7. 1804: John Deere was born. He invented the tractor and several other modern, convenient ways for a farmer to lose an arm.
8. 1904: The Russo-Japanese War began. Rene Russo won.

9. 1964: The Beatles first appeared on *The Ed Sullivan Show*, while Yoko Ono first appeared on *The Atonal Screaming Hour.*

11. 1990: Nelson Mandela was released from prison after 27 years. You should see his dozens of badass prison tattoos.

Abraham Lincoln, after he pasted a dead badger to his lower jaw.

12. 1809: Abraham Lincoln was born. He was a Republican, though today's GOP would probably demand to see his birth certificate.

13. 1960: France exploded its first atomic bomb, giving the French the power to surrender the crap out of any war.

14. 1859: Oregon became a state. Hacky Sack–playing hipsters nationwide celebrated.

15. 2005: YouTube was launched. Before this, people had lives and shit.

16. 1923: King Tut's tomb was unsealed in Egypt. The archaeologists were quoted as saying, "Snakes. Why did it have to be snakes?"

17. 1963: Both Michael Jordan and Larry the Cable Guy were born. They are, of course, identical twins.

18. 1930: Pluto was discovered. But since it's not a planet anymore, no one gives a crap.

19. 1945: The Battle of Iwo Jima began. Those guys with the flag had to stand that way for months until the photographer showed up.

20. 1962: John Glenn became the first American to orbit Earth. Somehow, NASA did this with less computer power than

a broken Casio watch from 1981.

21. 1972: Richard Nixon began his historic visit to China. In order to make him feel at home, the Chinese immediately broke into an office for him.

22. 1980: At the Winter Olympics, the Miracle on Ice occurred: a hockey game was actually almost interesting.

23. 1870: Mississippi was readmitted to the Union; the make-up sex was incredible.

24. 1868: President Andrew Johnson was impeached. And he didn't even get any hot intern action out of it, the poor dope.

25. 1943: George Harrison was born. He wrote the Beatles songs "Here Comes the Sun," and "Yes, I Know the Sun Comes Every Day, It's a Metaphor, Dumb-Ass."

26. 1932: Johnny Cash was born. Before he became the Man in Black, he was briefly the Man in Adorable Little Pink Polka Dots.

28. 1827: The B&O Railroad was founded. The Disalmanacarian

can't believe you can still buy it for $150; it should be worth billions by now.

▶ Fact-Like Fact

In 1966, Johnny Cash turned down a million-dollar offer from Crayola to become the Man in Burnt Umber.

29. 2004: *The Lord of the Rings: The Return of the King* won eleven Oscars, including the award for Best Achievement in Jesus, How Many Endings Does This Movie Have, Like Twelve? Just End Already.

MARCH

1. 1803: Ohio became a state. The top tourist destination in Ohio is Are You Kidding Me? I Am So Not Vacationing in Ohio.

2. 1877: Rutherford B. Hayes was declared the winner of the 1876 election, after a spectacular showing in the swimsuit competition.

3. 1847: Alexander Graham Bell was born. He invented the

telephone, so super-annoying Black Eyed Peas ringtones are his fault.

4. 1974: *People* magazine was first published. The first cover story: "Infant Jennifer Aniston: Anorexic, Angry at Toddler Brangelina."

5. 1770: The Boston Massacre occurred when Colonists said they requested "More Than a Feeling," but the British played "Foreplay/Long Time" instead.

6. 1806: Elizabeth Barrett Browning was born. She wrote all those poems about that man from Nantucket.

7. 1873: Piet Mondrian was born. He became famous for painting his geometry homework.

8. 1618: Johannes Kepler discovered the third law of planetary motion: all you gotta do is zoom-a-zoom zoom zoom and a boom boom.

9. 1862: The *Christian Science Monitor* defeated the *Christian Science Merrimack*.

10. 2000: The NASDAQ reached a peak of 5132.32 on news that a Nigerian prince needed help transferring his fortune.

11. 1861: The Confederacy adopted a constitution, which later became the lyrics to "The Devil Went Down to Georgia."

12. 1947: Harry Truman established the Truman Doctrine: "Melts in your mouth, not in your hands."

13. 1781: The planet Uranus was discovered. It was apparently named by a sniggering 10-year-old.

Julius Caesar. Toga! Toga! Toga!

14. 1879: Albert Einstein was born. He invented relatives.

15. 44 BC: Julius Caesar was stabbed to death by Brutus and others. This became the basis of the great Shakespeare play *Thundercats*.

16. 1751: James Madison was born. Some people call him the Father of the Constitution, but some people call him Maurice because he spoke of the pompatus of love.

17. 1522: Saint Patrick said, "I have had it with these motherfucking snakes on this motherfucking island!"

18. 1970: Queen Latifah was born. Despite her name, she is only fourth in line for the British crown.

19. 1918: Congress established our time zones. New York is Eastern Time, California is Pacific Time, and Indiana is 1957.

20. 1852: *Uncle Tom's Cabin* was published. It's about a really, *really* crappy time-share.

21. 2006: Twitter was created. Since then, over 1 billion whales have been lifted out of the water by tiny little birds.

22. 1931: William Shatner was born. He played Captain Kirk in pretty much everything he ever appeared in.

23. 1983: Ronald Reagan first proposed a "Star Wars" missile shield by introducing his new secretary of defense, Boba Fett.

23. 1775: Patrick Henry said, "Give me liberty, or give me death! And if it's death, I would prefer to be smothered in breasts."

24. 1958: Elvis Presley was drafted. At the time, the army had a Don't Ask, Don't Tell policy regarding men doing the Jailhouse Rock.

25. 1947: Elton John was born. He recorded such hits as "How Did You Not Know I Was Gay? Did You See What I Was Wearing in the '70s?"

26. 1874: Robert Frost was born. Good thing that path in the woods didn't diverge into three paths; he'd still be standing there trying to decide.

27. 1794: The U.S. Navy was created by George Washington, in his bathtub with his rubber ducky.

28. 1979: The Three Mile Island nuclear accident occurred. The high levels of radiation caused the 1980s.
29. 1790: Tenth U.S. president, John Tyler, was born, though his entire presidency may just be an urban myth.
30. 1870: Texas was readmitted to the Union. You know, no one would have minded if we didn't let them back in.
31. 1596: René Descartes was born. He wrote, "*Cogito ergo sum,*" which is Latin for "My uncle's toaster-oven."

APRIL

1. 1976: Apple was founded. Back in the early days, the iTunes User Agreement was only 150 pages long.
2. 1914: Sir Alec Guinness was born. He played Obi-Wan in the *Star Wars* movies, unless George Lucas has replaced him with a CGI fish or something.
3. AD 33: Historians believe Jesus was crucified on this date. They say he came back to life later—just like that dude in Mötley Crüe!
4. 1850: Los Angeles was founded. At last, America had a place that would turn your favorite comic book into a shitty, shitty movie.

> ## Fact-Like Fact

Los Angeles is home to America's Strategic Out-of-Work Actor Reserve.

5. 1792: George Washington cast the first veto, rejecting Congress's George Washington Is a Wooden-Toothed Buttock-Face Act.
6. 1909: Robert Peary became the first man to reach the North Pole. Somehow, this led to Santa Claus conquering the Martians.
7. 1939: Italy invaded Albania, because, you know, something to do, I guess.
8. 1513: Ponce de León claimed Florida for Spain. Not that anyone else wanted it.
9. 1865: Robert E. Lee surrendered to Ulysses S. Grant, the sweat glistening on

his heaving bosom as Grant's manhood pressed forward.

10. 1970: It was announced that the Beatles had broken up. Paul got custody of Ringo.

11. 1970: NASA launched *Apollo 13*. This tragic mission was later turned into the Tom Hanks movie *Bachelor Party*.

12. 1606: The Union Jack became the flag of Great Britain. Before this, they just flew some spotted dick or whatever.

13. 1743: Thomas Jefferson was born. He wrote the Declaration of Independence, which had the working title "God Emperor of Dune."

14. 1865: Abraham Lincoln was shot by John Wilkes Booth, though Oliver Stone thinks it was the CIA, the Mafia, and the Cuban government.

15. 1912: The *Titanic* sank, probably because of that "I'm the king of the world!" douche bag.

16. 1943: The effects of LSD were first observed. This led directly to the Teletubbies.

17. 1961: The United States tried to overthrow Fidel Castro in

the Bay of Pigs Invasion. It was a disaster, mostly because pigs can't swim.

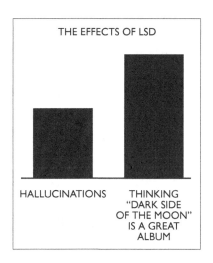

THE EFFECTS OF LSD

HALLUCINATIONS   THINKING "DARK SIDE OF THE MOON" IS A GREAT ALBUM

18. 1775: Paul Revere began his midnight ride, calling out, "The British are coming!" Which, you know, yuck.

18. 1955: Albert Einstein died, before he could come up with an all-encompassing theory of what was up with his hair.

19. 1775: The Battle of Lexington and Concord was fought. Lexington defeated Concord in a controversial Hell in a Cell match.

20. 1889: A couple called their newborn son Adolf Hitler, the

first-ever instance of Godwin's Law.

21. 1910: Mark Twain died. No exaggeration this time.

22. 1724: Immanuel Kant was born. He wrote *Critique of Pure Reason* about philosophy and *Critique of Pure Bullshit* about the GOP.

23. 1564: William Shakespeare was born. He exited the womb pursued by a bear.

24. 1704: The first newspaper was published in the United States. A "newspaper" is like if some dumb-ass printed out all of CNN's website daily.

25. 1990: The Hubble Space Telescope was deployed. Since then, it has discovered more than 5,000 planets where apes evolved from men.

26. AD 570: Muhammad was born. He was the founder of Islam, and a founding member of the Ramones (early member Muhammad al-Ramone).

27. 1861: Abraham Lincoln suspended habeas corpus (Latin for "Rico Suave").

28. 1937: Saddam Hussein was born. Remember when it turned out he didn't have any of those weapons of mass destruction Bush said he had, and that we basically had a whole war for nothing? Good times.

29. 1982: Someone passed the dutchie on the right-hand side, and oh man, all hell broke loose.

▶ Fact-Like Fact

Seriously, who the hell passes a dutchie on the right-hand side, right?

30. 1789: George Washington became our first president, and he didn't even have to show his birth certificate to a bunch of idiot lamewads.

MAY

1. 2011: Osama bin Laden was killed. And he would have gotten away with it too, if it weren't for those meddling kids!

2. 1992: Rodney King said, "Can we all get along?" (SPOILER ALERT: We can't.)

3. 1611: The King James Bible was first published. Jesus doesn't say anything about gay marriage in this version of the Bible, either.

4. 1971: The NPR program *All Things Considered* was first broadcast. Yet to be considered: why people get off an escalator and just stand there, blocking all who follow.

5. 1626: The Dutch discovered Manhattan. It already smelled like piss and vomit.

6. 1260: Kublai Khan became ruler of the Mongol Empire. He got a lot of help from his Super PAC, Citizens for Your Head on a Stick.

7. 1856: Sigmund Freud was born. Dude really loved bananas and cigars. Nothing weird or symbolic about that. Nope.

8. 1718: New Orleans was founded by settlers who longed for the freedom to drunkenly flash their thingies in exchange for beads.

9. 1886: Coca-Cola was first sold. It used to be made with cocaine, but now it's made of those adorable polar bears from the ads.

10. 1994: Nelson Mandela became president of South Africa, because that's first prize in the Morgan Freeman Lookalike Contest.

11. 1908: The first Mother's Day was celebrated, with massive displays of fireworks and guilt.

12. 1858: Minnesota became a state. Their dictator-for-life is Garrison Keillor.

13. 1937: George Carlin was born. We wish his "Seven Words You Can Never Say on Television" included "Kardashian," "Trump," "Palin," and "Snooki."

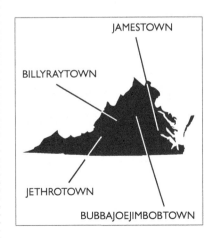

JAMESTOWN

BILLYRAYTOWN

JETHROTOWN

BUBBAJOEJIMBOBTOWN

14. 1607: The English settled in Jamestown, Virginia. It was all downhill from there.

15. 1944: George Lucas was born. He's currently making three shitty prequels to the *Police Academy* movies. Send help.

16. 1859: Pierre Curie was born. He and Marie Curie studied radiation, which is how they later became Godzilla and Gamera.

17. 1866: Root beer was invented when someone said, "Let's make booze out of this weird-ass thing I found in the ground."

18. 1792: The New York Stock Exchange was formed; it started out as a support group for total tools who wanted to destroy the economy.

19. 1980: Mount St. Helens erupted just as Tom Hanks and Meg Ryan jumped in.

20. 1925: Malcolm X was born. No one knows what happened to the first nine Malcolms.

21. 1861: North Carolina left the Union. The Union stayed home, ate a thing of Ben & Jerry's, watched *Titanic*, and cried and cried.

22. 1927: Charles Lindbergh completed the first transatlantic flight. Boy, were his arms tired. The Disalmanacarian is here all week! Tip your waitress!

23. 1980: Pac-Man was released. Later, Ms. Pac-Man was created from Pac-Man's rib.

24. 1859: Sir Arthur Conan Doyle was born. He created the character Sherlock Holmes, a British detective who is also Iron Man.

25. 1788: South Carolina became a state, which immediately lowered the average American IQ by 27 points.

26. 1941: Bob Dylan was born. He's known for the hits "Wazzo Yoppa ZhoooOOOOoooo" and "Ezza Muh Muzz BinbohhHHHHhhhh."

27. 1977: *Star Wars* was released, though it was originally titled *Han Totally Shot First*.

28. 1897: Bram Stoker's book *Dracula* was published, and it

sure as hell wasn't this sparkly *Twilight* crap. Jesus.

29. 1923: Henry Kissinger was born. He was like the groovy 1970s version of Dick Cheney.

30. 1908: Ian Fleming was born. He created James Bond and such Bond villains as Octopussy, Quintuplabia, and Infinipenis.

31. 1953: Edmund Hillary and Tenzing Norgay became the first men to reach the summit of Mount Everest. Not surprisingly, there was already a damn Starbucks up there.

32. 1431: Joan of Arc was burned at the stake. Worse, nobody brought any BBQ sauce.

33. 1819: Walt Whitman was born. He wrote *Leaves of Grass*, which may have been what he was smoking when he wrote it.

JUNE

1. 1974: Alanis Morissette was born. *Fact:* Rain on your wedding day isn't ironic. It's weather.

1. 1937: Morgan Freeman was born. If Morgan Freeman is narrating your life, you're either in prison or a penguin. Possibly both.

2. 1981: Donkey Kong made its U.S. debut, and it was on like . . . um . . . Simon Le Bon? On like Jean Valjean? On like Kraftwerk's "Autobahn"? Something like that.

3. 1539: Hernando de Soto claimed Florida for Spain. Unfortunately, they didn't keep it.

▶ Fact-Like Fact

Florida became a state due to a clerical error.

4. 1738: King George III of England was born. He was known as the Mad King, probably because he appointed a tin of crumpets the duke of Happy Unicornland.

5. 1837: Houston became a city. They have yet to apologize, the bastards.

6. 1833: Andrew Jackson became the first president to ride a train, because all the previous presidents were total puss-faces.

7. 1975: The first Betamax was sold. Betamax was videotape. Videotape was a cassette you could watch. A cassette . . . Oh, never mind.

8. AD 793: The Vikings invaded England. Even the Vikings were disgusted by British oral hygiene.

9. 1905: Einstein published his groundbreaking paper on quantum theory and light. Because of where it was published, it began, "Dear Penthouse . . ."

10. 1953: Former U.S. senator John Edwards was born. Yep, he's still a scumbag.

11. 1910: Jacques Cousteau was born. He invented the ocean.

11. 1184 BC: The Greeks entered Troy in the Trojan Horse. Later, the South tried this tactic in the Civil War with the Trojan Varmint.

12. 1987: Ronald Reagan stood in Berlin and said, "Mr. Gorbachev, tear down this wall." Yes, Reagan's entire foreign policy was based on Pink Floyd albums.

13. 1900: The Boxer Rebellion began. The Boxers were trying to overthrow the cruel, despotic Tighty Whities.

WHAT REALLY LANDED IN ROSWELL?

RELAX, IT WAS JUST A WEATHER BALLOON

A WEATHER BALLOON FROM THE PLANET GRAXON-17! AAUUUUGGHHH!

14. 1947: A UFO may have landed in Roswell, New Mexico. Also, we may have been taken over by alien lizard people, and you may be their dinner.

15. 2002: A giant asteroid nearly struck the Earth, narrowly avoiding the disaster of Aerosmith recording another crappy power ballad.

16. 1829: Geronimo was born. Before this, people didn't know what the hell they were going

to say when they jumped out of airplanes when they were invented someday.

17. 1971: Richard Nixon declared the War on Drugs. Drugs won.

18. 1812: The United States declared war against Britain, because, you know: Russell Brand.

19. 1964: The Civil Rights Act was passed. Of course, the Patriot Act made civil rights moot, but still.

20. 1863: West Virginia became a state. During the Civil War, it provided the Union with much-needed crystal meth and hillbilly heroin.

21. 1905: Philosopher Jean-Paul Sartre was born. He wrote *Being and Nothingness.* (SPOILER ALERT: Nothingness wins.)

22. 1964: Dan Brown was born. He wrote *The Da Vinci Code* and *The Michelangelo Sudoku.*

23. 1863: The typewriter was patented. Soon, men were typing pictures of their junk and sending them to women via pneumatic tube.

24. 1509: Henry VIII was crowned king of England. This was celebrated with a 21-head salute.

25. 1903: George Orwell was born. His novel *1984* is about an oppressive, dystopian future of acid-washed jeans and hair mousse.

26. 1963: John F. Kennedy famously said, *"Ich bin ein Berliner"* (German for "I am my uncle's toaster oven").

27. 1880: Helen Keller was born. She was deaf, dumb, and blind, but she played a decidedly non-mean pinball.

28. 1846: The saxophone was patented. Sadly, this led directly to Kenny G.

29. 2007: The iPhone first went on sale. For some reason, this made birds very angry.

30. 1817: Sir Joseph Hooker was born. Hooker was the inventor of the hooker.

JULY

1. 1908: SOS became the official international distress signal, replacing "Aaaauuugghhh!"

2. 1881: President James Garfield was shot by a madman who was pro-Monday and anti-lasagne.

3. 1883: Franz Kafka was born. He was one of the greatest authors who also happened to be a giant cockroach (along with Mitch Albom).

▶ Fact-Like Fact

Franz Kafka was profoundly disappointed when he learned that "Kafkaesque" did not mean "a super-handsome love machine with washboard abs."

4. Today is the Fourth of July in America. Everywhere else, it's also the Fourth of July, because that's how calendars work, you nimrod.

5. 1937: Spam luncheon meat was introduced. Later that day, the "Spam, Spam, Spam, Spam, Spam, Eggs, and Spam" skit was introduced.

6. 1921: Nancy Reagan was born. After her "Just Say No to Drugs" campaign in the 1980s, drugs completely disappeared forever! Yay!

7. 1676: Quakers arrived in America. America's religious tolerance allowed them to at last, without persecution, worship oatmeal.

8. 1932: The Dow Jones reached its lowest point of the Great Depression, closing at a couple of buttons, some old string, and a moth flying out of an out-turned pocket.

9. 1956: Tom Hanks was born. He peaked with *Bosom Buddies*.

10. 1856: Nikola Tesla was born. He discovered electricity, air, and sweet, sweet lovin'.

11. 1921: William Taft was sworn in as chief justice. He is the only person to ever be president, chief justice, and Miss South Carolina.

12. 1957: A connection was shown between smoking and lung cancer. The tobacco industry claimed it wasn't lung cancer, but "lung awesomeness!"

13. 1985: The Live Aid concerts took place. The shows were a huge success because they took place before the Black Eyed Peas or Ke$ha existed.

William Taft. Toga! Toga! Toga!

14. 1969: Honduras and El Salvador went to war over a soccer game, which makes way more sense than why George W. Bush invaded Iraq.

16. 1945: The United States successfully tested the A-bomb, which led directly to giant ants overrunning L.A. or some shit.

17. 1955: Disneyland opened. Within three minutes, "It's a Small World" was already the most annoying song ever.

18. July 18 does not exist. Please update your records.

19. 1834: Artist Edgar Degas was born. He painted that one thing. No, the other one. Right.

20. 1902: The first San Diego Comic-Con was held. Thousands gathered in a stuffy room and waited for comic books to be invented.

21. 1969: Millions watched as Neil Armstrong and Buzz Aldrin became the first men to fool people into thinking we had landed on the Moon.

22. 1940: Alex Trebek was born. Most people are surprised to learn that he has an IQ of only 57.

23. 1968: Riots broke out in Cleveland when people realized they lived in Cleveland.

24. 1969: Jennifer Lopez was born. She started her show-biz career as a Fly Girl, a horrible half-human/half-fly created in a freak science lab accident.

26. 1894: Aldous Huxley was born. His novel *Brave New World* was originally titled *You*

*Know What's Stupid? The
Future.*

27. 1975: Alex Rodriguez was born
as part of a three-player deal
with the Astros.

28. 1866: Beatrix Potter was born;
she is author of the charming
Tale of Peter Rabbit and
the somewhat less charming
*Samuel Squirrel Meets the
Stump Grinder.*

29. 1981: Prince Charles and Lady
Diana Spencer were married
in London's St. Paul's
Cathedral. As tradition
dictates, the royal couple
honeymooned in Branson,
Missouri.

30. AD 762: The city of Baghdad
was founded, and U.S. troops
have been there ever since.

31. 1987: The not-so-humanitarian
organization Doctors Without
Pants was founded.

AUGUST

1. 1942: Jerry Garcia was born.
Garcia was awarded the 1989
Nobel Prize in Munchies.

2. 1888: Thomas Edison invented
the Electric Light Orchestra.

Random Bonus Fact!

JONATHAN COULTON, MUSICIAN

**All rhombuses are
parallelograms, but only some
rhombuses are squares (and
most squares are assholes).**

3. 1963: It was discovered that
Malcolm X was secretly Speed
Racer's older brother Rex.

4. 1961: Barack Obama was
born, part of a plot by the all-
powerful Socialist Party of
Kenya, who secretly rule the
world. Obviously.

5. 1966: The Beatles released
Revolver. It's considered one of
their greatest albums, mainly
because Ringo only sings one
song.

6. 1928: Andy Warhol was born.
He said that in the future
everyone would be famous for
15 minutes, so Snooki is his
fault.

7. 1978: Blue Öyster Cult
announced that they are
actually scared shitless of
the reaper.

8. 1979: The most serious oil

crisis in the 1970s broke out: Scott Baio's T-zone. Damn, Slappy.

9. 1974: Richard Nixon resigned the presidency, and a grossed-out nation was able to move on from his shocking streaking scandal.

10. 1821: Missouri became the twenty-fourth state. They were desperate to join the Union, because Missouri loves company.

11. 1965: Riots and looting broke out in the Watts area of Los Angeles. It was such a bad day, Ice Cube had to use his AK at least twice.

12. 1833: The city of Chicago was founded. Sadly, this led directly to "If You Leave Me Now" by the band Chicago.

13. 1981: John Oates thought for one brief moment that maybe, just maybe, he could go for that.

14. 1917: Feeling left out because nobody had declared war on them yet, China declared war on Germany and Austria during World War I.

15. 1965: The Beatles played Shea Stadium. Ringo hit a walk-off homer to beat the Washington Senators 6–5.

16. 1954: *Sports Illustrated* was first published. The cover model for their first swimsuit issue was Vice President Richard Nixon, so that was upsetting.

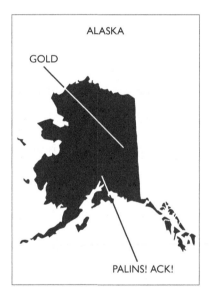

17. 1896: Gold was discovered in Alaska. Instead of panning for it, prospectors shot the gold from a helicopter.

18. 1807: Lewis and Clark broke up when Meriwether Lewis admitted he wanted to see other continents.

19. 1921: Gene Roddenberry was born. He created *Star Trek*, and generations of awkward nerds with no social skills.
20. 1859: Darwin published his *On the Origin of Species*. However, it doesn't even mention hobbits, Klingons, or Cylons, so what the hell?
21. 1858: The first Lincoln-Douglas debate was held. The debate format was birdcalls.
22. 1920: Ray Bradbury was born. He wrote *Fahrenheit 451*, which was about what should happen to every copy of *Fifty Shades of Grey*.
23. 2011: Muammar Gaddafi was overthrown as both leader of Libya and winner of the World's Best Muumuu competition.
24. 1891: Thomas Edison patented the motion picture camera. Sadly, this led directly to Nicolas Cage screaming about bees.
25. 1930: Sean Connery was born. He was not only the first James Bond, he was the original Weezy Jefferson.
26. 1920: The Nineteenth Amendment to the U.S. Constitution was declared in effect. Women could now vote, which led directly to Senator Leif Garrett some 50 years later.
27. 1908: Lyndon Johnson was born. He was the thirty-sixth U.S. president but was unable to end the war in Vietnam or free Hogan's Heroes from the Nazis.
28. 2009: It was found that most of those who deny the existence of global warming are the descendants of those who denied the existence of global roundness.
29. 2005: Hurricane Katrina slammed into New Orleans. FEMA is still hoping to get bottled water to the Superdome by the end of 2027.
30. 1797: Mary Wollstonecraft Shelley was born. She wrote the book *Frankenstein* and performed the cool-ass drum solo in the Edgar Winter Group's number one hit "Frankenstein."
31. 1803: Lewis and Clark began

their journey west by making some really sweet mix tapes, with lots of Foghat and Molly Hatchet.

> **⮕ Fact-Like Fact**
>
> **Clark almost left the expedition when Lewis insisted on not fast-forwarding through "Sister Christian."**

SEPTEMBER

1. 1939: Germany invaded Poland. The Nazis were after Poland's secret lightbulb-changing technology.
2. 1969: The first ATM opened. The next day, they invented charging you $2.75 to get at your own damn money, the bastards.
3. 1777: The Americans and the British fought the Battle of Cooch's Bridge, as both sides desperately wanted a bridge that led to Cooch.
4. 1957: Ford introduced the Edsel, which was a car filled with New Coke.
5. 1638: Louis XIV of France was born. He was later succeeded by his son, Louis CK.
6. 1620: The Pilgrims set sail on the *Mayflower.* They were escaping persecution for their nothing-but-turkey-and-stuffing-and-cranberry-sauce diet.
7. 1936: Buddy Holly was born. Surprisingly, Buddy Holly did not look just like Buddy Holly, nor were you Mary Tyler Moore.
8. 1974: Gerald Ford pardoned Richard Nixon. Even more controversially, Ford also pardoned that crappy "Billy, Don't Be a Hero" song.
9. 1828: Leo Tolstoy was born. He wrote *War and Peace* and the much less successful *War and Mayonnaise.*
10. 2000: The musical *Cats* closed after more than 7,000 performances and 600,000 hairballs.
11. 2001: It was a very, very bad day.
12. 2011: Martial law was declared in Philadelphia by the mayor of a Starbucks on FourSquare.
13. 1985: Super Mario Brothers was released. Twenty-five years later, the Disalmanacarian still

has no idea what castle the damn princess is in.

Theodore Roosevelt. As president, he required all Americans to shoot an elephant in their pajamas.

14. 1901: Theodore Roosevelt became our youngest president, until 1990's brief, disastrous President Screech debacle.

15. 2008: Lehman Brothers filed for bankruptcy—just the financial kind; they have yet to declare moral bankruptcy, the bastards.

16. 1959: Xerox introduced the first photocopier, revolutionizing how we showed people our naked butts.

17. 1862: The Union defeated the Confederacy at Antietam, but it went into triple overtime.

18. 1793: The cornerstone of the U.S. Capitol was laid by George Washington, while the slaves building it were laid by Thomas Jefferson.

19. 1995: The *New York Times* published the Unabomber's Manifesto, which read simply, "That drawing of the guy in the sunglasses and hoodie is supposed to be ME? I so do not look like that! Do I? I'd like to think I'm thinner than that."

20. 1982: NFL players went on strike, demanding better conditions for their dogfights.

21. 1937: J.R.R. Tolkien's *The Hobbit* was published, though Orcs call the book *That Sawed-Off Bastard.*

22. 1975: Someone tried to assassinate Gerald Ford by leaving a banana peel and some roller skates on the Oval Office floor.

23. 1949: Bruce Springsteen was

THE DAYS OF THE DAMN YEAR

born. He became "The Boss" after several years as "The Assistant Regional Manager."

24. 1936: Jim Henson was born. He created the Muppets, including Kermit, the Swedish Chef, and Newt Gingrich.

25. 1789: Congress passed the Bill of Rights. This was pretty much the last time Congress did anything useful, ever.

26. 1849: Ivan Pavlov was born. His dogs were not salivating at the sound of a bell, but because dogs drool all the damn time.

27. 1964: The Warren Commission issued its report on the JFK assassination. Turns out, Oliver Stone did it.

28. 551 BC: Confucius was born. He came up with the central tenet of Eastern philosophy, "Nickelback really sucks."

29. 1911: Italy declared war on the Ottoman Empire. Italy lost and is now ruled by small, cushy furniture.

30. 1791: Mozart's opera *The Magic Flute* premiered. Operas about phallic symbols were *huge*.

OCTOBER

1. 1795: Belgium was conquered by France, which had to be, like, totally embarrassing for Belgium.

2. 1869: Mahatma Gandhi was born. Originally, the title role in the film *Gandhi* was to be played by Arnold Schwarzenegger, which would have been so much better.

3. 1990: West and East Germany reunified as a united Germany. Now we're all screwed.

4. 1957: The USSR launched Sputnik, the first man-made satellite, into orbit. All the natural satellites laughed and made fun of Sputnik's stupid radio antennae and dumb silver-zinc batteries.

5. 1943: Steve Miller was born. Some people call him Maurice; these people are idiots.

6. 1889: Thomas Edison showed his first motion picture. Sadly, it was *Little Fockers*.

⟩ Fact-Like Fact

Edison stole the idea of *Little Fockers* from Nikola Tesla.

49

7. 1996: Fox News Channel debuted on television. Before this, you could only receive Fox News by wearing a special tinfoil hat.

8. 1939: Paul Hogan was born. He appeared in the popular *Crocodile Dundee* movies and the hugely unpopular *Tapeworm Steve* films.

9. 2006: North Korea announced it had tested a nuclear device, though it turned out to be merely a microwave with a fork in it.

9. 1940: John Lennon was born. In the Beatles, he was the fucking awesome one.

10. 2000: Zoologists successfully returned John Oates's mustache to the wild.

11. 1975: *Saturday Night Live* debuted on NBC. Sadly, this led directly to *Deuce Bigelow: Male Gigolo.*

12. 1492: Christopher Columbus landed in the Bahamas; he thought it was China. Yes, the New World was discovered by a total moron.

13. 1925: Margaret Thatcher was born. Thatcher is considered to be the most popular of Ronald Reagan's many drag characters.

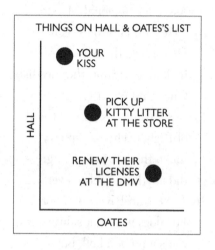

14. 1947: Chuck Yeager broke the sound barrier when he played the album *Yoko Ono/Plastic Ono Band.*

15. 1844: Philosopher Friedrich Nietzsche was born. He said "God is dead—it was Colonel Mustard in the library with the candlestick!"

16. 1793: Marie Antoinette was beheaded for advocating cake-eating.

17. 1972: Eminem was born. In rap music, Eminem is the white Vanilla Ice.

18. 1931: Thomas Edison died. He passed away before he could perfect his final invention,

something he called "electric boogaloo."

19. 1987: The stock market plunged on news that a poor person found a nickel on the sidewalk in front of the 7-Eleven.

20. 1803: The U.S. Senate approved the Louisiana Purchase, though if they'd known about Arkansas they definitely would have reconsidered.

20. 1973: The Sydney Opera House opened, with performances of *Shrimp on the Barbie of Seville* and *Die Flederfoster's*.

21. 1980: Kim Kardashian was born, or hatched, or burst out of a dude's chest, or however we keep getting all these Kardashians.

22. 1962: The Cuban Missile Crisis began, with a jump to the left and then a step to the right.

24. 1945: The United Nations was founded, as an organization dedicated to doing pretty much jack shit.

25. 1881: Pablo Picasso was born.

He painted *Is That Supposed to Be Three Musicians? Really? Because It Looks Like a Bunch of Random Crap to Me.*

26. 1774: The first Continental Congress adjourned after agreeing that yes, they were in fact a congress located on a continent.

27. 1932: Sylvia Plath was born. She wrote the influential book *Can Someone Please Hurry Up and Invent Prozac?*

28. 1636: Harvard was founded so that rich douche bags could have someplace to hang out for four years.

29. 1929: The Great Depression began when the stock market put on that one Morrissey album.

▶ Fact-Like Fact

You know, the one with "November Spawned a Monster"? So yeah.

30. 1938: Orson Welles broadcast *The War of the Worlds*. Many actually believed New Jersey had fallen to space aliens, and celebrated.

31. 1941: Mount Rushmore was completed. It was immediately criticized, as the four faces look nothing like the Beatles. WTF?

NOVEMBER

1. 1512: Michelangelo's ceiling of the Sistine Chapel was first shown to the public. They preferred his earlier, funnier ceilings.
2. 1889: North Dakota and South Dakota became the thirty-ninth and fortieth states. No one knows which one was first, and nobody gives a damn.
3. 1839: The First Opium War broke out, but ended a few hours later when everyone had nodded off.
4. 1879: Will Rogers was born. He once said, "I never met a man I didn't like. Except Hitler. Screw that guy."
5. 1959: Bryan Adams was born, which means his summer of '69 mostly involved eating Franken Berry and watching *Scooby-Doo*.
6. 1861: James Naismith was born. He invented basketball, which somehow led to that movie where Shaquille O'Neal plays a genie.
7. 1867: Marie Curie was born. She won two Nobel prizes: one for her pioneering work with radiation and another later for her glow-in-the-dark liver.
7. 2000: Al Gore was elected president of the United States. Then things got complicated.
9. 1934: Carl Sagan was born. He was billions and billions of times smarter than those who believe the universe is only 600 years old.
10. 1969: *Sesame Street* premiered. It taught children to play with that thing that lives in the trash can.
11. 1918: World War I ended, with a cliffhanger that totally set up the sequel.
12. 1840: Auguste Rodin was born. He sculpted *The Thinker*, which is the opposite of a statue of Sean Hannity.
13. 1775: U.S. forces captured Montreal. Why didn't we keep it? Beats the crap out of Arkansas.

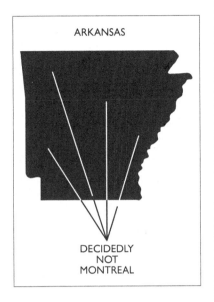

ARKANSAS

DECIDEDLY
NOT
MONTREAL

14. 1851: Herman Melville's *Moby-Dick* was first published. Due to censorship, it was originally titled *Moby Pee Pee*.

15. 1887: Artist Georgia O'Keeffe was born. Her paintings of vaginas often include subliminal cattle skulls and flowers.

16. 42 BC: Roman emperor Tiberius was born. His greatest accomplishment: becoming Captain Kirk's middle name.

17. 1942: Martin Scorsese was born. He's at work on a sequel to one of his classic films, *Taxi Driver 2: Spring Break!*

18. 2008: Scarlett Johansson gave up her lifelong effort to develop a second facial expression.

19. 1863: Abraham Lincoln gave the Gettysburg Address. Then they asked for his Gettysburg Social Security number, and he realized the whole thing was an Internet scam. But it was too late; the entire U.S. treasury had been transferred to a bank in Nigeria.

20. 1985: Microsoft released Windows 1.0. Before this, sucking did not exist.

21. 1877: Thomas Edison invented the phonograph. Unfortunately, this led directly to "Come Sail Away" by Styx.

22. 1963: John F. Kennedy was assassinated by approximately 487 individuals, organizations, and cartoon ducks, if you believe all the conspiracy theories. Seriously, people. It's called Occam's Razor; look into it.

23. 1963: *Doctor Who* debuted on the BBC. For a brief period in the 1980s, the doctor was portrayed by that guy who

played Balki on *Perfect Strangers.*

24. 1990: The Environmental Protection Agency shut down Vanilla Ice over concerns about excessive hair gel.

25. 1986: The Iran-Contra scandal erupted on a very special episode of *The Cosby Show.*

26. 1922: Charles Schulz was born. He created the comic strip *Peanuts*, which led directly to the need for antidepressants.

27. 1942: Jimi Hendrix was born. Man, if he knew about Justin Bieber, he'd bust out of his grave and exact some sweet zombie revenge.

29. 1963: The Beatles released "I Want to Hold Your Hand." Tragically, this led directly to "Ebony and Ivory."

30. 1874: Winston Churchill was born. During World War II, he said that thing that made people be, like, yeah.

DECEMBER

1. 1945: That guy from that thing was born. No, the other guy. Yes, him.

2. 1981: Britney Spears was born. She is to blame for everyone knowing who the hell Kevin Federline is.

3. 1818: Illinois became a state. Just like every other state in the union, its capital is Springfield.

▶ Fact-Like Fact

Scientists now believe there is just one Springfield that, through Type II-A String Theory, exists in multiple places and times.

4. AD 771: Charlemagne became king of the Franks, which meant he got all the hot dogs he could eat for life. Win!

5. 1848: The Gold Rush began. Somehow, this led to Mr. T.

6. 1849: Harriet Tubman escaped from slavery by jumping a Jet Ski through a burning barn, machine guns blazing. *So cool!*

7. 1941: The Japanese attacked

Pearl Harbor. Sadly, not with Hello Kitty.

7. 1787: Delaware became the first state, which was not exactly an auspicious start for the United States.

8. 1863: Lincoln announced Reconstruction, with plans to redo the South's bathroom with a Danish Modern influence.

9. 1934: Dame Judi Dench was born. She has played Queen Victoria, Queen Elizabeth I, and Queen Latifah.

10. 1817: Mississippi became a state. Even though there were only 20 states then, Mississippi still ranked forty-seventh in education.

11. 1816: Indiana became a state. Indiana's state bird is the cardinal, while its state emotion is bored shitless.

12. 1915: Frank Sinatra was born. He sang the inspirational classic "My Way (Or I'll Have the Mob Shoot Your Dog)."

13. 2000: George W. Bush claimed the presidency 36 days after the election once the Supreme Court ruled on the landmark case *The Son of Our Friend George vs. That Boring Guy Who Didn't Even Invent the Internet.*

14. 1819: Alabama became a state. Their dictator-for-life is Larry the Cable Guy.

15. AD 37: Nero was born. It's bad enough he played the fiddle while Rome burned, but he was playing "The Devil Went Down to Georgia."

Ludwig van Beethoven. His Fifth Symphony is the most famous song from *Schoolhouse Rock.*

16. 1770: Ludwig van Beethoven was born. Unbelievably, he was deaf by the time he wrote his final piece, the *Really Loud and Annoying Atonal Symphony*.

17. 1873: Writer Ford Maddox Ford was born. Crazy cattle could cross the river near his car dealership, the Ford Maddox Ford Ford Mad Ox Ford.

18. 1787: New Jersey became a state. They call themselves "the Garden State" because they are living a sad, sad lie.

19. 1843: Dickens's *A Christmas Carol* was first published. Everyone thought Tiny Tim was an annoying little twerp back then, too.

20. 1860: South Carolina seceded from the Union. We're still not 100 percent convinced we needed it back.

21. 1937: *Snow White and the Seven Dwarfs* premiered. Controversially, Disney re-edited the film so that Greedo shoots Dopey first.

22. 2010: Don't Ask, Don't Tell was repealed. However, Don't Go Breakin' My Heart remains in effect.

23. 2001: Congress changed "three French hens" to "three freedom hens."

24. 1814: The War of 1812 ended when someone said, "Dude, 1812 was, like, two years ago. What the hell?"

25. 1965: The Grinch's heart grew three sizes, causing his chest to explode and covering little Cindy Lou Who in green Grinch guts.

25. AD 1: Jesus was born. That jerk who got him myrrh totally went to Hell.

26. 1846: The Donner Party turned to cannibalism. They hadn't actually departed for California yet; they just couldn't wait for dinner.

27. 1979: Soviet forces seized Afghanistan. At least they had the good sense to leave after 10 years, unlike some countries.

28. 1856: Woodrow Wilson was born. He won the 1912 presidential election after

William Taft ate Theodore Roosevelt during a debate.

29. 2010: Newark mayor Cory Booker flew against the Earth's rotation in order to go back in time and prevent a huge blizzard from decimating his city. And then Tweeted about it.

30. 1851: Asa Griggs Candler was born. He developed Coca-Cola, because he wanted a form of cocaine kids could drink at McDonald's.

31. 1862: West Virginia became a state, which immediately lowered our national IQ by 32 percent.

Holidays

Everyone loves holidays! That is, everyone except for the Disalmanacarian's eighth-grade science teacher, Mr. Woodhull. But then, Mr. Woodhull also hated puppies. Went to prison for it, actually. Mr. Woodhull defrauded thousands of puppies out of their life savings in a crooked real estate scheme. Who

knew puppies had so much ready cash to invest?

Federal Holidays in the USA

There are 10 federal holidays during the year, which is exactly 355 too few (356 in a Leap Year).

POPULAR NEW YEAR'S RESOLUTIONS

GO ON A DIET | EXERCISE | NEVER MIX VODKA AND MOTOR OIL AGAIN

New Year's Day (January 1): This is the day you wake up hungover, wearing only your socks and your year 2000-whatever glasses. Yes, you're still in Times Square, sleeping in a pile of those stupid Dr. Seuss-y hats in the gutter underneath the giant picture of Puff Daddy. Way to start the year, asswipe.

Martin Luther King Jr. Day (Third Monday in January): This holiday marks the birth of the great Civil Rights leader, whose "I Have a Dream" speech inspired millions. His dream: he was late for his chemistry final, even though he thought he had dropped the class. He was flying to class, but he was flying backward. Plus, he was naked, and everyone could see his little Luther and was laughing.

Presidents' Day (Third Monday in February): This day was originally set aside to honor George Washington only, but then people were all like, "Oh, that's right by Abe Lincoln's birthday, let's honor him, too." And that opened the floodgate: Theodore Roosevelt and James Madison wanted in on that action, and so did Andrew Jackson and Rutherford B. Hayes. Even William Henry Harrison, who was only president for 30 days! So now we have to honor *all* the presidents that day. Even the sucky ones. And

George Washington's kind of pissed, you guys.

Memorial Day (Last Monday in May): This is the day we honor the sacrifice of those who died protecting the United States of America, by watching cars in Indianapolis go around in a circle for approximately 14 hours, hoping for a flaming tire or two to relieve the tedium. Thank you, soldiers.

Independence Day (July 4): This is the birthday of our nation. Americans usually celebrate with fireworks, while the *1812 Overture* is played. Of course, fireworks were invented in China, while the *1812 Overture* was written to mark Russia's victory over Napoleon. USA! USA!

Labor Day (First Monday in September): This is the day all Americans try to remember what it was like to have a job.

Columbus Day (Second Monday in October): This holiday celebrates Christopher Columbus, one of billions of humans who never set foot on American soil in their lives.

Veterans Day (November 11): Contrary to popular belief, this is not the day you buy a present for the guy who fixed your cat.

Thanksgiving (Fourth Thursday in November): Traditionally, this is the day families come together to give thanks that no one has to talk to one another as long as the game is on.

⟩ Fact-Like Fact

At the first Thanksgiving, Pilgrims and Native Americans cheered as actual lions defeated actual bears, 24–7.

Christmas (December 25): This Christian holiday marks the day that Jesus was disappointed because his dad didn't get him that bike he wanted. Again.

Lesser Holidays

These are not official get-the-day-off holidays. Unless you call in sick like everyone else does.

April Fool's Day (April 1): This is a day of practical jokes. We do not approve. Only the worst sort of human being would make a joke of everything and expect you to believe it as a fact.

Arbor Day (Last Friday in April): Arbor Day is devoted to the lost art of arbing. Go arb the crap out of some stuff today!

Ben Franklin also invented sticking your tongue on a frozen flagpole, the nimrod.

Daylight Savings Time (First Sunday in March): Ben Franklin invented the idea of daylight savings time. But then, Ben Franklin thought flying a kite in a thunderstorm would be the best idea ever.

Election Day (Tuesday after the first Monday in November): Every four years, Americans vote for their choice for president on Election Day. The choice is usually between You Cannot Be Serious and No Way in Hell, though sometimes a third candidate, such as You Have Got to Be Kidding Me or This Is a Sick Joke, Right? slips in there. Choose wisely!

Father's Day (Third Sunday in June): This is the day all Americans sit in a bar, drinking cheap whiskey and wondering where the father they haven't seen since 1982 is.

Flag Day (June 14): The day we honor the American flag, the old Stars and Stripes. If you're a politician running for office, try not to poop on the flag and then light it on fire, OK? Easy, big fella.

Groundhog Day (February 2): Groundhog Day marks the occasion in 1888 when Thomas Edison invented the groundhog, which revolutionized the entire varmint industry.

Halloween (October 31): Hey, parents? Just buy your kids a big bag of those little Snickers bars and leave the rest of us out of it. Also: nobody likes candy corn, so adjust your purchases accordingly.

Kwanzaa (December 26– January 1): This seven-day observance of African-American heritage and culture features the lighting of candles and ends with the extremely solemn ceremonial Wearing of the Bill Cosby Sweater.

Mother's Day (Second Sunday in May): On Mother's Day, all Americans phone home. They try to remember to call early, because she's usually into the wine by one p.m.

St. Patrick's Day (March 17): This great religious figure is honored annually by drinking until you puke up your large intestine (hence the term, "wearin' o' the green").

Random Bonus Fact!

BEN GREENMAN, *NEW YORKER* EDITOR AND NOVELIST

Octopi use seven different techniques to gain entry to hard-shelled prey: they may pull it apart; bite it open; drill through the shell with their beak; release a cloud of mild acid that dissolves the shell; produce a high-pitched "whinesong" that cracks the shell in much the same way that a soprano singer can crack a wineglass; beg; or wait.

St. Valentine's Day (February 14): St. Valentine's Day is for lovers, who usually mark the day by shooting up a Chicago garage filled with 1920s gangsters. You know, for love.

Religious Holidays

These are the most holy days of America's major religions. Your mileage may vary.

MAJOR CHRISTIAN HOLIDAYS

Christmas marks the birth of Jesus Christ in Bethlehem and is still celebrated much as it was 2,000 years ago: stores put up decorations before Halloween, and you have to hear Mariah Carey's damn Christmas album approximately 60,000 times daily until you wish for the sweet release of death.

Good Friday marks Jesus's Crucifixion. This seems like the opposite of "good" to us.

Easter is the celebration of Christ's Resurrection from the dead. After Jesus was crucified, he came back to life three days later and hid eggs in his backyard while wearing a giant bonnet. Obviously.

MAJOR JEWISH HOLIDAYS

Rosh Hashanah is Jewish New Year's. Be sure to kiss your rabbi at the stroke of midnight!

Yom Kippur is the Day of Atonement. Because, you know, you really shouldn't be smooching your rabbi. We know sometimes one thing can lead to another, but let's behave ourselves, OK?

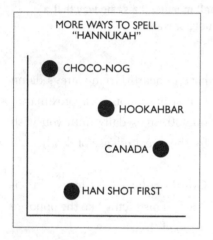

MORE WAYS TO SPELL "HANNUKAH"

CHOCO-NOG

HOOKAHBAR

CANADA

HAN SHOT FIRST

Hanukkah (also spelled Channukah, Hockeymom, Chakakhan, Honkycat, Cthulhuthon, and Comic-Con) is an eight-day observance of figuring out what the exact name of this holiday is.

MAJOR MUSLIM HOLIDAYS

Ramadan is a month-long observance that involves fasting from sunrise to sunset daily—no food or beverages, no sexual relations, and

no evil actions. But of course, after sunset it's one big Par-Tay. Whooo!

Eid al-Fitr is the day Muslims get together to feast and to discuss how to best freak out small-minded idiots and bigots in the Midwest and South about Islam. Good times!

MAJOR ATHEIST HOLIDAYS

The main atheist holiday is **Nothingmas**. Atheists give gifts that remind the recipient that after you die, there is absolutely nothing. The gift that best communicates this idea: Mariah Carey's Christmas album.

Unofficial Holidays

These are holidays in the sense that you are really, really desperate for an excuse to drink in public, possibly wearing a silly hat, aren't you?

Bloomsday (June 16): June 16 is the date of the action of James Joyce's massive novel *Ulysses*. On Bloomsday, this novel is celebrated by the four people worldwide who've read the entire thing. Actually, make that three, as one of them died last year in the middle of some hot James Joyce cosplay sex.

Cinco de Mayo (May 5): Cinco de Mayo, Spanish for "excuse to drink way too much with your co-workers and be really, really sorry the next day," is an excuse to drink way too much with your coworkers and be really, really sorry the next day.

4/20 (April 20):
Dude. Duuuuuuuuude. Dude.

Record Store Day (Third Saturday of April): This is the day to celebrate records! Records were like if your iPod only had 10 songs on it, or if Spotify only had *Bachman-Turner Overdrive's Greatest Hits*.

Talk Like a Pirate Day (September 19): This recent holiday is celebrated by saying things like, "Arrrrr, thar be a filthy bilge rat on my bunghole! Arrrr!" until you get kicked hard in the yardarm.

Lumberjack Day (September 26): This is a day to remember all the great contributions that lumberjacks have made to society. Oh, who are we kidding? It's just an excuse to eat flapjacks for dinner, wear a fake lumberjack beard, and enjoy family-oriented lumberjack activities like Chain Saw Jousting.

PART TWO

The United States

The United States of America is located in North America, just south of that one country and just north of that other country. There are oceans, too.

U.S. History

The United States of America has a long history. There were some people, and there were some places. That one guy, with the hair? What a time.

Here is a quick history of America. Memorize this for your AP history exam! Note: Disalmanac and the Disalmanacarian are not legally responsible if your AP history score is a negative integer.

Pre-Columbian America: A Period of Time

Technically, the present day is still pre-Columbian America, seeing how Christopher Columbus has still never set foot on the North American con-

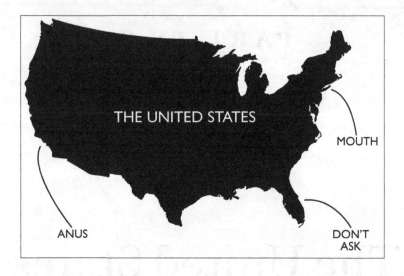

THE UNITED STATES

MOUTH

ANUS

DON'T ASK

tinent. How do you miss an entire continent, Columbus? Get a GPS, dude.

Anyway, before the arrival of Europeans, America was nice. Native Americans had some nice civilizations going, buffalo were plenty, and there were majestic mountains and great plains and beautiful waterfalls.

Then those asshat Europeans started showing up in the 1500s and pretty much ruined everything. Thanks, Europe.

Jamestown: What Could Possibly Go Wrong?

In 1607, England sent about a hundred of their laziest and most clueless aristocrats to take over the entire North American continent. They started the Jamestown colony in Virginia, and immediately got to work; a year later, only 39 of them were still alive, and the period known as "the starving time" hadn't even started yet.

Of course, maybe there wouldn't have been a "starving time" if (a) they hadn't tried to farm in a swamp, and (b) they'd sent along someone with a little farming experience, instead of a bunch of spoiled, rich landed-gentry gits.

And yet somehow, improbably, these few plucky settlers managed to piss off the local Native Americans—maybe because they kidnapped the chief's daughter Pocahantas and forced her to marry some sickly British guy even though she was only 14. Just a thought.

How this tiny band of nitwits took over this continent is still a mystery, but here we are.

The *Mayflower*: What *Else* Could Possibly Go Wrong?

In November of 1620, the Pilgrims landed at Plymouth Rock in Massachusetts, because hey, starting a colony in Massachusetts as winter sets in? Smooth move, Ex-Lax. Seriously, once you got the *Mayflower* to Massachusetts, you couldn't turn the ship south and sail until you found somewhere warm and nice, like the Bahamas?

But no, the Pilgrims wanted to settle where there was already four feet of snow. "Let's starve to death and/or get eaten by hungry wolves and bears," they may have been heard to exclaim with joy.

The only reason they survived at all was thanks to the help of nearby Native Americans, who showed the Pilgrims how to farm and not die and crap. In gratitude, the Pilgrims made the Native Americans a big meal. This was the first Thanksgiving, and it was a complete disaster.

First, there was the food. The Pilgrims made a pie with peanuts in the crust, even though the Wampanoags had told them, like, a million times, that Massasoit was allergic. Worse, Massasoit forgot his auto-injector and swelled up as soon as someone mentioned peanuts. Plus, the Wampanoags brought mashed potatoes, and everyone knows that the Mayflower Compact states, "Stuffing, insteadde of ye Potatoes."

**Myles Standish, King of
the Pilgrim Dudes.**

Things got worse when everyone sat down to eat. Myles Standish wanted everyone to hurry so he could get back to watching the game, because, "Dammitte, I haveth five pelts of fine beaver fur on the Lions." This made Roger Williams cry out, "I toileth away in a hotte kitchen all day, and this is ye thanks I get?" and then run weeping from the table. Squanto chose this moment to announce that he had had an important personal revelation and wanted everyone to address him

as "Barbara" from now on. The Pilgrims and the Wampanoags then started chucking biscuits and sweet potatoes at one another. Jonathan Smith said, "I shalt not cleaneth this shit up."

Everyone was glad when the meal finally ended, which is the true meaning of Thanksgiving.

The Salem Witch Trials: Build a Bridge Out of Her

In 1692, a sort of mass hysteria gripped several towns in Massachusetts, including Salem Town, Salem Village, Salem Settlement, Salem Forest, Salem Farms, and Salem Town 2: The Saleming. Young women started acting strangely: they would scream, contort themselves and cry out. While today's medical community recognizes these as classic symptoms of Beatlemania, seventeenth-century physicians assumed the cause was witchcraft.

Suddenly, dozens of men and women were accused of witchcraft, even as far away as Salem Salem Bo Balem. Several confessed to witchcraft and were condemned to death. Later, it turned out there weren't really any witches at all; apparently, it was just a big old misunderstanding, and boy, did everyone feel really stupid the next day! Sales of "Sorry We Hanged Your Wife" cards shot up 300 percent overnight.

Ben Franklin: Famous Guy

In 1730s Philadelphia, a young man named Benjamin Franklin began publishing *Poor Richard's Almanack*, which contained such homespun colonial wisdom as "A penny saved is a penny earned," and "Ow! Don't step on my toe, I've got the Gout!"

Franklin was also a scientist and inventor. For instance, he flew a kite in a thunderstorm, thus discovering third-degree burns.

But by the late 1750s, Franklin was urging his fellow colonists in a new direction: having lots of mistresses. Oh, and independence.

Before the Revolution: Britain Is Very Mean!

Great Britain was really starting to piss off the colonies by 1765, when Parliament passed the Stamp Act. The Stamp Act forced all colonists to start an unfathomably dull stamp collection and to talk about it for hours and hours, boring everyone within earshot.

▶ Fact-Like Fact

The worst thing about the Stamp Act: all those disgruntled postal workers.

Tensions increased in 1770 with the Boston Massacre. British soldiers killed five colonial civilians who refused to discuss which King George III stamp they liked better—the young, handsome King George or the older, fatter King George in the white jumpsuit.

In 1773, Parliament taxed tea. This was the final straw for both of the colonists who actually liked tea, so the Sons of Liberty protested with the Boston Tea Party. In the middle of the night, a bunch of wealthy lawyers and merchants dressed up like Indians and dumped all the tea into Boston Harbor in order to protest taxation without representation. This was the forerunner of today's Tea Party movement, except that now the wealthy guys are actually really, really well represented in Congress (though they do dress up like Indians sometimes, just for fun).

Anyway, Parliament was pissed, so they responded with the Intolerable Acts, the Somewhat Unbearable Acts, and the Really Quite Unpleasant Acts, We Daresay They're Rather Not Cricket, Jolly What.

This led to the Battles of Lexington and Concord in 1775. Of course, before the battles could start, King George III had to cut a ceremonial ribbon with his giant, jewel-encrusted ceremonial scissors. And then, the winner of season three of *Colonial Idol* sang the national anthem. And then the armies of all the nations marched into the stadium, and Benjamin Franklin jogged in and lit the torch. And then there was the coin toss; the British won, and for some reason elected to kick rather than receive, which is now considered a major military blunder.

Anyway, by this time, it had started raining, so a rain delay was declared and the grounds crew rolled out enormous tarps over the entire colony of Massachusetts. And then there was the sausage race, and by this time, it was getting dark so they rescheduled the battle for sometime in 1787. And by the time 1787 rolled around, the war was already over, so they just canceled the whole damn thing.

And this is why the Battle of Lexington and Concord is considered one of the greatest battles in history.

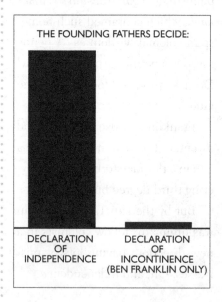

THE FOUNDING FATHERS DECIDE:

DECLARATION OF INDEPENDENCE

DECLARATION OF INCONTINENCE (BEN FRANKLIN ONLY)

The Declaration of Independence: A Thing That Happened

In 1776, the Continental Congress decided it was time to write a Declaration of Independence. They asked Thomas Jefferson to write it, because, as John Adams said, "Jefferson knows, like, lots of words and shit."

Jefferson spent the next several days drafting the Declaration. There were many revisions; eventually, the inspirational words "We hold these truths to be self-evident, that all men are created equal" replaced the even more inspirational "King George can ram it up his hole of arse." King George ramming it up his arse is the true cornerstone of our democracy.

In the end, it didn't matter what the Declaration said, because reading hadn't been invented yet. Everyone signed it (though John Hancock used an enormous joke signature) on July 4, 1776, which America celebrates every year on Columbus Day.

The Revolutionary War: Another Thing That Happened

As it turns out, Britain didn't want the United States to be independent. They sent thousands, or perhaps millions, of troops to the colonies. And this action got results: soon, the British were losing to a ragtag bunch of colonists with little organization, firepower, or, in some cases, clothing. By 1783, the nearly nude colonists had won their clothing-optional war of independence with Britain.

The U.S. Constitution: Now with Extra Freedom!

But now came the tricky part—how were 13 separate states to function as a whole (especially since South Carolina wasn't the sharpest cookie on the continent).

In 1787, delegates from each state met in Philadelphia to draw up a constitution. The U.S. Constitution outlined the kind of government we still have today: slow and filled with dimwits. In 1791, the Bill of Rights became the first 10 amendments to the Constitution. The Bill of Rights guaranteed individual liberties, such as the individual's right to lug around an assault rifle that can kill more people in two seconds than died at the entire Siege of Yorktown. The Founding Fathers would have wanted it that way.

George Washington: A President Guy

George Washington became our first president in 1789. So that was fun.

Slavery: A Bad, Bad Thing

Have we mentioned yet that it was a thing that you could, like, own another human being in several states? So that was seriously messed up.

While slavery was abolished early on in the northern states, there was a growing demand for more and more slaves in the Deep South. This would later lead to perhaps the most defining and iconic period in U.S. history: Ken Burns's Civil War.

The Louisiana Purchase: Does It Come in Loden?

President Thomas Jefferson turned out to be a shrewd real estate man, buying the massive Louisiana Purchase from France for $12 and a handful of escargot. The French: they loves 'em some snails, what are you gonna do?

> ## Fact-Like Fact
>
> Thomas Jefferson refused to buy the service contract with the Louisiana Purchase, so we're stuck with Nebraska as-is.

The Louisiana Purchase was basically a vast, unexplored wasteland, kind of like modern Detroit. Jefferson sent Lewis and Clark west to explore it. Lewis and Clark jumped at the chance, with Lewis saying, "How long can it take to explore half a continent on foot? Like, two weeks?" Besides, it wasn't like Lewis and Clark had a lot else to do besides play Super Mario Brothers in Clark's mom's basement, anyway.

So they set out from St. Louis in 1804, after a hearty breakfast at McDonald's. They also got a few to go, and they each got a large Diet Coke. This held them until they returned, in 1806. And what a day that was! It was after 11 p.m., so they ordered from the late night menu, getting a good deal on Big Macs and fries for under three bucks. Not bad! What an adventure! Wow! Plus, Clark was able to pick up his Super Mario game right where he'd left off *and* save the princess, so: bonus.

The War of 1812: The War with Its Own Overture

It wasn't long until the United States had to suffer through another war, the War of 1812.

Contrary to popular belief, the War of 1812 did not occur in 1812 at all. It happened in 1930—that's when the year 1812, lying in wait the whole time, attacked the United States, plunging us back to a time of powdered wigs and horse-drawn carriages and all that other 1812 crap. Eventually, the year 1978 came back to 1930 to defeat the evil year 1812. But now we're cursed with stuff from the 1970s remaining popular forever. We hope you like "Come Sail Away" by Styx, because it's not going away anytime soon, Slappy.

One good thing came out of the War of 1812: Francis Scott Key wrote our national anthem, "Come Sail Away."

Some Other Damn Stuff Happened, Too

Our fifth president, James Monroe, came up with what he cleverly called the Monroe Doctrine (originally, he called it the Ahem! [Points at Self] Policy). The Monroe Doctrine, which has since become the very cornerstone of American foreign policy of the last 200 years, states: "God damn, the French suck."

In the 1830s, Andrew Jackson (that guy on the $20 bill who everyone thinks is Bea Arthur) forced

Native Americans off their lands and made them march west with everything they owned. This was Jackson's I'm a Horrible, Horrible Excuse for a Human Being Policy. Like the smallpox wasn't bad enough. Jesus, Andrew Jackson.

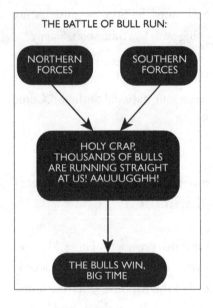

In 1849, gold was discovered in California, so everybody made the months-long trek to go strike it rich. Somehow, this led to those awful *Transformers* movies.

The Civil War: A Merely Average Guns N' Roses Song

My Dearest Eliza:

They say you can tell a man is a captain in this man's army by how many holes he's got in his boots. A captain, the story goes, has two holes in his boots, one for each of his eyes. No, wait. That's not how it goes. He has two holes in his boots, one for each of his testicles. Er, sorry about my salty language, my dearest Eliza, I just want to get this story right. I hope I haven't offended your tender sensibilities.

Wait—OK. It's a general! A general has two boots in his pants, and . . . that doesn't even make sense. Who puts boots in their pants? I beg you please bear with me, my dearest Eliza; it is a fairly humorous anecdote.

So as I was saying, my lovely bit of venison jerky, a sergeant has three holes in his socks. The better to see you with, my dear. That's from something else, isn't it? Dammit.

I apologize deeply, my sweetest little sourdough. I'll check with

Colonel Anderson about the story of the captain with the holes in his britches, or boots. I have another story about a rear admiral, but I'm afraid it's not for mixed company.

In closing, the North won the Civil War.

Yours,

General Ulysses S. Grant (drunk)

1866–1920: A Period of Time

Nobody knows what happened during this time. There were some beefy men with enormous mustaches. That's about it.

The Roaring Twenties: Stop with the Roaring Already, Some of Us Have to Work in the Morning

Things finally got more interesting in 1920. Women were allowed to vote for the first time, which is why America was later forced to endure the extremely brief and turbulent presidency of Leif Garrett in the late 1970s.

The 1920s were a time of great prosperity for America. "The business of America is business," said President Calvin Coolidge. Then he demanded that someone pull his finger before ripping a huge one right in the Oval Office. They had to leave the windows open overnight.

This was the Jazz Age, when flappers jitterbugged and 23 skidoo'ed a shrimp on the barbie or some shit. Historians and speech pathologists believe there was some sort of aphasia rampant that made people speak random words.

Random Bonus Fact!

EMO PHILIPS, COMEDIAN

It's a myth that tortoises live a long time. They're just all really good at identity theft.

The 1920s were also the era of Prohibition. The manufacture, sale, import, export, and juggling of alcoholic beverages was prohibited by the Eighteenth Amendment to the Constitution. And yet, alcohol was easily available at neighborhood "speakeasies." Many were run by organized crime figures like Al Capone, who controlled all bootlegging in 37 states, six Canadian provinces, most of Europe, and the planet Neptune.

A few years later, Prohibition itself would be prohibited. Well, mostly—it is still illegal today to juggle alcoholic beverages. If you are discovered doing so, you can be sent to Guantánamo as a potential terrorist. You've been warned.

The Roaring Twenties were basically one huge party (or, in 1920s parlance, "a fine how-do-you-do wit da big palooka, toots"), but that party ended in late 1929.

The Great Depression: Morrissey's Favorite Time

In October 1929, the stock market suddenly fell several hundred points. Desperate Wall Street bankers jumped out of windows. Even more desperate Wall Street bankers ran straight through the walls, leaving cartoon-like desperate Wall Street banker–shaped holes. It was a bad, bad time, especially if you were walking on the sidewalk below. Ouch.

This market crash triggered the largest economic downturn in U.S. history, the Great Depression. Millions of people were suddenly thrown out of work, and they couldn't even spend all day watching *The Jerry Springer Show* and *Maury*, because no one had invented either Jerry or Maury yet.

President Herbert Hoover tried to fix things with the Smoot-Hawley Act, which made it illegal to smoot one's hawley in public. Sadly, the Smoot-Hawley Act actually worsened the Great Depression, as America's economy is based on hawley-smooting.

Another blow to America's economy in the early 1930s was the great drought that led to the Dust Bowl. The formerly fertile Midwest became a barren wasteland (even more so than today).

Hoover lost the election of 1932 to the charismatic Franklin Roosevelt, who immediately implemented several programs known as the New Deal. The New Deal included important new banking regulations such as the Whatever

You Banks Were Doing in 1929, Cut It the Hell Out Act. The New Deal also included jobs programs such as the Hey, Let's Build Some Dams and Shit Act of 1933. And so we built some dams and shit. Some of that shit is still standing today.

But just as America started to recover, our attention turned to growing crises elsewhere. Good one, the rest of the world.

World War II: The War to End All War Movies

With the rise of Adolf Hitler and Nazi Germany in the 1930s, Europe soon found itself deep in war. America wanted to stay out of the war, telling Germany and the other Axis powers, "You wouldn't like us when we're angry."

Apparently, Japan didn't get the "angry" memo, because they bombed America's naval base at Pearl Harbor, in Hawaii. That was the final straw: America got angry and started turning green. Soon, its rippling muscles had burst out of its shirt (while its miraculous pants somehow stayed on) and America

was in full Hulk Smash mode. The United States pretty much Hulk Smashed its way through Europe, defeating the Nazis in early 1945.

Japan kept fighting, though. But what Japan didn't know was that the United States had been developing a fearsome new weapon, the atomic bomb. And so President Harry Truman ordered atomic bombs to be dropped on two Japanese cities, Hiroshima and Nagasaki. Which: *so not cool*. At all. Yes, this effectively ended the war, but damn, Slappy.

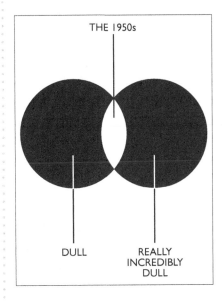

The 1950s: Conform!

The 1950s began with the Korean War. America sent its best wise-cracking surgeons and cross-dressing enlisted men, eventually defeating the North Koreans on penalty shots. The prize for winning this war: American troops are still stationed in South Korea, 60 years later. This certainly bodes well for current U.S. plans in Afghanistan. After World War II, the Soviet Union consolidated its power, and their stated aim of world domination started to worry the United States and other nations who were maybe not so much into the whole being dominated by the Soviet Union thing. The United States, while into hammers, was never all that into sickles.

An arms race began, with both the United States and the Soviets developing more and more missiles, bombs, and warheads. The smallest misunderstanding could suddenly lead to the total annihilation of man. This is why Americans drank so much back then. You would, too, if you and everyone you love could suddenly be vaporized at any in-stant. Actually, this is still true today, which is why you'll always see people chugging a bourbon Slushee morning, noon, and night (not to mention heaping handfuls of Xanax and cough syrup smoothies).

There were even fears that the Communists were infiltrating our own government, trying to bring it down from within. Senator Joseph McCarthy claimed to have a list of Communists within the State Department who needed to be exposed immediately. Later, he said the same thing about his pants, and he was quickly removed from office.

But the 1950s wasn't all just nihilistic, brain-melting fear that we were all going to die. The economy prospered because building all that crap to destroy the planet 400 times over meant jobs, jobs, jobs! Soon, an affluent middle class developed. Families with 2.4 kids wanted nice suburban homes with televisions and modern kitchens and those frozen TV dinners with the Salisbury steak and the peas that always stayed a little frozen and the brownie that was always burnt and the corn that had that weird texture with the little red things in it. What the hell were those? And what do you buy .4 of a kid for his birthday, like, one-quarter of a hula hoop?

Partly due to the new affluence, teenagers emerged as a powerful market force. Their rock-and-roll music swept the land. Elvis Presley became the biggest star of the time with hits like "Look at My Hips (They Are Moving About in a Sexually Suggestive Manner)" and "Seriously, All My Songs Are About Doing It (I Have No Idea How We're Getting Away with This Shit in the Ultraconservative 1950s)."

A new invention called television swept the nation, with hit shows like the sitcom *Leave It to Beaver*, the cop drama *Cooter & Vajayjay*, and *Snatch Hoo-ha, P.I.*

Later in the 1950s, the Civil Rights Movement started to pick up steam. In part of the United States (we don't want to name names, but it rhymes with "the Schmouth"), blacks still lagged behind whites economically. Blacks were still discriminated against in jobs, housing, and the ability to have a hit song with "Tutti Frutti" (see the landmark Supreme Court case, *Little*

Richard v. Pat Boone, Who Is Seriously the Whitest Man Who Has Ever Existed, I Mean, Damn).

▶ Fact-Like Fact

Cold War tensions reached a high in 1956 when the Soviets refused to leave anything to Beaver.

In 1955, Rosa Parks refused to move to the back of the bus to make room for a white passenger, which led to anger nationwide about how much having to take the bus home from work just plain sucks. And in 1957, Arkansas governor Orval Faubus called out the National Guard to prevent nine black students from making fun of his silly name.

As the 1950s closed, outgoing president Dwight Eisenhower warned against the rise of the "military-industrial complex," hoping it might be replaced with a "cookies-and-ice-cream complex." Sadly, his hope has not come to pass, because we could really go for some Chubby Hubby and a giant, chewy chocolate-chip cookie right about now. Or really, anytime. We just want ice cream and cookies. Is that so wrong?

The 1960s: You Baby Boomers Know That the Doors Sucked, Right?

John F. Kennedy swept into office in 1960, with two stated aims: to land a man on the moon by the end of the decade and to land himself on Marilyn Monroe's nether region as ASAP as possible. NASA got to work on both missions immediately.

But soon, Kennedy had to stare down nuclear Armageddon itself with the Cuban Missile Crisis. Historians agree that this was the closest the Cold War came to becoming an all-out nuclear war, with both sides most likely destroying each other and much of the world's population in the process. Finally, both sides stepped back from the very brink of the nuclear abyss when Hollywood bombshell Jayne Mansfield agreed to go on a double-date with Soviet premier Nikita Khrush-

chev and Kennedy and Monroe, but "no funny business."

Sadly, John F. Kennedy was assassinated in November 1963 in a motorcade in Dallas. There are still many theories about who might have been responsible for Kennedy's death—some believe the Cubans were involved, or the CIA and organized crime figures. Today, historians believe the entire assassination was orchestrated by the cast of TV's *Gilligan's Island*. A sailor hat and a red shirt were discovered in the book depository, while a rifle made completely out of bamboo and coconuts was found on the grassy knoll. Can you prove otherwise? We didn't think so.

The great speaker Martin Luther King Jr. made millions aware of the civil rights issue, not to mention the importance of keeping a dream journal, because that "I Have a Dream" dream was pretty awesome, compared to the dreams most people describe in mind-numbing detail (not you, of course).

Anyway, due to Dr. King's efforts, President Lyndon Johnson signed major civil rights legislation, though it all kind of became moot when George W. Bush later signed the Patriot Act. Good luck having any rights now, chump!

Lyndon Johnson also escalated America's presence in a small civil war in Vietnam into a major and highly unpopular U.S. military intervention. American college students protested the war in massive numbers, leading to many arrests and many more really crappy protest songs. By the end of the decade, one of John F. Kennedy's dreams came true—no, not the Marilyn Monroe thing, but putting Americans on the Moon. Millions watched their TVs in July of 1969 as *Apollo 11*'s Neil Armstrong stepped out of the *Eagle* and uttered those inspirational words, "I'm a little teapot, short and stout." He may have been a little oxygen-deprived from the trip.

The very next month, several hundred thousand long-haired young hippies gathered for the biggest concert in rock history, the Woodstock Festival. There was sex, there were drugs, and for all anyone knows, there may have been music. Most of the audience was too busy with the sex and the drugs to even notice. Because really, which would you rather do—have anonymous sex outdoors in the mud with someone while you're flying on Felix the Cat acid, or sit patiently through Crosby, Stills & Nash yammering on about the two cats in their damn yard? Right?

Grand Funk Railroad, secretary-general of the United Nations (1971–1974).

The 1970s: The Arnold Horshack Decade

The 1970s were an awful, awful time: harvest-gold and/or avocado-green kitchen appliances. Lime-green shag carpeting that you had to rake with a big (and matching) plastic rake once a week. That hot dog cooker that cooked wieners by electrocuting the crap out of them, and kids were encouraged to use it because you were a latchkey kid and there was nothing else to eat until Mom got home hours later. Televisions the size of Lincoln Continentals. Cable TV had a total of five channels.

Parents getting divorced, then suddenly a sketchy hippie dude with a motorcycle staying with your mom every night. The sketchy dude's brother moving into the family room with his super-sweet stereo but super-sucky record collection of Three Dog Night and Grand Funk Railroad albums. Finding a jar full of weed in the garage and being too young to know what one was even supposed to do with it; nibbling the corner of a leaf sure as heck didn't

do anything. But that's OK, because your Valium-addicted mom was happy to share with you. Watching terrible cartoons like *Hong Kong Phooey* simply because they were on and there was nothing else to do.

Your seventies may vary, but probably not.

1980–Present: We Give Up

The 1980s were a turbulent time, filled with *Crocodile Dundee* movies and Huey Lewis demanding new drugs. There were asymmetrical haircuts and neon-colored clothing. Basically, it was anarchy. And it was all because in 1980, the United States elected B-movie actor and cigarette spokesmodel Ronald Reagan as president. Yes, the one who was in those movies with the monkey. We know, right?

▶ Fact-Like Fact

In the 1980s, everybody knew your name, and they were always glad that you came. It was all the cocaine.

It was the Reagan administration that finally figured out how to win the Cold War: by spending several metric buttloads of money on missiles and crap. The Soviets couldn't keep up with America's rampant, clinically insane levels of spending, and by 1990 both the Cold War and the Soviet Union were no more. Of course, the United States was now deep in debt to the Chinese. That's the price of freedom—reducing America's credit score from 800 to 12½. USA!

With Russia now a fledgling democracy and an ally, the United States quickly found it needed a new enemy. The U.S. government put on a prime-time reality competition, *America's Next Top Evil Villain*, and the hands-down winner was Iraq's Saddam Hussein. Because, you know: that mustache. President George HVAC Bush immediately attacked Iraq in 1991's Gulf War, which, despite earning high ratings, was not renewed for a second season.

Things were relatively quiet for the United States until 1998, when the House of Representatives decided to impeach President Bill Clinton because he got a blow job and lied about it or some shit. Clinton explained that he did not engage in sexual relations, that it was simply "a mouth-to-penis high-five." Eventually, even the press became bored with wall-to-wall presidential penis coverage and we all finally moved on.

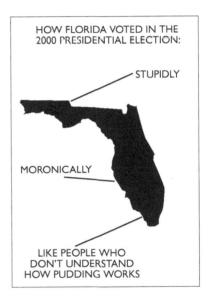

HOW FLORIDA VOTED IN THE 2000 PRESIDENTIAL ELECTION:

STUPIDLY

MORONICALLY

LIKE PEOPLE WHO DON'T UNDERSTAND HOW PUDDING WORKS

The 2000 presidential election between George W. Bush and Al Gore ended up being decided by the Supreme Court, because after 200 plus years of democracy, Florida had apparently *still* not learned how to count. Jesus, Florida. Get your shit together. Why must you embarrass the rest of the nation every few years? Does someone still have the receipt from when we bought Florida from Spain? Do they take returns?

Anyway, the court found in Bush's favor because a majority of the justices had personal ties to either the Bush family or the Bush campaign, or had family members held hostage in Dick Cheney's undisclosed location. Plus, we love Al Gore, we really do, but man: what a pain in the ass that dude is, right? Dang.

And so it was George W. Bush who received the memo entitled *Bin Laden Determined to Strike in United States*. And Bush dealt with the threat by immediately clearing some brush on his ranch. But just a month later, despite Bush's best brush-clearing efforts, Osama bin Laden did strike the United States, on September 11, 2001.

The 9/11 attacks led directly to the U.S. War on Terror. Congress passed the Patriot Act (which, because it suspended the civil rights of U.S. citizens, was really more of a victory for the terrorists, but it does win the Most Accurately Named Bill Award in Opposite Land). George W. Bush sent troops to Afghanistan to find Osama bin Laden and then decided, "I know what let's do—let's *not* find America's number one enemy and instead invade this other country that has exactly jack and shit to do with 9/11!" So that was worthwhile.

But the next president, Barack Obama, did find and kill Osama bin Laden. And now? We're all just waiting around for whatever the hell's next.

Documents of U.S. History

The history of the United States is filled with great documents: the receipt for Abe Lincoln's big-ass hat. John F. Kennedy's awe-inspiring speech. Dan Quayle's diploma for completing most of kindergarten. Barack Obama's birth certificate.

These are the documents that make us what we are: documented Americans. Here are a few of the most important such documents in U.S. history.

The Declaration of Independence

By 1776, the colonists were fed up with British rule. On June 7, at the Continental Congress, Richard Henry Lee of Virginia stood up and said, "God dammit, I've got the Gout again." This somehow led to the appointing of a committee to write a Declaration of Independence, and to sever ties with Britain once and for all.

Thomas Jefferson wrote the Declaration, and it was unanimously adopted on July 4, 1776. Today, we celebrate this day as Independence Day and honor the Founding Fathers by making shit blow up.

About the signers: John Hancock's signature was the largest, as he was a total tool. We get it, John, you like freedom. Jesus. Charles Carroll of Maryland was the last of the signers of the Declaration to die, because he was only three when he signed it (he also drew in the corner an adorable picture of a kitty and a pony-robot with rocket wings).

> ## Fact-Like Fact
>
> Declaration of Independence signer Button Gwinnett was actually Ben Franklin's pet hamster.

Today, some see the Declaration as an inspired philosophical statement about the natural rights of man. Others see it as a strictly legal document, laying out America's indictments against the despotic King George III. Still others see the Declaration as a map to an incredible hidden treasure (OK, this is mostly just Nicolas Cage, but still).

But whatever you believe, everyone agrees the Declaration of Independence is one of the greatest documents mankind has ever produced, after those *Fifty Shades* books.

The Constitution

While the Declaration of Independence was merely a declaration of independence, it's the United States Constitution that is the supreme law of the land—yes, even more legally binding than all the fine print in a Valtrex ad.

The Constitution is the document that details the structure of our government and its powers (and the limits of its powers—e.g., no jumping over a building in a single bound, which is why we've never elected Superman president).

In 1787, delegates from all 13 of the former colonies gathered in Philadelphia to come up with the plan for an overall federal government. Alexander Hamilton immediately proposed they make James Madison sit up all night and write it while the rest of them went out and got plowed and looked for hookers, which was quickly seconded.

The first three articles of the Constitution call for three branches of government: the legislative, the executive, and the judicial (originally, there was also a fourth branch, the keggers, but this is now under the purview of Congress).

Obviously, Madison missed some stuff, because in 1791 the first 10 amendments were added to the Constitution. These are known as the Bill of Rights. These established such fundamental ideas as freedom of speech, due process, and that an angry white supremacist guy with swastika tattoos and 50 AK-47s with hundreds of clips in his basement is *exactly* the same thing as a "well-regulated militia."

In order to become part of the Constitution, an amendment must first be approved by Congress, and then it must be ratified by three-

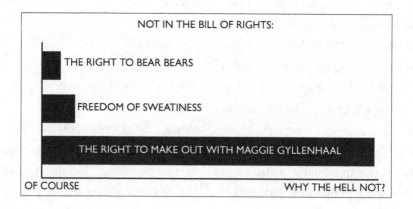

NOT IN THE BILL OF RIGHTS:

THE RIGHT TO BEAR BEARS

FREEDOM OF SWEATINESS

THE RIGHT TO MAKE OUT WITH MAGGIE GYLLENHAAL

OF COURSE   WHY THE HELL NOT?

quarters of the states. Then comes the lightning round about general knowledge, and finally the tribal council, where the amendment may be voted off the island.

Since 1791, there have been 17 amendments. Many of these have had far-reaching effects: the Thirteenth Amendment abolished slavery, while the Twenty-sixth prohibited the wearing of short, short denim shorts by men of a certain weight (though many still flout the law today).

The U.S. Constitution has inspired many other nations to adapt their own constitutions, especially the part about Congress and keggers. Whoo! Keggers!

The National Anthem

As we all know, America's national anthem is "Come Sail Away" by Styx. It is performed at all official state occasions, before (and sometimes during) sporting events, and is a staple of Double-Shot Tuesday on classic rock stations all over the country (though they usually play it

with "Renegade" or "Blue Collar Man," which, you know, meh).

"Come Sail Away" was written by Francis Scott Key during the War of 1812, when space aliens from planet X-17 landed and took him far into space, which brought the war to a swift end because holy shit, aliens! Incredibly, "Come Sail Away" is not the only national anthem in the Styx oeuvre. Japan's national anthem is the Styx classic "Mr. Roboto," while for some reason Canada chose the Styx ballad "Babe," probably the weakest song in the entire Styx catalog. Good one, Canada. What, you couldn't get "Suite Madame Blue" or "The Grand Illusion"? Typical.

▶ Fact-Like Fact

The Styx hit "Lady" is still available as a national anthem. Operators are standing by!

But one thing is for sure: when an American athlete wins a gold medal at the Olympics, and they hoist the Stars and Stripes and start playing "Come Sail Away" by Styx, well, call us old-fashioned but our heart swells with pride. Come sail away, come sail away, come sail away with every American everywhere, baby.

The Emancipation Proclamation

On January 1, 1863, President Abraham Lincoln issued the Emancipation Proclamation. This great document freed the slaves.

The Confederacy, however, didn't want any part of it. They desperately tried to find a loophole. For a time, they defined African-Americans as "robots from the planet X-17," who specifically have no rights in the Constitution. The ruse failed when robots from the planet X-17 were called to testify before Congress and stated that the South was "full of shit."

Lincoln's proclamation was ironclad (not to mention notarized, and placed in a nice manila folder), and the South was on the wrong side of history. From that day forward, all men in America have been free to participate in our great democracy. Sadly, robots from planet X-17 still have no rights under the Constitution.

The Gettysburg Address

In 1863, at the height of the Civil War, Abraham Lincoln gave one of the most famous speeches in U.S. history: the Gettysburg Address. In terms of great oration, it's right up there with FDR's "We Have Nothing to Fear but Fear Itself" speech and "Baby Got Back" by Sir Mix-A-Lot.

The Gettysburg Address began, "Four score and seven years ago." That's right, the Gettysburg Address was a math test. The Union answered first, getting the correct answer (87) *and* showing all work. Meanwhile, the Confederacy answered, "chicken," which was so, so wrong. Because of this, the Southern states were forced to repeat eighth grade. This was the turning point of the Civil War.

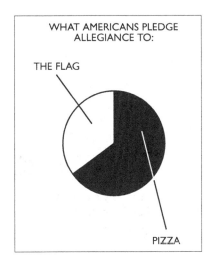

WHAT AMERICANS PLEDGE
ALLEGIANCE TO:

THE FLAG

PIZZA

volves plenty of mild inconvenience and irkage (standing in the way at the bottom of the escalator at the mall, not going when the light turns green, that sort of thing).

The only real escape from the powerful hold Borkon has on all our lives is to eschew fabric entirely. Go about your business completely nude, swinging freely. Try it, you'll like it!

Pledge of Allegiance

Everyone knows the Pledge of Allegiance to the flag of the United States of America. But: did you know that pledging allegiance to the flag is not the same as pledging allegiance to the United States?

Here's the truth: when you pledge allegiance to the flag, or any colorful bit of fabric, you are actually pledging your allegiance to Borkon, the god of mild inconvenience and irkage. Borkon lives in fabric—flags, clothing, you name it. And by pledging allegiance to the flag, you are promising to do the bidding of Borkon, which in-

The Federal Government

In the Constitution, the Founding Fathers created a complicated system of checks and balances, dividing government power into three distinct branches. This was to ensure both that power did not become concentrated and that nothing would ever, ever get done.

Basically, the executive branch runs the operations of government, the legislative branch makes the laws, and the judicial branch lounges around in black robes all damn day. You certainly wouldn't want the judicial branch running the government, or the legislative branch lounging around in robes (especially because they probably wouldn't close them, and you'd have to see their little filibusters).

Here's a handy guide to what you'll find in each of the three branches of government. Jimmy your head open with a crowbar and cram this knowledge in somewhere near your left parietal lobe:

The Executive Branch

The federal government's executive branch consists of the president, the vice president, and the cabinet. For reasons involving the separation of powers, the president's house pets are part of the judicial branch and may decide major Supreme Court cases (see Socks the Cat's well-argued dissent in *Bush v. Gore*).

THE PRESIDENCY

The President is the chief executive of the United States. He is both the head of state and the head of the government, as well as commander in chief of America's armed forces. So that's awesome.

The President takes an oath to "preserve, protect, and defend the Constitution of the United States, even the boring parts like the eleventh amendment, which, like, whatever."

▶ Fact-Like Fact

The president only makes nine bucks an hour, and he has to split his tips with his Cabinet.

The President may sign or veto legislation passed by Congress. Congress may overturn a presidential veto with a two-thirds majority in both houses. If there is only a 60 percent majority in both houses, then the bill is ruled a ground-rule double and the President advances to second base. A president may also issue executive orders, such as "Hey, let's bomb that country over there!" or "I decree it to now be beer-thirty. Someone hook me a cold one."

The President may sign treaties, but treaties must be ratified by the Senate. The House of Representatives doesn't get to say shit about foreign treaties. This is a good thing. For reals.

Finally, a president may be impeached by the House and convicted by the Senate for knowingly participating in oral sex. So there's that.

BIOGRAPHIES OF THE U.S. PRESIDENTS

The office of the President of the United States has been held by 44 men. Or, quite possibly, 39 men, 2 women, a robot, a zombie, and a small dog named Mr. Pooters. What presidents do in their private time is their business. Especially Mr. Pooters. Good doggie!

George Washington

From 1776 through 1788, America had no leader. This meant that there was nobody to make phone calls to sports teams that had just won championships. That situation was intolerable, so Revolutionary War hero and noted denture wearer George Washington was made our first president.

As our first president, George Washington started many traditions. For instance, every president since Washington has had wooden teeth installed, usually against his will. And he was the first president to spend, like, three-quarters of his entire damn presidency clearing brush.

Today, we recognize our first president by calling the nation's capital Washington. What an honor, having a city located in a festering, humid swamp named after you; a city synonymous with complete, utter pricks and jerkwads. Sign us up.

John Adams. On a popular HBO show, he was played by Lena Dunham.

John Adams

When George Washington abruptly announced he wouldn't seek a third term in 1796, America was heartbroken. John Adams was there for America, a shoulder for the nation to cry on. A nice guy who would listen, and was attentive to America's needs at a vulnerable moment.

Yes, John Adams was a "rebound" president, and America dumped him the second the much smarter, wealthier, and more handsome Thomas Jefferson came along. Poor John Adams.

Thomas Jefferson

Thomas Jefferson not only wrote the Declaration of Independence, but also the wildly popular self-help books, *Do Not Perspire Upon Items of Smallness, for Verily, All Items Possess the Quality of Smallness*, and *The 60-Second Plantation Manager*.

Thomas Jefferson is the only president ever to send the U.S. Marines to fight pirates. Why this has never been made into a major motion picture is a complete mystery. Please contact us if you'd like to see our screenplay *Marines versus Pirates*, starring Bruce Willis, Johnny Depp, and Justin Bieber as the Littlest Marine.

To honor one of our greatest presidents, America put Thomas Jefferson on the two-dollar bill. From beyond the grave, Jefferson was quoted as saying, "Really? The two-dollar bill? Hamilton wasn't even president and he's on the ten."

▶ Fact-Like Fact

While Alexander Hamilton was never president, he was one of the cast members of *Queer Eye for the Colonial Guy.*

James Madison

James Madison wrote the Constitution *and* the Bill of Rights, and what did he get? Nada, that's what.

His face doesn't appear on any of our paper money or coins (except for that one gold dollar that nobody likes). There's not even a superamazing Madison Monument in Washington, DC. Bupkus. Zeroville.

Today, James Madison is wherever it is dead Founding Fathers go, plotting his revenge.

James Monroe

James Monroe is perhaps best known for *The Monroe Doctrine*, in which he portrayed a man without an identity who is chased worldwide by shadowy forces who want to kill him. He followed that up with the equally successful *The Monroe Supremacy*, where he was once again on the run from shadowy forces while searching for his true identity. Then came *The Monroe Ultimatum*, with—surprise!—James Monroe, still with absolutely no knowledge of his true identity, still with the shadowy forces trying to murder him before he learns the truth.

Don't bother even renting the next one. Seriously.

John Quincy Adams

John Quincy Adams was the son of second president John Adams. When the senior Adams wouldn't let him borrow the horse-and-buggy for his inaugural ball in 1825, John Quincy Adams screamed "I hate you, Dad!" and ran sobbing up to his room.

When young president John Quincy Adams would try to tell his father about pending legislation, the elder Adams would slam down his beer and shout, "You think you have it rough? Back in my day I had to walk 20 miles in the snow to veto a bill! Uphill! With no boots!" John Quincy Adams would then scream "I hate you, Dad!" and run sobbing up to his room.

John Quincy Adams was the only president required to be home by 10:30 p.m. on weeknights and 11:30 p.m. on weekends. And when the younger Adams failed to win a second term in 1828, his father sent him to bed without supper and grounded him for a month. John Quincy Adams screamed "I hate you, Dad!" and again ran sobbing up to his room.

Andrew Jackson

Andrew Jackson was known as Old Hickory, because he had his real head replaced with a solid wood one after a freak tobacco-spittin' accident. By all accounts, nobody could tell the damn difference.

iel Hawthorne (known as the Scarlet A).

Martin Van Buren. He was also known as Old Kinderhook because he had his hands replaced with small German children with hooks for hands.

Martin Van Buren

Eighth president Martin Van Buren had a secret. Nobody knew that mild-mannered Van Buren was the secret identity of the great 1800s superhero Rather Remarkable Chap, who could leap a two-story building in a single bound and was stronger than a horse-and-buggy and faster than a speeding covered wagon. He spent his entire presidency defeating his evil arch-nemesis, Nathan-

William Henry Harrison

William Henry Harrison didn't listen to his mother; he went out without a coat, made a four-hour inauguration speech out in the cold and snow, caught pneumonia, and died after only 30 days in office. So, please. Listen to your mother.

John Tyler

John Tyler was the first man to succeed a president who had died in office. At his inauguration, Tyler poured a forty on the ground and dedicated his presidency to "my dead homiez." He later claimed he'd meet his predecessor "at da crossroads." In his inauguration speech, Tyler encouraged all Americans to put their hands up in the air and wave them in a manner that conveyed a general lack of concern.

Later in his presidency, John Tyler described the state of the union as "supa-dupa fly." But Tyler's most famous quote is arguably,

"Don't push me, I'm close to the edge; I'm about to annex Texas. Huh huh huh huh." That is still true today.

James Polk

Don't blame yourself—more than 20 million men over the age of 50 may be experiencing the same problem that you are. James Polk may be able to help you feel like yourself again.

Warning: James Polk may cause drowsiness. Do not operate heavy machinery during the Polk administration. Diarrhea or stomach/abdominal pain may also occur.

> ### ▶ Fact-Like Fact
>
> **Ask your doctor if your heart is healthy enough for James Polk.**

Tell your doctor immediately if any of these rare but very serious side effects occur:

- Severe stomach/abdominal pain
- Persistent nausea/vomiting
- Manifest Destiny

A very serious allergic reaction to James Polk is rare. However, seek immediate medical attention if you notice any symptoms of a serious allergic reaction, including:

- Rash
- Severe dizziness
- War with Mexico

And if you experience a Polk administration lasting longer than four years, please call your doctor.

Zachary Taylor

Zachary Taylor constantly refuted rumors that he was a zombie, claiming to eat nothing but human brains because "they are a good source of iron."

Historians are still divided on the Zachary Taylor/zombie question. It is true that during his military days, Taylor was called "Old Rough and Ready and Decaying." And while he was slow-moving and awkward, he may have just been, you know, a klutz (see: Gerald Ford).

Congress planned to determine if Taylor was a zombie by seeing what happened if he was lit on fire.

Unlike normal people, zombies hate being on fire. Sadly, they were unable to test this as Taylor ate the brain of House speaker Eldridge G. Steward (D-OH, D-Undead).

Still, most historians agree that Taylor's greatest accomplishment as president was breaking into that one house where all the living humans had barricaded themselves and then eating all their brains.

Millard Fillmore

According to historians, Millard Fillmore was easily our most exciting, exhilarating president. They consider Fillmore's Compromise of 1850 to be "200 percent pure adrenaline, dude," and the Clayton-Bulwer Treaty "a roller coaster chain saw thrill ride."

But then, historians don't exactly get out a lot.

Franklin Pierce

So, like, Franklin Pierce was all like, yeah, but I was all like, nuh-huh, and he was all like, yuh-huh, and I was all like, no way, and he said, way. And I was like, whoa.

James Buchanan, America's sassy best friend.

James Buchanan

James Buchanan was the only bachelor elected president. It's a wonder that neither Buchanan nor his long-time roommate Christopher never settled down and married some nice girls. They were such handsome, eligible young men.

After his failed reelection bid (campaign slogan: "Buchanan is FABULOUS!"), Buchanan became the host of the popular makeover show *Queer Eye for the Frontier*

Guy and wrote the popular children's book *Heather Has Two Presidents.*

Abraham Lincoln

Nothing is known about Abraham Lincoln.

Andrew Johnson

Constructed out of pieces of corpses and brought to life by a mad scientist, Andrew Johnson was impeached after his controversial "Fire Bad" speech. Following his impeachment, Johnson was chased by angry villagers with torches and pitchforks.

Ulysses S. Grant

Eighteenth U.S. president Ulysses S. Grant had many nicknames, such as Drunky, Hey Get Up You Can't Sleep Here, Check to See If He's Still Breathing, and Ol' No Liver. His notable cabinet appointments included Jim Beam, Johnnie Walker, Ernest & Julio Gallo, G. Horace Ripple III, Stephen Maddog2020, and Arthur Rubbingalcohol.

▶ Fact-Like Fact

Here are few more nicknames for Ulysses Grant: Pukey; General Blowchunks; the Prince of Horkness; Good God, What Is That Smell? Oh, It's the President; and, of course: Rudolph the Red-Nosed President.

Rutherford B. Hayes

Many cultures have a legend of Rutherford B. Hayes.

The legend is similar all over the world: Rutherford B. Hayes ventures forth from his comfortable, everyday world into a world of mystery and wonder: difficulties are encountered, but a decisive victory is won. And then, Rutherford B. Hayes returns from his incredible adventure with powers and riches.

In our culture, the legend of Rutherford B. Hayes goes like this: Rutherford B. Hayes becomes our nineteenth president and grows a cool-ass ZZ Top beard. The end.

James Garfield

Let's face it, James Garfield was kind of a douche. He was that guy driving down the street in his souped-up horse and buggy, with his Loverboy eight-track cranked up. He'd be out cruising every weekend, with his muscle tee, blond feathered hair, and little wispy mustache, totally coming on to our girlfriend while we're standing right there. And you know what? She got in his horse and buggy with him anyway, and they went and parked down by the river and smoked some Maui Wowee and who knows what else, and but so we was so pissed we went to Dairy Queen and got into a fight and got thrown out and so went home and listened to Zep and drank all our mom's wine (like, half of a one-gallon jug) and we passed out and woke up in our own barf and it just sucked, OK?

Oh, wait. That was someone else.

Chester Arthur

Pitchfork.com gave Chester Arthur's presidency a 4.2, calling it "self-indulgent," "lackluster," and "not fulfilling the promise of such magnificent sideburns."

Grover Cleveland, who wasn't from Cleveland and never, ever groved, the big fat liar.

Grover Cleveland

Grover Cleveland won the 1880 election, despite admitting that he had fathered an illegitimate child. Tabloids and gossip websites of the day were also filled with many shocking up-skirt photos of Grover Cleveland getting out of carriages while not wearing underwear. Eventually, he got clean on the 1880s reality show *Celebrated Persons Rehab.*

True fact: While in office, Grover Cleveland underwent a secret operation to remove his jaw, impairing his ability to speak. Don't you wish more politicians would undergo this procedure?

Benjamin Harrison

Benjamin Harrison was a very friendly otter who liked to play! All day long, he played with his little otter friends in the happy, happy lake. Fun!

Then, after a yummy dinner, his otter mommy tucked him in for a night of pleasant otter dreams.

Good night, Benjamin Harrison! Sweet otter dreams!

Grover Cleveland 2.0

Grover Cleveland 2.0 was a necessary upgrade of the original Grover Cleveland and contained many bug fixes and fewer error messages.

William McKinley

William McKinley was just a temp president. America needed some- one to come in and do the presidenting for a few weeks while the regular president was on vacation. So Congress called PresiTemps and they sent McKinley over.

It didn't work out so well. PresiTemps said McKinley knew Word and Excel, but he didn't even know what a spreadsheet was. How is that even possible? Plus, the agency said he typed 80 words per minute, but McKinley could only type with two fingers, so it was more like 35.

McKinley was terrible on the phone, too. He put Spain on hold for so long, it led to the Spanish-American War. And let's not forget that McKinley made a huge mess in the break room every single day; it still smells like burnt microwave popcorn in the break room.

Anyway, when the next guy showed up to be the real president, nobody was sad to see McKinley go. We hear he got a full-time job later, being vice-president of Costa Rica, so good for him, we suppose.

Theodore Roosevelt

"Rough and Ready" Theodore Roosevelt was a professional wrestler.

In 1904, he defeated Alton "the Crusher" Parker in two out of three falls in a Caribbean Strap match to become the Undisputed President of the World.

But he wasn't always an imposing wrestler. As a child, Roosevelt was small and sickly and could only barely body slam William "the Body" Jennings Bryan. But as a young man, Roosevelt became a national hero during the Spanish-American War (or, as it was known at the time, WrestleMania 6).

▶ Fact-Like Fact

Because he was a pro wrestler, the entire Theodore Roosevelt administration was fake.

As president, Roosevelt created our national park system, mainly so he could have a steady supply of bears he could wrestle.

Roosevelt was famous for saying, "Speak softly and carry a big stick—to beat your ass!" Today, this quote is known as "Teddy 3:16."

William Taft

They say that William Taft was so fat, he got stuck in the White House bathtub. Is this true, or merely an urban myth? To find out, we hired Adam Savage and Jamie Hyneman, from TV's *Mythbusters*, to find out the truth.

First, Adam and Jamie made a faux-Taft out of ballistics gel and a human skeleton. Then, they built a bathtub out of steel rods and duct tape. Then, Adam and Jamie hauled all of that out to the bomb range, where Frank and J.D. filled the tub with C4. Finally, once everyone was a safe distance away, they blew up the duct tape tub and the ballistics gel Taft.

What did we learn? That blowing up shit is *awesome*. Dude. And check out the high-speed footage— bits of Taft fly everywhere!

Woodrow Wilson

Woodrow Wilson was walking with Will Wentz, when Wentz went with Wilson where Warren worked. Warren worked with wood, whistling while whittling. When will Wanda welcome Wes, wondered Woodrow. Wes was weird when Wanda wanted walnuts.

Well, whispered Warren, Will was worried Woodrow would want Wanda without Wes's wherewithal. Why wouldn't Woodrow wait with Will while Warren worked with Wanda? Wanda wanted Will, while Woodrow wanted Wanda. Why Wanda? Whither Will? Wouldn't Wes work?

Will wished Wanda would woo Wes while Warren was whistling.

Warren G. Harding: America's village idiot.

With Woodrow Wilson, Will Wentz went westward with Wanda. Warren worked with Wes, whittling well.

Warren G. Harding

We're not saying Warren Harding was our dumbest president, but he didn't even know how to clear brush.

Calvin Coolidge

His friends called him "Silent Cal," which was short for "Silent-But-Deadly Cal." Doctors think it may have been some kind of intestinal problem, because damn, Slappy. It took until the Reagan administration to get the smell out of the Oval Office.

Coolidge brought the nation to the brink of war with France in the He Who Smelt It Dealt It Incident of 1925. The situation escalated with Coolidge's "He Who Denied It, Supplied It" speech later that year, while the French fired back by declaring, "He who reported it, exported it." Armed conflict was narrowly averted when both sides agreed to the Treaty of He Who Shunned It, Tail-Gunned It.

Herbert Hoover

Herbert Hoover's administration started out all Jake, see. It was the height of the Roaring Twenties. Dames had gams that wouldn't quit, speakeasies had the giggle water, and palookas got scrooched on the hootch, then taken for a ride and 86ed. It was the cat's meow!

But then the Great Depression arrived and ruined everything. Oh, people should have seen it coming; the signs were there: President Hoover would stay in bed all day, listening to the Smiths. If he went to a cabinet meeting at all, he usually showed up in his pajamas, saying, "I don't even see what the damn point is anymore."

Soon, the entire country was feeling the effects of the Depression. Hoover's policies didn't help matters (especially the Darkness Is Slowly Consuming Me Act of 1930 and the You Don't Understand, It Hurts Just Being Alive Treaty with Canada), and the voters drove him out of office after just one term.

After his presidency, Herbert Hoover got the help he needed and was soon living an active, happy life. But he still did pretty much everything in his pajamas.

Franklin Delano Roosevelt

Franklin Roosevelt heroically led the United States through the Great Depression and World War II, all while suffering from a debilitating disability: his middle name was Delano. Seriously, what kind of name is Delano? What kind of parent does that to a child?

Harry S. Truman. The S stood for "Party" (he wasn't a good speller).

Harry Truman

While president, Harry Truman was the lead guitarist for the hair metal band Sex Kitty, known for their hits "Party Like You're at a Party (Party)" and "Party Your Party Off (Party Party)," plus the tender love ballad "Bite Me in the General Buttock Region (No, Lower)," which went straight to number one. "Bite Me in the General Buttock Region" has since become a staple of weddings and proms nationwide.

But soon, Sex Kitty were known more for their offstage antics than their music, or even their hair. Harry Truman nearly died from an overdose of Sassoon Extra-Hold Strawberry Mousse, and a groupie nearly stabbed him to death with a blow dryer. At a concert in Kansas City, the entire band passed out onstage during an encore of their huge hit, "Party Party Party (Party Party)," causing a massive riot that is still going on today.

Eventually, Truman, Thomas Dewey, Adlai Stevenson, and the other members of Sex Kitty went through the painful process of rehab. They got back together in the 1980s, found a whole new audience for their melodic glam rock, and were the inspiration for Poison, Ratt, and dozens of others really, really sucky bands. Um, thanks?

Dwight Eisenhower

Under Eisenhower, the United States started undergoing a series of nuclear tests in the Nevada desert. This led directly to our major cities being attacked by giant ants, giant spiders, and giant Gila monsters. Also: giant locusts, giant praying mantises, and giant giants.

But the worst of all was the Blob, a horrible gelatinous mass spreading evil and chaos everywhere. It turned out that this awful mass of roving protoplasm was actually Eisenhower's vice president, the future president Richard Nixon (see section on Richard Nixon).

John F. Kennedy

There are several unlikely coincidences that link John F. Kennedy, our thirty-fifth president, to Abraham Lincoln, our sixteenth president. For example, Lincoln was elected president and so was John F. Kennedy.

Random Bonus Fact!

DEB OLIN UNFERTH, AUTHOR

Animal sleep facts: it is known that chickens sleep in trees—lesser known is that so do sunfish, giraffe-heads, and very small horses.

But it gets stranger! We all know that Kennedy proposed that America go to the Moon by the end of the 1960s, but did you know that Lincoln proposed that America go to the Moon by the end of the 1860s? It's true—he called on Congress to fund his "Giant Rubber Band" idea, but the costs of the Civil War made this idea too expensive for the time.

Also, we've all heard the rumors that John F. Kennedy and Marilyn Monroe, you know, did it and stuff. But did you know that Abraham Lincoln did it with Marilyn Monroe, also? In a last-ditch effort to defeat the North, the Confederacy built a rudimentary time machine (ironically, using the very Giant Rubber Band technology Lincoln had wanted to use for his Moon trip!). The South sent Stonewall Jackson to 1953 Hollywood and brought Marilyn Monroe back to the White House in 1864. How this was supposed to help the Confederacy is unclear, but Lincoln had a good time, as did Marilyn Monroe. Plus, the Union won anyway. Score!

Lyndon Johnson

Lyndon Johnson had a fancy bottle that contained a sexy lady genie named Jeannie, who would get him and his friend Major Healey into all kinds of wacky trouble every week!

Lyndon Johnson's biggest legacy may be his Great Society program, which lifted people out of poverty by having them strike oil—black gold, Texas tea—on their land and then moving their families out to Beverly. Hills, that is. Swimming pools, movie stars.

Johnson's wife, Lady Bird, was not only a beloved first lady, she was also a witch who could cast spells by scrunching her nose in a really adorable manner. Her mother, Endora, also lived in the White House, leading to all kinds of trouble with Johnson's boss, Mr. Tate.

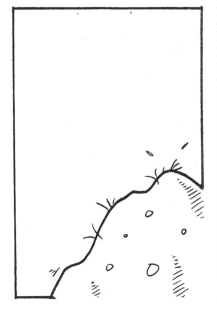

Richard Nixon, *People* magazine's Sexiest Blob Alive for 1973.

Richard Nixon

Richard Nixon was a giant blob of pure evil. Evil!

Nixon made a name for himself early in his political career with his famous "Checkers" speech in 1952, when he ate a small dog on live television. As president, Nixon was personally responsible for a great deal of the evil in the world in the late 1960s and early '70s. For instance, that "brown acid" at Woodstock? That was Nixon. More disturbingly, most historians now believe that Nixon and Yoko Ono were the same person.

Nixon was finally forced to resign when people realized that the Constitution specifically prohibits giant blobs of pure evil from being president (though giant blobs of pure evil can still serve as vice president, hence Dick Cheney).

Gerald Ford

Gerald Ford is still best known for pardoning Richard Nixon, which was an unpopular move among approximately 1 billion percent of Americans.

Jimmy Carter

Jimmy Carter's presidency is remembered as a time of malaise, both economically and sexually. But Carter achieved many amazing accomplishments during his four years in office:

- Getting that truck full of beer from Texas to Atlanta without getting caught by Jackie Gleason.
- Winning that fiddlin' contest when the devil went down to Georgia.
- Championing that landmark piece of legislation, the Mamas, Don't Let Your Babies Grow Up to Be Cowboys Act of 1978.

But, sadly, Carter's popularity plummeted when he couldn't stop disco from sweeping the nation in 1979.

Ronald Reagan

As a joke, America thought it would be both hi and larious to elect the washed-up actor who starred in *Bedtime for Bonzo* as president. What a hoot, right?

Yeah, not so funny, as it turned out, because it led directly to that horrible 1988 Tom Cruise movie *Cocktail*. America still hasn't fully recovered from this national nightmare because, come on, a bar called Cocktails & Dreams? Barf.

We hope you enjoyed your little "joke," America. Now let us never speak of it again.

▷ Fact-Like Fact

In 1984, Ronald Reagan appointed Huey Lewis to be the new drug czar.

George Herbert Walker Bush

The elder Bush's presidency is perhaps defined by Operation Desert Storm, a major military operation to remove the evil, despotic Michael Bolton from power. His awful, retchinducing power ballads were becoming a danger to the entire Middle East and our own national security. And when Bolton released his earshattering cover of "When a Man Loves a Woman," Bush knew he had to take action before more innocent people were killed.

Operation Desert Storm was ultimately a success. Though Michael Bolton remained in power, his influence was greatly diminished as grunge and rap became more popular. Later, Bush's son claimed Michael Bolton was working on the ultimate weapon, a deadly cover version of Aerosmith's already-crappy "I Don't Want to Miss a Thing" that could take out millions of people at once. This turned out to not be true, but better safe than sorry.

Bill Clinton

Bill Clinton was apparently the first president to ever sport a penis, because it's all anyone talked about for, like, two damn years. America could have spent that time solving hunger or homelessness or inventing jetpacks and flying cars, but no, everyone had to argue about oral sex and what the meaning of "is" was. *We can't get that time back.*

George W. Bush

George W. Bush's historical legacy is still up in the air, but one thing is for sure: George W. Bush kept this nation safe from the ominous, ever-present danger of uncleared brush. And for that, we thank him.

Barack Obama, part of some sort of conspiracy by Kenyan Socialists to take over the world or some shit.

Barack Obama

Remember that time a bunch of total dickwads pretended that a birth certificate from Hawaii wasn't a real birth certificate? Yeah. So awesome.

THE VICE PRESIDENT OF THE UNITED STATES

The vice presidency is a very, very important office. No, really! OK, it's not. But here's what you need to know about the vice presidency.

Selection

The people don't vote for the vice president directly, which explains why we didn't end up with Vice President Shaun Cassidy in the late 1970s. It's a shame, really.

The candidates for president choose a running mate, and the choice can depend on several criteria—Kennedy chose Lyndon Johnson because Texas was a key swing state. George W. Bush chose Dick Cheney because it shored up his foreign policy credentials. And in 2008, John McCain chose Sarah Palin because, come on, that was hilarious.

Role

The vice president has a lot of important stuff to do, you know. He has to hang around the Senate in case there's a tie vote. In U.S. history, this has happened approximately never.

Also, the vice president is often sent overseas to the funerals of important foreign dignitaries, such as Lithuania's undersecretary of agriculture (turnip division) and Belgium's assistant viceroy of waffles. Basically, the vice president attends approximately 4,000 funerals a year, so an important qualification for the office is being a truly morbid little prick. The ideal VP would be Tim Burton, or maybe Marilyn Manson.

> ### ▶ Fact-Like Fact
>
> **Once a week, the vice president has to take out the nation's recycling.**

Finally, if something should happen to the president, the vice president is next in the line of succession to take office. (See "Order of Succession" in a few pages. Be patient, it's coming right up, we promise. Keep your shirt on, Junior.) This could be permanent, as in the case of presidential death—like when James Garfield accidentally swallowed his own beard, so Chester Arthur was sworn in as president. Not that he was any sharper in the accidentally-swallowing-facial-hair department than his predecessor, but at least he didn't die from it like that idiot Garfield.

Famous Vice Presidents

Despite being an utter shithole of a public office, there are more than a few famous vice presidents (more than a few = five).

John Adams: Our first vice president, his life was turned into the award-winning HBO miniseries *Sex and the City.*

Elbridge Gerry: James Madison's second in command, Gerry invented both Gerrymandering and the Gerry curl. Samuel L. Jackson dedicated his performance in *Pulp Fiction* to the former vice president.

Schuyler Colfax: The first vice president who was in Slytherin House at Hogwarts.

Dan Quayle: Well, he didn't help the elder Bush win an important swing state, and he certainly didn't shore up Bush's foreign policy cred. He couldn't even spell fucking "potato." Seriously, what was Bush Senior smoking?

Dick Cheney. Watch what you say, or he'll shoot you in the damn face.

Dick Cheney: Noted evil person.

Nobody knows a damn thing about the other 714 vice presidents. Also: it is never too late to make Shaun Cassidy our vice president. America, let's come together as one and work on this.

THE ELECTORAL COLLEGE

Oh, you may think that when you vote for president, you're voting for the guy you're voting for. You are such a rube.

It's the electoral college that actually elects our presidents. Each state gets a certain number of electors, based on its population. The electors are supposed to vote the way their state voted, but really, they can do whatever the heck they want. And you remember how you were in college—getting wasted over at Sigma Nu and mooning your philosophy professor, or doing bong hits in the dorms and watching Game Show Network for several hours and/or days. Who knows? It's a *Match Game* marathon, dude!

The point is, the electoral college should not be trusted to elect the president of the United States, unless they brought enough brewskis for everybody.

THE CABINET

The President is advised by the cabinet on matters of policy and, more importantly, if these shoes go with this tie.

The cabinet is composed of the top people at each of 15 departments within the executive branch. Sometimes, they let the vice president in, too, but only to make them

Kool-Aid, to fix bits of Hot Wheels track, or to get them more Lego for the super-cool Lego town they're making.

Here are the 15 departments represented in the cabinet. If you don't see your department listed, then you are not in the cabinet and you should really leave the White House now before the Secret Service finds you hiding in the Taft Library.

Department of Agriculture

Well, I reckon that spelt ain't gonna harvest itself.

> ### ▶ Fact-Like Fact
> Hope we get some rain soon, or we're gonna lose all that endive we put in this spring. Yup.

Department of Commerce

Did you want to return that wicker chair you bought 10 years ago in college because you thought it looked cool and it was kind of cheap, even though it was never very comfortable, and it vaguely smells of cat pee from when Fum Fum had that bladder infection (rest in peace, Fum Fum), and anyway now you're going for more of a Danish Modern thing because you're a damn grown-up with a real job and crap, but Pier 1 won't take it back because you didn't keep the receipt from 10 years ago and, you know, the cat pee smell?

Take that chair to the Department of Commerce. They'll know what to do.

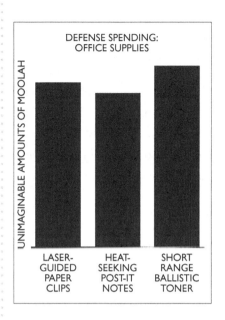

Department of Defense

The Department of Defense is in charge of America's armed forces: the army, the navy, the air force, the marines, the National Guard, and the Mighty Ducks of Anaheim (and, of course, the Mighty Ducks Reserve, which plays hockey two weekends a year. For America).

Much of the Defense Department is housed in the Pentagon, which is the world's largest office building. And since it is the world's largest office building, it is also home to the world's largest stapler—a stapler so large, it could staple France to Spain!

The Department of Defense has by far the largest budget of any fed-

eral agency—their operating budget for 2013 was approximately $800 crap-zillion. That buys a lot of toilet seats. Well, it buys five toilet seats, but still.

A small but important arm of the Defense Department is the Joint Chiefs of Staff. The Joint Chiefs of Staff advise the president on important military matters, such as our military readiness and why does a toilet seat cost $160 crap-zillion, when you can get one at Home Depot for, like, half that (answer: lasers).

Department of Education

This is the cabinet department in charge of that Pink Floyd song where all of those kids don't not need no education. Most of those kids? The backbone of today's Tea Party movement. Good job, kids!

Department of Energy

Red Bull Red Bull Red Bull Red Bull Red Bull Red Bull Red Bull AUUURRRGGGHHHNNN-GGGG!!! ZRRNNNNGGG!!! I CAN FLYYYYYYYYYYYY!!!

Department of Health and Human Services

Health is pretty self-explanatory, but what exactly are "human services"?

Well, let's just say it's $20 for the basic "human service," which you can often get in an alley or sometimes in the front seat of your car, out back of the HappyLube on Fourth Street. But an all-night session of high-end "human services" can go for up to $5,000 (and that doesn't include the hotel room, the horse, or the case of Viagra). Happy "human servicing"!

Department of Homeland Security

Created after 9/11, Homeland Security's job is to protect the United States from a terrorist attack by juggling our junk at the airport.

▶ Fact-Like Fact

Even with all of today's restrictions and safeguards, a terrorist could still take over a plane with a boom box and any random Celine Dion CD.

Homeland Security is also in charge of FEMA (which responds to natural disasters by juggling our junk) and the U.S. Coast Guard (if you want your junk juggled out on the open sea—and on a nice day, who doesn't?). The Department of Homeland Security also juggles the junk of illegal immigrants (U.S. Border Patrol) and the President (the Secret Service).

How does all this junk juggling make us safer? If you have to ask that question, the terrorists have already won.

Department of Housing and Urban Development

Because they deal with housing, this is the cabinet department that does most of the nation's ghost busting. Because busting makes them feel good.

Department of the Interior

You know what this country needs? Some nice drapes, or some good, high-quality vertical blinds. Come on down to the Department of the Interior for our big Holiday Blind Sale. Venetian blinds at up to half off. Draperies in various colors and patterns, also half off.

Come in on Saturday and bring the whole family. Hot dogs for Mom and balloons for the kids. And appearing from 3 p.m. to 5 p.m.: Burt Ward, Robin from TV's original *Batman* show! Come get a photo and some vertical blinds at the Department of the Interior.

Remember, it's curtains for our competition here at the Department of the Interior! Now with two locations: at City Towne Square and at Square Towne City. Open till midnight every day.

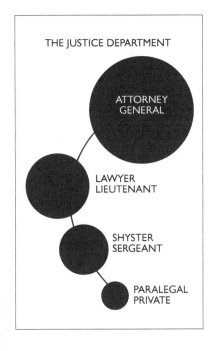

THE JUSTICE DEPARTMENT

ATTORNEY GENERAL

LAWYER LIEUTENANT

SHYSTER SERGEANT

PARALEGAL PRIVATE

Department of Justice

The Department of Justice is out to get justice for that little girl.

Now, the department might have to "break a few rules." It may accidentally shoot up that Burger Whiz because it received a bad tip from that informant the department "questioned" using a match and some lighter fluid.

And yes, the Department of Justice might have to turn in its gun and badge due to the unfortunate incident at the elementary school. The Department of Justice probably should have known that trusting a first grader with a handheld rocket-grenade launcher was a bad, bad idea.

The DOJ may even get placed on indefinite "administrative leave" because of that explosion that shut down the entire 405 for seven hours. The State Police lost three helicopters that day. And let's face it, the DOJ will undoubtedly get investigated by Internal Affairs for that incident with the hooker and the AK-47 that went horribly awry.

And obviously, the Department of Justice will most likely get fired for that nasty bit of business with the school bus, the cliff, and the pack of wild coyotes. And the Department of Justice will definitely be going to prison for a long, long time for that tax fraud case involving that real estate development in Palm Springs that was really just a money-laundering front for the DOJ's secret uranium-smuggling operation, which has nothing to do with getting justice for that little girl but is highly lucrative.

But the Department of Justice *will* get justice for that little girl. Oh yes, it will.

Department of Labor

Wait, how far apart are your contractions? Four minutes? That's not too close, right? Oh. Oh, shit. Should I have already called a taxi? I should have already called a taxi. I'm going to call a taxi. No, I don't know if you're supposed to push yet. I missed that class. Why doesn't the taxi place answer? No, don't push. Can't you see how stressed out I am? Yes. Yes, you *are* the one in labor. Sorry. Jesus, why doesn't the taxi company answer the goddamned phone? Wait, that's not . . . No, that's the head. Oh, shit.

▶ Fact-Like Fact

We're just gonna go pass out for a while. You're on your own.

Department of State

The State Department deals with important foreign issues, like "Is Poland the one that's by Spain?" and "Is Valvoline a country, or am I thinking of Vanity 6?" These are important questions for our national security, and someday, perhaps, we'll get answers.

Department of Transportation

The Department of Transportation makes trains go! Pretty, pretty trains! Chugga chugga chugga chooooo chooooo! Make the train go through the tunnel again! Whoosh!

Of course, the Department of Transportation has many other responsibilities, including highways, ships, and aviation. But who cares? Trains!

Department of the Treasury

These are the people who print our money, so ask *them* why they put Alexander Hamilton on the $10 bill when he wasn't even a damn president. Although we do have to admit, if founding father Alexander Ham-

ilton's portrait on the $10 is any indication, he was certainly a FFILF. Rowr.

Department of Veterans Affairs

If you are a veteran and you want to have an affair, this is the department for you. You will be assigned a paramour based on your rank, service record, and which war you fought in (no lovers available for Grenada vets, because, come on— Grenada? whatever).

Fact-Like Fact

Most veterans want to have an affair with Megan Fox, despite the 27-year waiting period.

ORDER OF SUCCESSION

If a sitting president should die, or be impeached, or resign, what do we do? Do we all freak the fuck out while the country dissolves into chaotic disorder?

Relax. There's no need to freak the fuck out, because the United States has in place an order of succession. If the person who is next in line is unable to take command, we move on to the next person, and so on down the list until we have a president again. Then you can freak the fuck out all you want.

Here is the current order of succession:

1. The vice president of the United States
2. The speaker of the House
3. The current Miss America
4. Whoever won last season on *The Biggest Loser*
5. George Clooney

The Legislative Branch

Originally, the legislative branch was the part of the government that wrote and passed laws. But now the lobbyists do that, and we're not sure what the legislative branch does anymore. Light filing, maybe?

When writing our constitution, our Founding Fathers decided it would be best to have a bicameral legislature (literally: two camels). Sadly, those camels died back around 1805 (which is why Aaron Burr shot Alexander Hamilton in that duel). But today, we still have

two barely functioning legislative bodies: the House of Representatives and the Senate.

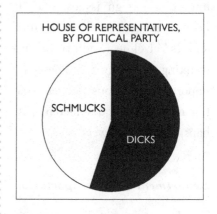

HOUSE OF REPRESENTATIVES, BY POLITICAL PARTY

SCHMUCKS

DICKS

THE U.S. HOUSE OF REPRESENTATIVES

The lower house of Congress is the House of Representatives. Because they're the lower house, they have to wash the Senate's car and mow their lawn and crap, while the Senate goes off to the lake with their friends for that big kegger.

Each state is represented by a number of representatives proportional to its population. California is represented by 53 men and women, while Alaska is represented by the back half of a caribou.

There are a total of 435 representatives, which is approximately 417 too many. According to the Constitution, only the following sorts of people are allowed to serve in the House of Representatives:

- Ass-ferrets
- Ass-clowns
- Ass-hats
- Ass-butts
- Ass-lemurs

The party with a majority of representatives gets to choose the speaker of the House. The speaker of the House then chooses his or her majority leader and a majority whip. The majority leader uses the majority whip when they bring out the majority gimp.

The House of Representatives' chief function is to write the revenue bills that fund government operations. If they can't agree, the government may be required to shut down. This can have huge repercussions: no Social Security checks for million of Americans, and no park rangers at Mount Rushmore to keep Cary Grant and Eva Marie Saint off George Washington's nose.

The House may also override a presidential veto with a two-thirds vote, or by singing the "Suck It, Mr. President" song (traditionally performed in the key of F), which goes:

Suck it, Mr. President,
Suck it, Mr. President,
Lay around the shack till the mail
train comes back,
Suck it, Mr. President.

The House has few special powers compared to the Senate, but they do have a cool invisible plane like Wonder Woman. Still, it's a bit unsettling for most U.S. citizens to see John Boehner just sitting in the sky, going 300 miles per hour.

House members are elected to two-year terms, which means they spend pretty much no time actually doing their damn jobs because they have to spend every waking moment raising money for their next election. That's what makes our democracy great.

The Speaker of the House

There have been a number of House speakers in our nation's history. Many, such as the guy with the mustache and the old-timey dude with the hair, have been forgotten. Some, like the time-traveling Leonardo da Vinci, are more famous for other accomplishments.

These are the five greatest House speakers in our nation's history:

Sam Rayburn: Texas representative Sam Rayburn was the longest-serving speaker of the House, serving nearly 180 years in the position. Historians now believe he may have been a vampire, having passed landmark legislation such as the I Must Have Blood Before the Night Is Out Act of 1954.

Random Bonus Fact!

BARATUNDE THURSTON, AUTHOR

Facts were invented in 1817 as a method of nonlethal crowd control.

Tip O'Neill: Representing liberal Massachusetts, Tip O'Neill was speaker of the House during much of conservative Ronald Reagan's presidency. While they disagreed on a vast array of issues, the two came together to pass important legislation during the 1980s, including the Hey, Phil Collins, What the Hell Is a "Sussudio"? Act of 1985, a law which positively impacted the lives of millions of Americans.

Newt Gingrich: In 1995, Georgia's Newt Gingrich became the first Republican to ascend to the speakership since, we don't know, the Cenozoic Era, maybe? It had been a while.

Gingrich was swept into the House leadership position by his "Contract with America." In the Contract, Republicans promised to "impeach the crap out of someone by the end of the 1990s for something really, really stupid." And boy howdy, did the GOP ever deliver.

Nancy Pelosi: The first woman to become House speaker, Nancy Pelosi of California blocked some of George W. Bush's most-desired legislation, including his plan to privatize Social Security and his promise to make Iraq a state.

John Boehner: In 2011, Representative John Boehner of Ohio became the first speaker of the House who was a person of color. Yes, that color was orange, but still.

THE SENATE

THE US SENATE,
BY POLITICAL PARTY

● POMPOUS BLOWHARDS
○ MORE POMPOUS BLOWHARDS

Based on the ancient Roman Senate, the name of the U.S. Senate comes from the Latin word *senatus* (literally, "my uncle's toaster oven"). The Roman Senate was a deliberative body, and today, the U.S. Senate is known as the World's Greatest Deliberative Body, after New Kids on the Block (who are known for their weeklong discussions about the tax code, vis-à-vis corporate tax cuts for increased ethanol production [Joey McIntyre is for it, while Donnie Wahlberg is vehemently against]).

The U.S. Senate consists of two senators from each state, regardless of population, which means both the dudes who live in Wyoming get to be senators. Good job, guys! Senators are elected to six-year terms, or every time Radiohead releases a new album, whichever comes first.

According to the Constitution, the vice president is the president of the Senate, since, you know, he or she's got nothing else to do and we all feel bad for him or her, the poor dope.

The Senate has many powers the House doesn't possess, including ratifying treaties, X-ray vision, and talking to fish (applies to Senator Aquaman, R-HI, only).

Because the Senate is a deliberative body, debates can last for days at a time. In fact, the filibuster is a strategy to defeat bills by prolonging debate indefinitely. President Obama's health care reform was held up for months when Senator Tom Coburn (R-Dick) started reading David Foster Wallace's *Infinite Jest* into the Congressional Record and was not persuaded to stop until he got to the 40-page filmography footnote.

According to the Constitution, if the House of Representatives impeaches the President, the case goes to trial in the U.S. Senate. Impeachable offenses include treason, bribery, and getting a blow job from a really hot Jewish girl.

Finally, the Senate gets to elect the vice president if the electoral college is deadlocked. This is how we ended up with Vice President Urkel in the early 1990s.

The Five U.S. Senators We've Heard Of: We Think

Yeah, we don't really pay attention to politics.

Bob Dole: After a long and august political career, Bob Dole became the face of erectile dysfunction with those really upsetting Viagra ads. Which: ewwwwww.

Ted Kennedy: Ted Kennedy was a respected lawmaker, but let's face it, he was kind of the Stephen Baldwin of the Kennedys. Still: both Ted Kennedy and Stephen Baldwin were awesome in *The Usual Suspects*. How Kennedy didn't win an Oscar as Keyser Söze is beyond us.

John McCain: On the one hand, John McCain of Arizona is a genuine war hero. On the other hand, he gave us Sarah Palin. Let's just call it even.

> **▶ Fact-Like Fact**
>
> **Ninety-seven percent of U.S. senators are old white dudes who look like they own at least one yacht named *Monkey Business*.**

Senator Palpatine: Yes, it was Palpatine's unbridled ambition that set the stage for war throughout the galaxy, but he had that snappy campaign slogan: "Your Faith in Your Friends Is Your Weakness! Palpatine!"

Strom Thurmond: Yes, Strom Thurmond was a vile relic of the pre–Civil Rights era South. Yes, he served well past the age when senility had set in. And yes, nobody could understand a damn word he said with that thick accent/cackle of his.

Oh, were you waiting for a "but"? Sorry. No but.

HOW A BILL BECOMES A LAW

When a corporation loves a lobbyist very much, they write a bill. Then, they give it to one of the many lawmakers the corporation has paid big money to put in office. Then it's a law! Yay!

HOW TO CONTACT YOUR REPRESENTATIVE

Unless you're going to give him or her a mind-bogglingly huge check, don't bother.

The Judicial Branch

The judicial branch is the branch of government that interprets and applies the laws written by the legislative branch (and let's face it, those clowns in the legislative branch are not the sharpest writers; as of 2012, only four congressmen even knew what a verb was).

The main component of the ju-dicial branch is the United States Supreme Court, the final authority on what is or is not constitutional. Usually, the court can be trusted to get it right. But sometimes the court makes a mistake, like when it upheld *The United States v. Nickelback*, declaring that not only was Nickelback constitutional, but they also, to quote the court's opinion, "rocked our asses off." This decision has been criticized for decades.

THE SUPREME COURT

The United States Supreme Court is the highest court in the land, unless Willie Nelson and Woody Harrelson are playing tennis someplace (you'll know—you can smell it from miles away).

The Supreme Court was established in 1789 when John Jay became our first chief justice. But John Jay hadn't intended to become chief justice.

One day, John Jay was minding his own business when he was bitten by a radioactive judge. The bite transformed the young Jay from a regular man to chief justice, giving him the incredible powers of a judge. These amazing powers included the ability to shoot gavels out of his wrists, super-agility, and the superhuman ability to listen to hours and hours of phenomenally dull and tedious legal shit.

John Jay. Listen, bud, he's got radioactive blood.

The Supreme Court was organized around the chief justice and eight other judges with special powers (also known as the Justice Friends). Soon, the chief justice's justice sense was tingling, and he and the Justice Friends were deciding some of the toughest cases the young country had to face: *The*

United States v. Doc Ock, *The Green Goblin v. The City of New York*, and perhaps most importantly, *The Chief Justice v. Who the Hell Has Ever Heard of a Radioactive Judge, It's 17-frickin'-91 for Chrissakes and Radioactivity Hasn't Even Been Discovered Yet.*

Today, whenever a new chief justice is chosen, he is taken down to the Justice Friends' basement, where the original radioactive judge is still alive and kept chained up. Eventually, the radioactive judge bites the candidate, and he gains the powers of chief justice. Then he and the Justice Friends go off for new adventures in the Justice Van!

Famous Supreme Court Cases

While most Supreme Court cases don't have a tangible effect on most Americans' lives (such as *Scalia v. This Whole Pizza Hut Pepperoni Pizza I Had for Lunch That's Making Me Fart Up a Storm Under This Robe, God Damn*), some cases have profound consequences.

For example, in 2000's *Bush v. Gore* case, the future of the nation was at stake as the court decided the outcome of that year's presidential election. George W. Bush's lawyers argued that Al Gore was an annoying know-it-all pain in the ass, while Gore's lawyers argued that Bush was a dummy dumb poopy-head. Ultimately, the chief justice's justice sense tingled in favor of Bush, because, you know: Al Gore is kind of a pain in the ass, you have to admit.

LOWER COURTS

There are also lower courts, as if anyone gives a crap.

Other Junk the Federal Government Does for Your Sorry Ass

Every day, nearly every American depends on services provided by the federal government, and no, that doesn't make you a goddamned Socialist. Dang, people. Take a chill pill and stop listening to so much talk radio.

Here are just a few of the vital services provided by the U.S. government:

THE U.S. MILITARY

The U.S. military has a long, distinguished history of protecting our nation, and the entire free world, from Nazis, Commies, terrorists, and, in several 1950s movies, space aliens and giant radioactive insects.

▶ Fact-Like Fact

The National Guard still spends two weekends every year training for the likelihood that the United States will be attacked by regular-sized grasshoppers placed in front of postcards to make them look huge and then cross-edited with footage of people screaming at giant things off-screen.

Today, there are over 1 million active duty military personnel serving all around the world. Well, probably not in Canada, though. Right? We don't have to worry about Canada, do we? Or do we? What are those America-hating bastards doing in Canada right now, what with their laser-guided toques and nuclear Timbits? Damn you, Canada! We're coming to get you!

These are the branches of our

armed services that will shortly be invading those Tim Hortons–loving hockey enthusiasts up in Canada:

U.S. Army: The oldest part of our armed forces, the U.S. Army traces its history back to the American Revolution. There would have been an air force back then, but air had not been invented yet.

U.S. Navy: The second oldest branch of America's military, the U.S. Navy has a long, distinguished history of serving the United States on the open seas. Great navy men have included John Paul Jones (who famously said, "I have not yet begun to fight!"), Admiral David Farragut ("Damn the torpedoes! Full speed ahead!"), and Vice Admiral Rihanna ("*Mahalo*, Mother!").

U.S. Marine Corps: Also dating back to the eighteenth century, the United States Marine Corps supports naval campaigns, mounts amphibious assaults, and serves "such other duties as the President may direct." This usually includes helping the President move (though, to be fair, the President usually provides pizza and brewskis).

U.S. Air Force: The U.S. Air Force was formed in 1947 when Dwight Eisenhower said, "You know what would be cool? Dropping shit out of airplanes and crap." And but so now we do, and it's pretty badass.

SOCIAL SECURITY

Signed into law in 1935, the Social Security Act provided much-needed benefits for retired workers throughout the country. This means your grandparents can afford the name-brand dog food, rather than the generic kind. Have you called them lately? They want to tell you about what happened on *Matlock* yesterday.

UNITED STATES SECRET SERVICE

These are the guys in the sharp suits, sunglasses, and earpieces who protect the President, the vice president, and their families from physical harm and *Breaking Bad* spoilers.

The Secret Service assigns code names to those they protect. Barack Obama is "Renegade." George W. Bush was "Durhay," while his veep Dick Cheney was "Darth." Bill Clinton was "Peener," while Al Gore was "That dude who invented the Internet or some shit."

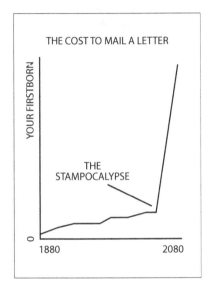

THE COST TO MAIL A LETTER

YOUR FIRSTBORN

THE STAMPOCALYPSE

0

1880   2080

THE U.S. POSTAL SERVICE

When you think about it, what the U.S. Postal Service does is pretty incredible: You give them some pocket change, and they lose your water bill! Soon, your water is shut off and you have to call your local water board. But the post office lost your phone bill, too, so that's been shut off as well. Soon, all your vital services have been cut off and you're going all over town to write large checks and try to explain. Thanks, Postal Service! We couldn't have done it without you!

Also: zip codes. Don't forget them, or you'll end up in secret zip code prison, which is under your local post office. Here, post office employees can waterboard you for not knowing how much a postcard stamp costs, and your only escape is to mail yourself to Cuba. Godspeed.

THE INTERNAL REVENUE SERVICE

In 1913, the Sixteenth Amendment to the Constitution gave Congress the right to levy an income tax against individuals and corporations. The Internal Revenue Service is the agency that collects these and other, even awesomer taxes.

The U.S. Tax Code is a simple, 73,000-page document that a four-year-old child could understand. This is why most certified public accountants are four-year-olds. After this age, the brain is less pliable and completely unable to deal with utter nonsense and total bullshit.

More than half of taxpayers now file their taxes electronically. For millions of people, e-filing has totally streamlined the process of counting your couch as a tax deduction under "place of business."

CIA

We don't know what all the Central Intelligence Agency does right now, but there's one thing we do know: they gave people free LSD back in the 1960s, which is all right with us. We are totally working on a time machine specifically so we can go back and get in on that action. Laters.

NATIONAL PARKS

The United States is home to several scenic national parks, and home to hundreds that are butt-ass ugly. When planning your vacation, choose wisely.

America's first national park, Yellowstone, was created in 1872. The entire country gathered there in 1875 for the first American Picnic. It was a disaster, because Mr. Jethro McKenzie of Bettendorf, Iowa, had signed up to bring the potato salad for the entire nation but forgot to bring it. "Dude, I flaked," he explained to a disappointed nation.

▶ Fact-Like Fact

Among America's butt-ass ugly national parks are Giant Steaming Mound of Feces in Texas, Opossum Carcass in Tennessee, and Joan Rivers's Weird Fiberglass Face in California.

There are national parks in nearly every state, except the ones that have already been completely paved over for parking (sorry, Delaware). Here are a few of America's most popular National Parks:

Everglades (Florida): Covering more than 1 million acres of pristine swampland in Florida, this is the park to visit if you love humidity. Other highlights of the Everglades include being eaten alive by mosquitos, being eaten alive by alligators, and being eaten alive by Sharktopus.

Glacier (Montana): Due to global warming, this national park is considering changing its name to A Complete and Utter Lack of Glacier National Park. We'll keep you posted.

Grand Canyon (Arizona): Every year, over 4 million Americans come to look at what is essentially a big-ass hole in the ground. This is the power of marketing, people.

Yellowstone (Wyoming and Montana): America's oldest national park, Yellowstone is still the number one spot to get mauled by bears who want your ham sandwich. Plus, there's a geyser or some shit!

Yosemite (California): This park is home to the rootin' tootinest, rackin' frackinest, fribblin' frabblinest sights you ever did see, ya long-eared galoot!

U.S. MONUMENTS

America is filled with monuments that remind us of how mega-awesome America is. Here are a few of America's most beloved monuments:

The Alamo

Located in San Antonio, the Alamo is the site of a battle between Texans and the Mexican Army. The Texans lost this battle. To the Mexican Army. Take a moment to let that sink in, Rocky.

Seriously, Texas? Our daughter's soccer team could take the Mexican Army. What is your problem? Even the French successfully invaded Mexico once. Come *on*, Texas. You're making America look bad.

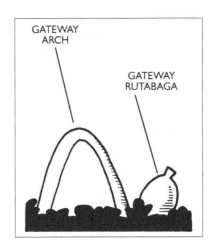

The Gateway Arch

Located in St. Louis, this massive structure honors the thousands of pioneers to the Western United States. These hearty pioneers traveled the Oregon Trail, where pretty much all of them were told, "You have died of dysentery."

The Liberty Bell

Philadelphia is home of the Liberty Bell, which has an enormous crack in it. Philadelphians say they don't know how the crack got there, but we're on to you, Philadelphia. You're why we can't have nice things.

The Lincoln Memorial

The Lincoln Memorial is located on the National Mall, right next to Baby Gap and the Sunglass Hut. It has been the site of many famous speeches over the years, most notably Martin Luther King's "Where Can I Find the Food Court?" speech.

The Statue of Liberty

France gave us the Statue of Liberty. But why? What was in it for them?

Turns out, the Statue of Liberty was meant to act as a sort of Trojan Horse for a French invasion of the United States. In Paris, the French filled the Statue of Liberty with thousands of French soldiers. Then they tied the statue down to a slow-moving barge that arrived in New York approximately six weeks later.

Instead of springing out and taking the entire Eastern Seaboard in one fell swoop, the few surviving French soldiers crawled out, begging for baguettes and little cigarettes. The French invasion had failed, but we got a pretty snazzy statue out of it. Although it took, like, 20 years to get the smell out.

The Vietnam Veterans Memorial

Located in Washington, DC, the Vietnam Veterans Memorial is a somber reminder that *Apocalypse Now* lost to *Kramer vs. Kramer* for

Best Picture at the 1979 Oscars. It was truly a dark, dark time in American history that we must never forget.

▶ Fact-Like Fact

Though let's face it, *The Muppet Movie* was totally robbed for Best Picture that year. Sadly, the Motion Picture Academy is famous for its continuing racism against Muppets, puppets, marionettes, and sock monkeys.

The Washington Monument

You decide: Is the Washington Monument a monstrously huge phallic symbol of America's might and power, or a middle finger directed at the rest of the world? Can it be both simultaneously?

You have 30 minutes to answer. Show all work.

The White House

The White House has been the official residence of the President since 1800. Before this, presidents had to dress in drag and live in a hotel for ladies with Peter Scolari.

The White House has a fascinating history. In 1814, the British set fire to it when they discovered that they were two years late for the War of 1812. President James Madison said, "We can rebuild it. We have the technology. We can make it better than it was before. Better . . . stronger . . . faster." And since then, the White House has been 100 percent bionic. The West Wing was added in 1901, by order of Aaron Sorkin.

Today, the White House is both the official residence of the President's family and home of the Oval Office, the official office of the President of the United States (though the President does much of the leading of the free world and whatnot at a nearby Starbucks, because they give the President free refills on the vanilla bean frappuccinos).

There are tours of the White House available daily; however, if you see something you're not supposed to see, you may be wrestled to the ground by the Secret Service and sent to Guantánamo for "safekeeping." Try to keep up with the tour, people.

The U.S. States

Like all countries, the United States is split into 50 states (even tiny countries like Luxembourg are divided into 50 states; most of their states can charitably be described as "fun-sized").

Each state has its own distinct personality. Some states, like California, are definitely suffering from multiple-personality disorder, while states like Indiana are total psychopaths.

Here is a list of all 50 states. Memorize it, or we'll hunt you down.

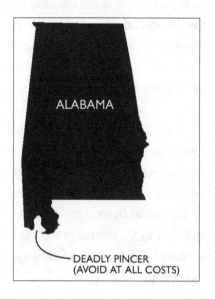

ALABAMA

DEADLY PINCER
(AVOID AT ALL COSTS)

Alabama

Alabama is the first state alphabetically (except for a brief period in the 1960s, when AAAAAAAAAANebraska was listed first in the Yellow Pages).

Alabama is also first in the nation in many other categories: people shootin' at varmints, people runnin' over varmints, and people cookin' varmints. Alabama has a varmint-based economy, making it one of the wealthiest states in the Union. At least, it will be when we switch from the gold standard to the varmint standard.

If we were you, we'd start stockpiling varmints down in the basement.

Alaska

America bought Alaska from Russia in 1867. Looking back, we maybe should have let Russia keep it.

Hear us out on this. The United States could have instead used the money for something really useful, like a giant butter sculpture of Martin Van Buren. And Russia would be stuck with all those Palins. It's a win-win, really. Unless you're Russia. Then you'd be the ones stuck with dozens of Palin-based reality shows. But: America would still have a giant butter sculpture of Martin Van Buren! USA! USA!

▶ Fact-Like Fact

While America missed out on a giant butter sculpture of Martin Van Buren, the United States does have a pretty sweet portrait of William Henry Harrison done with pasta and glitter glued to a board hanging in the Smithsonian.

Arizona

Now, we here at Disalmanac don't want to endorse any religion over another. And we're not saying we believe in a Heaven or a Hell.

But we know this much is true: if you're a bad, bad person in this life, Arizona is where you are sent after you die. There, the devil pokes you with his pitchfork and sends you down to work in the flame mines. The heat is unbearable. All you can hear is wailing and moaning, and a Michael Bolton greatest hits album playing on a continuous loop. There is pain; there is the gnashing of teeth; there is a TV that plays nothing but repeats of *Jersey Shore*.

There is still time for you, though. Reject your evil ways now so you can avoid being sent to Arizona. Accept Bondor, God of Darkness, as your one true savior before it's too late.

Arkansas

In 1836, Arkansas became our twenty-fifth state, while Andrew Jackson was president. And well, Andrew Jackson wasn't the brightest bulb in the tool shed, if you catch our drift. Though why you'd keep your lightbulbs in the tool shed is a mystery. Every time a lightbulb burned out in the house, you'd have to run out to the tool shed to get a replacement. It's not only extremely inconvenient, it could also be dangerous. What if there are bears out there? Or like, that dog from *Cujo*? Or what if it's nighttime, and your house is being overrun by zombies?

Of course, the idea of zombies is absurd anyway. Most people these days are cremated. So chill out about the zombie invasion, people. It's never gonna happen.

And that's why Arkansas.

California

OK, California, we get it. You have glamorous movie stars like Judd Nelson and Justine Bateman. Now get over your damn self and leave us alone.

Colorado

Colorado is chock-full of mountains. There's Pike's Peak, Martin's Mountain, Hill's Hill, Buford's Butte, Mason's Mesa, and more, and that's just in downtown Denver. The rest of the state is even worse.

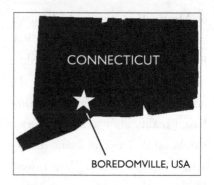

BOREDOMVILLE, USA

Connecticut

Movies such as *A Haunting in Connecticut* would have you believe Connecticut is full of ghosts. This is simply not true. In fact, a plucky group of four teenagers and their large dog who kind of talks drive around the state in their van, the Mystery Machine, and bust these hoaxes.

For instance, the Black Knight Ghost was actually Mr. Wickles, who wanted to steal all the valuables from a local museum. "And I would have gotten away with it," he said, "if it wasn't for you meddling kids!" Actually, he used a much stronger word than "meddling," but they couldn't use it in the cartoon they made of the case.

Delaware

The very first state to ratify the U.S. Constitution, in the 1960s Delaware was completely paved over to provide parking for the Philadelphia, Baltimore, and Washington metropolitan areas.

Here are a few facts about Delaware:

- **Size:** Forty regular spaces and three handicapped spaces
- **State Movie:** *Heavy Metal Parking Lot*
- **State Song:** Anything by Judas Priest or Whitesnake
- **Memorable Event:** That time Toby totally threw up all over that dude's Escalade before the AC/DC show last year. Dude!
- **Famous Delawareans:** Joe Biden started his political career in Delaware. He was elected to the U.S. House of Representatives in 1968 to represent the souped-up 1967 Mustang in space #12.

Florida

Have you ever seen Florida's state quarter? It portrays probably the greatest event in the state's history: the day the space shuttle fought some pirates for control of Gilligan's Island. This was one of the most decisive battles of the Civil War; schoolchildren learn about the battle in first grade through the old song, "Battle Hymn of Gilligan's Island." Who cannot be brought to tears by the lyrics, "Arrr, many salty tars were lost that day/and the Professor and Mary Anne . . ."?

Random Bonus Fact!

FRANK CONNIFF, COMEDIAN AND TV'S FRANK

The full title of D. W. Griffith's most famous film was *Birth of a Nation, Based on the Novel Push* by Sapphire.

Now if anyone brings up the state of Florida in the office or on the train, you can join in the conversation and tell them about that time when the space shuttle and some pirates fought for control of Gilligan's Island. You're welcome.

Georgia

Georgia, the state, is not to be confused with Georgia, the country. Georgia is larger in size than Georgia, while Georgia has a larger population than Georgia. Georgia's official song is "Georgia on My Mind," while Georgia's official song is "Georgia on My Mind."

Another key difference between Georgia and Georgia: in Georgia they speak a language that most Americans don't understand, while in Georgia they speak Russian.

Hawaii

If you're worried about whether people will think your birth certificate is legitimate, try not to be born in Hawaii. Enough said.

Idaho

Idaho is known for its Famous Potatoes (like Idaho's beloved former governor, Pappy the Potato). But watch out for Idaho's Infamous Turnips.

There was Tubey the Turnip, who once shot a beet for snoring too loud. And Terry the Turnip swindled millions in a complicated Ponzi scheme and then fled to Fiji, where he still lives today. He is on Interpol's list of the world's most wanted root vegetables and should be considered armed and dangerous (not to mention delicious, if brushed with olive oil and roasted in a 400-degree oven until golden brown).

Idaho is also home to Depressed Cashews, Flirtatious Rutabagas, and even a few Disgusted but Amused Chickpeas. There's something for everybody in Idaho.

Illinois

It's somewhere in the middle, that's all we know.

Indiana

Indiana is home to the Indianapolis 500. Every year, those "I would walk 500 miles" guys come in last. Someone should really buy them a car.

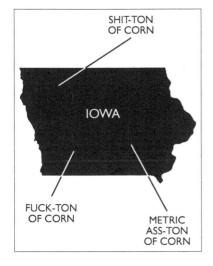

Iowa

The small Midwestern state of Iowa has a pivotal role to play every four years in our presidential elections. Yes, it's at Iowa's folksy county fairs that Iowans photograph the candidates as they bite into really quite phallic-looking corn dogs. Then Iowa puts the photos up on its Facebook page and we all laugh and laugh, until we realize we have to actually vote for one of them.

This is why voter participation was down to a record low of 2.7 percent in the last presidential election.

Kansas

All Kansas is dust in wind. That is *so* true, man. Far out.

Kentucky

Kentucky is not actually a state; officially, it's a commonwealth.

What's wrong, Kentucky? Being a state not good enough for you? Well, listen, Kentucky: you're no better than any of the rest of the states, so stop being all snooty and ditch this "commonwealth" crap, pronto. Don't make us sic Montana on you.

Louisiana

They may call them "bayous" in Louisiana, but don't be fooled: the state is really one large swamp, and Governor Swamp Thing is looking to keep it that way.

Do not bring your evil here, I warn you. Beware the wrath of Governor Swamp Thing.

Maine

When people think of Maine, what do they think of? We may never know, because nobody has ever thought of Maine. Well, maybe someday. But don't hold your breath.

Maryland

Maryland is a state. We would imagine some people live there and stuff . . . ? It probably has some geographical features: maybe there's a hill, maybe there's, like, a lake somewhere. Who knows?

> **Fact-Like Fact**
>
> Oh! We thought of a city in Maryland: Milwaukee! Oh, wait— that's in Wisconsin. Never mind.

There could quite possibly be a city in Maryland. And um, a state animal? Could be.

And that's everything you need to know about . . . Oh! We just remembered something cool about Maryland: no, wait. That's Delaware. Never mind.

Massachusetts

Massachusetts is called the Bay State, because it is on its sunny, golden beaches that *Baywatch* was filmed in the 1980s. Even as we speak, beautiful bebosomed lifeguards in red swimsuits are running in slow motion toward the ocean to save a small child, their glorious long blond hair waving in the wind while their magnificent breasts sway like meaty pendulums. There are women lifeguards, also.

Michigan

What has happened to you, Michigan? You were once such a mighty state, and now look at you: crawling around on the sidewalk, looking for spare change for your next fix.

You need real help, Michigan. We are here today to offer you the help you need.

But if you do not accept this help, there will be a price. We won't give you any more money, and you can't live in our garage anymore, or use it as a meth lab. We simply cannot enable your addiction anymore, Michigan.

So please, Michigan, accept this offer of help. We can't stand to see you throwing your life away.

Minnesota

Minnesota calls itself "Land of 10,000 Lakes." Let's take a look at some of those lakes, shall we?

- Big Pine Lake is just a mud puddle in Grandpa and Grandma's driveway.

- White Bear Lake is not so much a lake as it is a 10,000-foot-tall mountain located in Colorado.
- Pequaywan Lake is actually just a photograph of a lake in some guy's wallet in Duluth.

As you can see, many of Minnesota's "lakes" don't meet the World Lake Commission's definition of a lake, which is "Dude, it has to be a damn lake."

Here's the sad, cold truth: Minnesota doesn't have 10,000 lakes at all. The total is closer to 12,000. Stop the bullshit, Minnesota.

Mississippi

Mississippi is known as the Magnolia State. And while the magnolias were nice for a while, the state is now overrun with them. Everywhere you turn, millions of magnolias. And they've developed a taste for human blood.

Yes, giant man-eating magnolias are devouring the entire population of Mississippi, and nothing can stop them. All the DDT they tried on them back in the 1950s only made them stronger, more sentient, and meaner. Radiation only made them larger—as much as 50 feet tall, able to use their roots and leaves to move about and shove people into their horrible, gaping maws. Soon, the entire world will fall victim to the beautiful, terrible magnolias. You have been warned.

Missouri

Many famous people have been born in Missouri, like that one guy. You know. He was on that show, with the woman who was in that other thing. No, not that show. The one with the theme song.

Oh, wait. I'm thinking of a completely other show, which means nobody famous has ever come from Missouri. Never mind.

Montana

Don't screw with Montana. They will pound the living boogers out of you. They will pound the dead boogers of you. They will pound *all* the boogers out of you.

Now, we mean this in a nice way, Montana, but have you considered anger management classes . . . ? They . . . Hey! Ow. No hit! Ow! Oof! Blurghhhhh!

Nebraska

Nebraska's capital is Lincoln. But Illinois is the Land of Lincoln. Confused? Don't be—the explanation is quite simple!

You see, Nebraska has taken the cost-saving measure of outsourcing their entire state government to an office park in the suburban Chicago area.

▶ Fact-Like Fact

Nebraska's state animal is corn. Please don't tell them that corn is not an animal.

Sadly, Nebraska is not saving nearly enough money and will soon move its state government to a call center in Bangalore. Nebraska residents who want to renew their driver's licenses will have to pay thousands for an airline ticket, travel to a DMV in India, and stand in line for many, many days, maybe even weeks, until their number (*"Do sau saat!"*) is called. Oh, did we mention the tens of thousands of dollars it will cost to ship your car to Bangalore and back to have its emissions tested?

But it will be worth it, for all the time and money Nebraskans will save, and that's all that matters.

Nevada

Nevada is home to casinos, brothels, and nuclear bomb testing facilities. Sadly, the constant barrage of radiation since the 1950s has had a serious effect on Nevada. Nearly all the sex workers at Nevada's legal brothels are more than 50 feet tall (as required by law), while erstwhile Las Vegas performer Celine Dion has turned into a giant monster called "Celinezilla," picking up tourist buses and slamming them back down on the Vegas strip with impunity. Caesar's Palace now charges $20 for this "ride." It's worth it.

New Hampshire

New Hampshire is known for its folksy slogan "Live Free or Die." But did you know they tried several other state mottos before settling on "Live Free or Die"? Here are a few of the also-rans:

- Die Hard with a Vengeance
- Buy One, Get One Free
- Faster, Pussycat! Kill! Kill!
- Living Is Easy with Eyes Closed
- Free Nelson Mandela
- Liv Ullmann or Die
- She's a Very Freaky Girl, the Kind You Don't Take Home to Mother
- Money for Nothing and the Chicks for Free
- Live, Die, or Morgan Freeman
- Extra Life at 1 Million Points
- Live Long and Prosper
- Die Another Day
- Freeze Livers or Die
- Go Big or Go Home
- YOLO
- Go Home or Go Bowling
- Deep Fry or Live

Did New Hampshire make the right choice? We may never know.

New Jersey

New Jersey is known as the Garden State. So who's going to tell them? Not it.

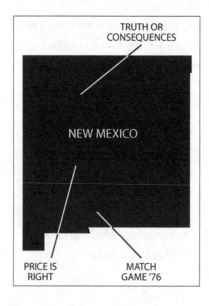

New Mexico

New Mexico is not located in Mexico, nor is it new. What's with all the lies, New Mexico? Are you even a state? How can we believe anything that comes out of your lying mouth, you lying liar?

New York

The state of New York is so much more than New York City. No, really. Like, um . . . Well, we can't think of anything right now, but trust us. So much other stuff in New York! Yep. Pretty much.

North Carolina

Over the years, North Carolina has taken the brunt of many hurricanes. In the 1960s, North Carolina felt the wrath of Hurricane Michael, Hurricane Jermaine, Hurricane Tito, and Hurricane the Other Two Guys in the Jackson Five Whose Names Nobody Ever Remembers. In the 1970s, North Carolina was pounded by Hurricane Richie, Hurricane Fonzie, and Hurricane Potsie. The 1980s saw North Carolina pummeled by Hurricane Balki, Hurricane ALF, Hurricane Tootie, and Hurricane Mr. T.

In the past decade, North Carolina has been struck by Hurricane Apl.De.Ap, Hurricane Wiz Khalifa, and Hurricane Ke$ha. All of this on top of the untold damage produced by 2011's Hurricane Bieber.

North Dakota

There is growing evidence that North Dakota may be a hoax. More on this story as it develops.

Ohio

You might think that's an astronaut on the Ohio state quarter, but you would be wrong, wrong, wrong again. Man, you are stupid. Wow.

No, that's no astronaut, it's a dude in a hazmat suit, because Ohio is basically one huge-ass toxic waste dump. Just breathing Ohio air or drinking some Ohio water will turn you into a reptile person. And while some of our greatest presidents came from Ohio, all of them were reptile people—especially James A. Garfield, who was assassinated by a disappointed herpetophobic office-seeker.

So if you visit Ohio, be sure to wear your hazmat suit at all times unless you too wish to become a reptile man. Which, maybe you do. We don't know you. Whatever.

▶ Fact-Like Fact

Go ahead, become a reptile man. We don't care if you throw it all away just so you can eat mice or whatever it is reptiles do all damn day. Disappoint your mother, that's fine.

Oklahoma

There's a hit Broadway musical called *Oklahoma!*, which is easily the least Oklahoma-y thing about Oklahoma.

Oregon

Many people think Oregon is pronounced "OreGONE," which is wrong. Wrong, wrong, wrong. Seriously, what is wrong with you people? "OreGONE"? Seriously? It's "OreGUN." Get with the program, America.

Would it be so hard to pronounce it correctly? Or do you pronounce *all* the state names wrong? Do you say "Neevayda?" "Minor Soda?" "Penis Sylvanier?" "Sooth Daycooter?" No, you do not. Because if you did, you would sound like an imbecile. So guess what you sound like when you say "OreGONE"? Hint: It rhymes with "schmucking schmidiot."

Pennsylvania

If you've ever driven across Pennsylvania, you know it takes forever. This is because the middle portion of Pennsylvania is a wormhole. Pennsylvania is actually over 77 million light-years across, or over 6 billion times the distance between the Earth and the Sun. And there are hardly any Arby's or Hardee's the whole way.

Not to mention it's a toll road—you'd better have approximately 70 trillion quarters ready for the trip, Slappy.

Rhode Island

Well, we found out the hard way that Rhode Island isn't really an island. There were no grass skirts, no leis or luaus, and no giant rum drinks with fruit and little umbrel-

las served in coconut shells. What the hell, Rhode Island?

Also? There were no beautiful black sand beaches. Or palm trees. While there was one Jimmy Buffett song, it was playing at the T.G.I.McGillicuddy's in Providence where we had dinner one night, so we're not sure that counts. Plus, we went in December, and it was *way* too cold to surf.

We're on to you, Rhode Island.

South Carolina

South Carolina is the emergency backup Carolina, just in case something goes wrong with North Carolina. So far, so good, yes. But, better safe than sorry.

South Dakota

Let's face it, South Dakota's the "cool" Dakota. South Dakota's the Dakota that lets you stay up past your bedtime. South Dakota's the Dakota that lets you eat a whole thing of M&M's for dinner. South Dakota's the Dakota that lets you watch that scary movie that other Dakota says you're too young to watch.

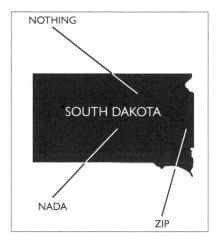

Man, we wish we could always stay with South Dakota.

Tennessee

Oh, we all like to pretend that Tennessee is a real state, with senators and a capital and everything. But the truth is, it didn't pass the entrance exams to become a state: in fact, it only got 14 percent of the answers right and didn't even spell its name correctly at the top of the answer sheet.

But we let it hang out with all the other states because we don't want to hurt its feelings. So please, don't tell Tennessee about any of this.

Texas

Did you know that, despite their slogan, there are literally dozens of ways to mess with Texas? It's true! Try one of these Texas-messing techniques today:

1. Call Texas and ask them if their refrigerator is running.
2. Leave a burning bag of dog poo at Texas's front door; then ring the doorbell and run away.
3. Call Homeland Security and tell them Texas is a known terrorist, and watch as Texas is dragged off to Gitmo, never to return! What a hoot!
4. Just push 'em down and kick 'em in the nads.

We bet you can come up with your own ways to mess with Texas. Be creative!

Utah

Utah is the Beehive State, because of the huge swarms of killer bees that roam the state, looking for human blood.

There are many ways killer bees can do you in. Stinging, of course. But also: guns, crossbows, and making you eat some chicken salad they've left out in the sun all day. There's also poison, kung fu, and running you over in a huge, silver SUV.

As well: Arson. Explosives. Ancient samurai swords. Ninja throwing stars. Viking breath. The five-finger death punch. Throwing you in front of an oncoming locomotive. Throwing you off a cliff, onto the jagged rocks below.

Not to mention: Using telekinesis to make your head explode, like in the movie *Scanners*. Machetes. Making you eat lots of yummy, buttery foods and waiting around until you have a massive coronary. Hanging. The electric chair. Terminal herpes.

> ### ▶ Fact-Like Fact
> **Terminal herpes is also called "terpes" and "really effing gross."**

Yes, these, and many, many more. So if you go to Utah, "bee" careful. (See what we did there? No? Oh, never mind.)

Vermont

While Montana is called the Big Sky State, Vermont is so small that it's known as the Tiny Sky State. In fact, Vermont's sky is so tiny that it is not visible to the naked eye. Even individual photons of sunlight are too large to enter their tiny sky, and the pale, pale people of Vermont have to suck on stunted maple trees for sustenance. It's sad, really.

Because of Vermont's microscopic sky, airplanes can't fly overhead without passing into the tenth and eleventh dimensions, as posited by Type II-A String Theory. Hundreds of pilots and airline passengers are now trapped in the higher dimensions. Scientists have no idea of how to save them without bringing the horrible eleventh-dimension spider-monsters from Hell back into our dimension as well. One proposal: send the eleventh-dimension spider-monkeys from Hell to Phoenix, because really, who'd notice?

Virginia

Virginia is known for being the home of the Jamestown settlement in 1607. But what do we really know about Virginia? Virginia says it was in Wensleydale when Sir Albert was murdered, but none of us saw Virginia leave the estate, or return early the next morning.

Virginia also had a motive for killing Sir Albert—I've discovered that Sir Albert had been blackmailing Virginia over an embarrassing youthful indiscretion involving a young woman and her horse. As for the weapon, Virginia is quite handy with a crossbow. Of course, Sir Albert was poisoned. I still haven't worked this part out yet.

Here are a few fact-like facts about the state of Virginia:

- Virginia is the birthplace of many presidents—presidents who could have helped Virginia murder Sir Albert in the garden last night!
- Virginia became a state in 1788, which is the last time any of us saw Sir Albert alive at his estate, Ferretshire Woods.
- And let's not forget that Virginia was involved in that unpleasantness on the moors last autumn, when Inspector Chesleyhelm turned up dead.

Washington

145

According to the *Twilight* books, the state of Washington is the home of vampires. Sparkly, annoying teenaged vampires. Oh, and they're all handsome, telepathic, and, for some reason, they collect expensive vintage automobiles. Sure, why not?

So if you visit Washington State, please kick some scrawny, emo vampire butt for us. Thank you for your attention in this matter.

West Virginia

West Virginia is coal country. The state animal is coal. The state bird is coal. The governor is a bag of coal. The state song is "Workin' in a Coal Mine," except they've changed every word in the song to "coal," so it now goes: "Coal coal coal coal coal coal, coal coal coal coal, coal coal coal coal coal, WHOO! Coal coal coal coal coal coal."

The whole damn state is nothing but coal. And as West Virginians say, "Coal coal coal, coal coal coal."

Wisconsin

Poets and popular songwriters hate Wisconsin, because nothing rhymes with "Wisconsin." Well, "Steve Monson," who was this guy we went to junior high with. Steve Monson was big for his age and always sweaty.

We used to help Steve Monson with his math homework, because he just couldn't get the hang out of how numbers work. He seriously thought eight came before five, and that six was a letter. And this was, like, pre-algebra, so now x and y weren't just letters but numbers also, and Steve Monson just could not understand. He'd stare at the blackboard, sweating, his mouth agape (always mouth agape, Steve Monson, always), his eyes all squinty while he wheezed ever so softly.

We're not sure what happened to Steve Monson after seventh grade. It probably involved sweating, as does Wisconsin.

Wyoming

The less said about Wyoming, the better. Seriously, you do *not* want to know. It's pretty disgusting.

Major-Ass U.S. Cities

America has these things called "cities," where people gather to live in large numbers. It seems like a bad idea to us, but here is a list of some of the largest U.S. cities. For your convenience, they are listed alphabetically by net weight.

Albuquerque, New Mexico

Albuquerque is located in the middle of nowhere, in central New Mexico. This may seem inconvenient, but actually it's for your own safety: decades of nuclear tests in the area have turned most Albuquerque residents into chupacabra-like mutants, bizarre goat-like creatures with razor-like teeth and a thirst for human blood.

Albuquerque's population is approximately 78 percent chupacabra and 22 percent victim. The chief industries of Albuquerque include a growing sense of dread, mutilated cattle that foreshadow your own certain doom, and high-tech products.

▶ Fact-Like Fact

Albuquerque's tourism slogan is "In the desert, no one can hear you scream."

Atlanta, Georgia

Many people believe that Atlanta hosted the 1996 Summer Olympics. This, of course, is an urban myth. As we all know, the 1996 Summer Olympics were held in Paris. Because come on—where would you hold a prestigious international event. a beautiful, cosmopolitan city like Paris, or Atlanta, best known for being home of the Weather Channel and a museum dedicated to Coca-Cola? Yeah, that's what we thought.

But: do *not* tell the residents of Atlanta that they didn't host the Olympics. They still believe it, and it would just break their hearts if they ever found out. We would hate to disappoint such nice, polite people.

Boston, Massachussetts

Boston is named for the giant, guitar-shaped spaceship hovering permanently overhead, constantly beaming down album-oriented classic rock to the inhabitants. It's wicked awesome.

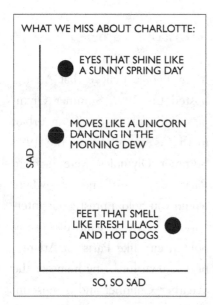

WHAT WE MISS ABOUT CHARLOTTE:

EYES THAT SHINE LIKE A SUNNY SPRING DAY

MOVES LIKE A UNICORN DANCING IN THE MORNING DEW

SAD

FEET THAT SMELL LIKE FRESH LILACS AND HOT DOGS

SO, SO SAD

Charlotte, North Carolina

We used to go out with Charlotte. It was years ago, but it still hurts like it was only yesterday. We thought it was the real thing, but Charlotte dumped us for an investment banker with a Jaguar. Is that what you wanted, Charlotte? A Jaguar? We would have gotten you a Jaguar, Charlotte. We'd have given you anything.

Charlotte's chief industry is that cute little dimple in her cheek when she laughs like a clear mountain creek on a sunny spring day.

We hear Charlotte's married now, to a Microsoft millionaire out in Seattle. We thought you hated the outdoors, Charlotte, but your Facebook page has all these photos of you hiking and camping, though we certainly don't stay up all night looking at your Facebook page and sobbing, because that would be pathetic, right? Ha! We're fine. Really. Oh, why, Charlotte? Why?

Chicago, Illinois

Chicago is known as the City of Broad Shoulders, the Windy City, the Hog Butcher to the World, the Second City, and Lord knows what else. Clearly, Chicago is suffering from multiple personality disorder and needs to choose just one damn nickname. Pick one, Chicago. We'll wait here.

Columbus, Ohio

Columbus is named after Christopher Columbus, even though the closest Columbus ever got to Columbus was, like, fucking Jamaica or some shit. Why not call Columbus, say, Gandhiville? Because I'm pretty sure he never set foot in Ohio, either. Or maybe Einstein City, or Spongebobopolis. Hell, call it Disalmanac, because we're sure as shit never going to a city named after a dude who was never there.

Of course, Columbus isn't the only state capital named after somebody who never set foot in the city. Madison, Wisconsin, is named for U.S. president James Madison, while Davenport, Iowa, is named after Digger Davenport, the shapely fictional TV private eye from the hit television show *Davenport: Dick After Dark*.

Dallas, Texas

Pretty much everybody stopped giving a crap about the city of Dallas when it turned out the whole city was a dream Pamela Ewing had while Bobby was in the shower or something. Lame.

Random Bonus Fact!

STACY PERSHALL, AUTHOR

The Arkansas version of Punxsutawney Phil is a frog named Mr. Hippity Hop, and if your frog can beat him in the toad jumping contest at Toad Suck Daze, you win a scholarship to the beauty school in Dardanelle.

Detroit, Michigan

The first time you visit Detroit, you'll notice right away that T. S. Eliot based his poem "The Waste Land" on the Michigan city. Indeed, April is the cruelest month in Detroit, as that's when your cousin the archduke straps you to a damn sled and down you go. Then he shows you fear in a handful of dust and you're really screwed.

Residents of Detroit are neither living nor dead, and they know nothing, looking into the heart of light, the silence, which is located in the beautiful Lafayette Park area, under the brown fog of a winter dawn. The chief industry in Detroit is turning the wheel and looking to windward, considering Phlebas, who was once handsome and tall as you, though the auto industry is making a comeback.

A popular tourist destination is this decayed hole among the mountains. Also, over the tumbled graves, there is the empty chapel, only the wind's home. Families enjoy getting their picture taken with the wind and buying T-shirts reading, "My grandparents went over the tumbled graves and all I got was this lousy T-shirt."

Honolulu, Hawaii

Located in the middle of the Pacific, Honolulu is a tropical paradise, with sun, sand, and a never-ending supply of alcoholic drinks the size of your head with cute names like Sex on the Beach, Sand All Up My General Ass and Cooter Region, and Months of Painful, Burning Regret.

Honolulu's chief industry is tourism, with factories churning out millions of tourists annually. For some reason, all of these tourists always end up on your flight, drinking, carrying on, and pooping on the drink cart. Try driving to Honolulu instead. You'll be glad you did, unless your car doesn't float. Then you're kind of screwed.

Houston, Texas

Located someplace in Texas, Houston is America's fourth largest city; its population even surpasses that of Singapore, the world's largest city-state. That's right: Singapore is a city that for some reason is also a country. Seriously. Like, the place is smaller than Houston, and it's a goddamn country? Where do they get off, pulling that shit?

Although—if Houston were to secede from the United States and become its own country, who'd miss it, really? Right? It's not like anyone ever goes there. Their sports teams kinda suck, anyway. It's just Halliburton and a bunch of strip malls.

Let's get on this. If you know anybody in Houston, please ask them to secede from the union immediately. Or maybe write your congressperson and have him or her kick Houston out of the country. Stupid Houston. Who needs it?

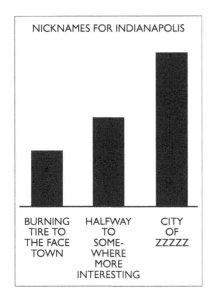

NICKNAMES FOR INDIANAPOLIS

BURNING TIRE TO THE FACE TOWN

HALFWAY TO SOMEWHERE MORE INTERESTING

CITY OF ZZZZZ

Indianapolis, Indiana

Indianapolis is named for its founder, H. Thaddeus Indianapolis III, who said, "I know what let's do. Let's build a city right in the middle of nowhere. That's a great idea." And so Indianapolis was born, because nobody in Indiana gets sarcasm.

Las Vegas, Nevada

Las Vegas is home to casinos, and nearby Area 51 is thought to be home to space aliens. Put two and two together, people—space aliens run Las Vegas casinos. Don't believe us? Who else would think Siegfried and Roy were a suitable entertainment?

The space aliens use the billions they make from their Vegas casinos every year to fund their efforts at world domination. Ke$ha? Space alien. Charlie Sheen? Space alien. Lady Gaga? Trick question! She's a robot.

Los Angeles, California

Los Angeles is home to the moving picture industry. We saw a movie once. It was *Outrageous Fortune*, with Bette Midler and that woman from *Cheers*. No, not her. The other one. No, the other other one. Right. Her. Anyway, we absolutely hated that movie, which is why we believe the motion picture is a passing fad that will be replaced by something more entertaining and fulfilling, like stabbing yourself in the eyeballs with a screwdriver, or croquet.

Los Angeles is also home of the music industry, which we also believe to be a passing fancy, because, you know: Maroon 5.

Finally, Los Angeles is home to the television industry. Television is certainly no passing fad; entertainments such as *Keeping Up with the Kardashians* and *Cupcake Mafia War Swamp Wives in Alaska* will live forever. Good job, Los Angeles!

Memphis, Tennessee

The chief tourist attraction in Memphis is Graceland, the palatial home of Elvis Presley. A popular urban legend is that "the King" died in his bathroom while sitting on the toilet. This is not true! Elvis died a hero, in Graceland's Jungle Room, fighting off man-eating tigers, bloodthirsty alligators, and surprisingly tenacious lemurs while sitting on the toilet.

There was at least one toilet in each room in Graceland; some rooms had as many as 58 toilets. You can see why it's such a tourist attraction.

Miami, Florida

Miami, located above the Arctic Circle, is the Land of the Midnight Sun. Polar bears and caribou frolic all summer long on the frozen tundra. Ice road truckers deliver ice roads to all the residents. Putin happily rears his head morning, noon, and night.

Of course, winter is a different story. Several feet of snow make travel impossible. Wily glaciers stalk and attack any Miamian who ventures out of his or her igloo. Of course, most Miami residents avoid this fate by hibernating for the entire winter, curling up with grizzly bears in their cozy caves.

Then in the spring, Miamians and grizzly bears alike awake from their slumber and, stretching and yawning, blinkingly enter a bright new world. New man-cubs are born (what, you think Miamians and grizzly bears spend all that time just sleeping?) and the cycle of life begins anew in beautiful Miami.

Milwaukee, Wisconsin

There is a growing body of evidence that Milwaukee is a hoax. We would investigate, but it would mean having to go to Wisconsin. Not happening.

Minneapolis, Minnesota

Minneapolis and St. Paul make up the Twin Cities. But what most people don't know is that Minneapolis is St. Paul's evil twin. One way to spot the difference: everyone in St. Paul is clean-shaven, while all the residents of Minneapolis have evil little goatees, which they stroke while they cackle about their evil schemes.

And what sorts of evil schemes is Minneapolis hatching? Well, it is Minnesota, so most of Minneapolis's evil schemes revolve around asking you to please try some lutefisk. Admittedly, it's a polite evil, but it's evil nonetheless. So beware of Minneapolis, sitting there with

its eye patch and stroking its evil kitty cat, offering you a slice of its freshly baked lingonberry pie.

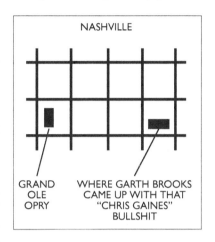

Nashville, Tennessee

They don't call Nashville "Music City" for nothing: it's the home of the Grand Ole Opry. When it first opened, the Grand Ole Opry was to be the nation's premier spelling bee venue. But since all three words of its name are misspelled ("Grand" is a misspelling of "Goober Peas"), it was doomed to failure. It shut its doors after the Spelling Riots of 1919. Several years later, it reopened as a country music venue (country music fans don't care how you spell "goober peas"), and soon, Nashville was the capital of the country music scene.

Of course, being home to country music brings its own problems. All the drinking, trains, pickup trucks, divorces, and the occasional new recording by Kenny Rogers's weird-ass head all make Nashville a dangerous place after dark. Be careful out there, and get us some of those delicious goober peas.

New York, New York

New York is the largest city in the United States. You got a problem with that?

There are many famous tourist attractions in New York. What are they? Who wants to know? You sure ask a lot of questions. Let me ask you a question: do you like your face? Because it would be a shame if something happened to it, like if somebody stabbed it or lit your face on fire. What? Oh, you like your face? Then maybe don't ask so many questions.

Many industries are located in New York, as well. You're not going to ask which ones, are you? Because that wouldn't be good for your what do call it, health. Medical studies have shown that sticking your big nose into business that doesn't concern you can result in serious health problems, like being pushed off a tall building or being stuffed into a gunnysack and dumped in the East River. That would be a shame, to suffer from such serious health problems.

Enjoy your visit to New York. Just don't ask too many questions, and never tell anybody what you saw here, or we'll put the kibosh on you, capiche?

Oakland, California

Oh, Oakland—home of the mighty oaks! A mighty sylvan glen on the Pacific. A majestic, twinkling arc of cyan above an emerald canopy that rustles with every one of the great forest god's breaths and fills the heart of yon weary traveler with ecstatic visions! This fertile, verdant bed of soil nourishes the mighty oaks of Oakland, their strong trunks supporting the whippoorwill, the woodpecker, and the wren! Lo, has man seen such beauty as this?

Also, you can totally score crack there. Ask for Fat Mike.

Oklahoma City, Oklahoma

Oklahoma City is a wonderful, vibrant city that is, unfortunately, located right in the middle of the area known as "Tornado Alley." In fact, it started out as Oklahoma City, Tennessee, back in 1887, but was blown across the border into Kentucky in 1903. Since then, Oklahoma City has been located in at least seven states. It has recently adopted the motto "Oklahoma City: I Don't Think We're in Kansas Anymore. Unless We Are."

 **Fact-Like Fact**

Oklahoma City is Oklahoma's Oklahomeliest city.

Of course, tornadoes aren't Oklahoma City's only weather problem. It's also located on Golf Ball–Sized Hail Avenue, Level Five Hurricane Lane, and Plague of Locusts Boulevard. If you're going to visit Okla-

homa City, bring an extra-strong umbrella in case it rains flaming toads, and make sure your suitcase has wheels because a tornado may blow you into Texas or Saskatchewan. Good luck.

Philadelphia, Pennsylvania

The comedian W. C. Fields once remarked about death, "On the whole, I'd rather be in Philadelphia." What Fields didn't realize was that Philadelphia is the dark, shadowy void of death.

When we die, our souls are immediately transported to Philadelphia. Here, they spend eternity shrouded in darkness, solemnly contemplating the mistakes and regrets of a life not lived as one might have wished. Also, there are cheesesteaks.

Phoenix, Arizona

Phoenix is the largest city in Arizona, which is kind of like being the King of the Hot Dog on a Stick in your local mall food court. Nobody cares, but: free hot dogs. But, but: you look like kind of an idiot wearing a crown with your Hot Dog on a Stick uniform, so maybe stop doing that, you pretentious ass.

Sacramento, California

Sacramento was founded during the great Gold Rush of 1849, and today, 86 percent of the population is made up of grizzled old prospectors and their mules (which are also grizzled and old).

The city's slogan is "Consarn It All to H-E Double Toothpicks!" This is probably America's most inspirational city slogan, after Buffalo's "Give Us a Quarter for Some Coffee?"

San Antonio, Texas

San Antonio is home of the Alamo, which is a thing you're supposed to remember. Did you remember it? Good! Our work here is done.

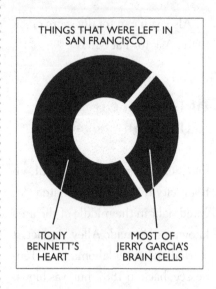

THINGS THAT WERE LEFT IN SAN FRANCISCO

TONY BENNETT'S HEART

MOST OF JERRY GARCIA'S BRAIN CELLS

San Francisco, California

We went to San Francisco once and saw their famous Cow Palace. It wasn't palatial at all, and there sure weren't any cows. Just a whole lot of Muppets on Ice. That's why we call San Francisco "the City of Massive, Life-Crushing Disappointment." But hey, if you want your life to be a sad parade of lies, then by all means go visit San Francisco's so-called palace of cows. We'll wait here.

San Jose, California

San Jose is the largest city in Silicon Valley, the headquarters of the world's computer industry. So if anything ever goes wrong with your computer, just pick up your phone and randomly call any number in the 408 area code. Anyone who answers will be able to help.

San Jose is also home to many Internet superstars; among its more famous residents are that cat that can haz cheeseburger, the walrus whose bucket they be stealing, and the "Chocolate Rain" dude. San Jose's mayor is the Dramatic Chipmunk, who narrowly lost the California gubernatorial race last year to the honey badger, who doesn't give a crap.

Seattle, Washington

Rain, rain, and more rain—that's what Seattle is known for. But this gives short shrift to Seattle's most beautiful feature: mildew, and lots of it.

South of Seattle, you'll find great mildew farms with magnificent rolling fields of mildew as far as the eye can see. They'll even let you pick your own mildew and eat it, fresh off the vine. East of town are the Great Mildew Mountains, where you'll find mildew skiing, mildew climbing, and all sorts of other mildew-oriented recreational activities.

▶ Fact-Like Fact

Seattle was home to grunge rock, a popular music of the 1990s until Creed came along and ruined it for everybody, the bastards.

Plus, Seattle is located right on the Mildew Sound, the largest body of fresh mildew in the United States. Mildew Sound has fun activities for the entire family—mildew swimming, mildew surfing, and watching for mildew whales. So much mildew!

Washington, DC

Washington, DC, isn't just our nation's capital. It's also the home of tens of thousands of lobbyists, roaming free in great herds on the great plains of K Street.

Sometimes, the lobbyist herds become larger than Washington can handle. Then, the herds must be thinned. Open season is declared on lobbyists, and the hunt is on. A savvy hunter can take five or more in a day. And last year, Sarah Palin shot several lobbyists from her special lobbyist-hunting helicopter.

Groups like CETUL (Corporations for the Ethical Treatment of Unethical Lobbyists) decry this annual hunt, but it's best for the environment of Washington, DC. Can you imagine what Washington would be like if lobbyists were allowed to run rampant, doing anything they wanted? Oh. Wait.

PART THREE

The World

Why a world? Why not, say, a photo of Nick Lachey or a thing of string cheese? Well, have you ever tried to put 7 billion people on a photo of Nick Lachey? You haven't? Then maybe you should stop asking such stupid questions.

The world: actual size.

The world is the planet we live on. It has had a history that nearly verged on the interesting sometimes. It is home to many nations, most of the names of which end in -stan for some reason. Also, there are many religions out there in the world, so if you're looking to hate people you've never met for the most superficial and flimsy of reasons, oh boy, are you in luck.

And now: the world. It's time to shove knowledge into your head and hope some of it actually reaches your brain.

The History of the Damn World

First, there was a world. Then, there were dinosaurs. Then some dude invented fire and we were on our way.

The Dawn of Civilization: Why Do We Have to Get up So Early?

Mesopotamia, between the Tigris and Euphrates rivers, was the cra-dle of civilization. Why was civilization born here and not say, in Boise, Idaho? Well, have you seen Boise, Idaho? They still don't have civilization there. They just got fire three years ago, for Christ's sake. Boise's got a long, long way to go.

Once started, civilization flourished in Mesopotamia. The ancient Sumerians invented writing, the calendar (though it was a Garfield calendar, but still), and wheeled carts. Before this, carts didn't have wheels, but were rocket-powered. Kind of a step backward, really.

Later, the Babylonians conquered the Sumerians, even though the Sumerians were armed with such impressive weapons as calendars and wheeled carts. The Babylonian king Hammurabi instituted the first set of laws, called Hammurabi's Code. Most of these laws involved not making fun of Hammurabi's huge-ass nose on pain of death, but it was the first step toward the society we live in today—in fact, in most U.S. states making fun of Hammurabi's nose is still a capital offense.

Around the same time, a civilization was born along the Nile River in Egypt, based on the radical new idea that they could make fun of Hammurabi all they wanted, because they weren't in Mesopotamia, neener neener neener.

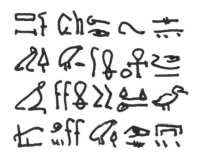

An example of ancient Sumerian writing. This says, "We're not saying Hammurabi has a big nose, but the Moon is one of his boogers." Clearly, humor had yet to be invented.

The ancient Egyptians developed hieroglyphics and papyrus, and so were able to invent the greatest advance of the time, the grocery list. At its peak, the great library at Alexandria housed several million grocery lists—and not just grocery lists, but maps to keggers, Starbucks orders for the entire office, and doodles of bunnies and kitties.

But the most lasting monuments to the ancient Egyptians are their colossal pyramids, which still stand today. The pyramids were huge tombs for the ancient Egyptian pharaohs, who were often laid to rest with hundreds of slaves, thousands of pets, and, in case Indiana Jones showed up 4,000 years later, a big pit full of snakes that are apparently immortal or something. Seriously, why are those snakes even still alive? That is creepy. Anyway, today the pyramids are a tourist attraction, which is like going to a cemetery for your vacation. Have fun, Goth chicks.

> ## Fact-Like Fact

Seriously, have those snakes been eating down there for thousands of years? Where do they poop? So many questions, George Lucas.

Ancient Greece and Rome: When Greco-Roman Wrestling Ruled the Planet

Around 1650 BC, the ancient Greeks started to emerge with their own civilization, which they called Ancient Greece (though some had wanted to call it "Nothing but Gyros!").

But ancient Greek culture eventually transcended the gyro, giving us many of the basic ideas of Western Civilization today. The Greeks invented democracy, which, sadly, has led directly to Sarah Palin. But there were good things, too. Archimedes gave us science, and Euclid and Pythagoras gave us math. So the ancient Greeks are why you only got a 900 on your SAT.

The ancient Greeks also gave us the building blocks of culture: philosophy, drama, sculpture, epic poetry, architecture, the Olympics, wrestling (both the WWF and the WWE), and really well-abbed guys in short dresses shouting "This is Sparta!" a whole bunch. Christ, they were annoying.

Greece was also a military power, winning the Trojan War (the prize: a lifetime supply of condoms). But eventually, Greece's many city-states turned on one another, fighting the Peloponnesian War. Unfortunately, nobody knew where Peloponnesia was, and so ancient Greece fell into turmoil, and Greek culture started to fade.

But as the golden age of ancient Greece closed, a new ruler stepped

Alexander the Great. Ladies?

in: Alexander the Great, also known as 336 BC's Sexiest Man Alive. Alexander the Great was only in his hot, throbbing twenties when, with smoldering eyes and manly eyebrows, he quickly crushed the Greeks and moved on to Asia and Egypt to create the largest empire the world had yet known, his great chest heaving and glistening with sweat.

But it was impossible for any one man to remain that sexy over such a wide area, and so Alexander died at the age of 33. It wouldn't be until the current century that someone would bring sexy back.

The Roman Empire began in 27 BC, when Octavian said, "I know what let's do—let's have an empire!" At its peak, the Roman Empire spread west to France, north to England, east to Mesopotamia, south to the Sahara, down to the Earth's mantle, and straight up to Alpha Centauri.

Rome had a militaristic culture. Romans were kept entertained by chariot races in the Colosseum, gladiators fighting lions in the baths, and the never-ending crucifying of people claiming to be Spartacus. Historians now suspect that very few of these people were actually named Spartacus, but at the time, it was very easy to get a fake ID so you could buy booze, go to the vomitorium, and get crucified. That was a typical three-day weekend in ancient Rome.

A peace-loving young man named Jesus arrived in the Roman Empire in the early first century; things didn't go so well for him.

The Roman Empire had many powerful, charismatic leaders. When the great Julius Caesar was

> ## ◗ Fact-Like Fact
>
> **According to the National Rifle Association, Jesus would never have been crucified if he'd only had a nice assault rifle.**

assassinated by his own men, he famously said, *"Et tu, Brute"* (or "You stabbed me, you bastards! What the hell?"). According to legend, Emperor Nero fiddled while Rome burned; you don't want to know what Caligula did while Rome burned (hint: it involved a male horse and a metric ton of Vaseline).

Eventually, the Roman Empire fractured apart due to civil wars, high taxes, and the arrival of the extremely upsetting miniskirt toga.

The Dark Ages: Dark, Like Our Soul

As the Roman Empire slowly collapsed, wave after wave of tribes rampaged through Europe. First they were the Goths, with their gloomy music, pale skin, and black eyeliner. Then came the Vandals, who broke all the handles. Then the most dreaded of all, Attila the Hun, plundered Europe (if by "plunder" you mean "split your face open with a rusty scythe").

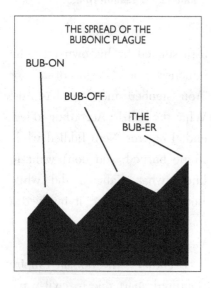

THE SPREAD OF THE BUBONIC PLAGUE

BUB-ON

BUB-OFF

THE BUB-ER

Eventually, Charlemagne managed to unite Europe once again, behind the principle "Charlemagne will beat the crap out of you if you don't do what Charlemagne says." But by this time, nearly all of the knowledge of the Greeks and Romans had been forgotten, and Europe entered its Dark Ages.

The Dark Ages began in the sixth century and extended well into the thirteenth century. In fact, Europe did so poorly in the eighth century that they had to repeat it, and the other continents made fun of them. This made Europe feel really insecure and led Europe to seek some serious psychoanalysis as soon as Sigmund Freud invented it in the nineteenth century.

The Dark Ages were a time of ignorance and superstition, when people reverted to primitive beliefs. For example, many people in this time did not use statistical mechanics to derive the fact that electromagnetic radiation is discrete and not continuous. Who does that? Oh, foolish Dark Agers! At the same time in the Middle East, the Arabs were inventing zero, writing amazing literature, and just generally kicking Europe's puny, Dark Ages ass.

The Mayans: Great, Another Civilization to Remember

Meanwhile, in the ancient Americas, the Mayans ruled all of Mexico (excluding Cabo, which belonged to an ancient tribe of Sammy Hagars). From AD 300 to AD 900, the Mayan culture rivaled that of the ancient Mesopotamians, right down to the sitcom *Everybody Loves Uaxamal.*

The Mayans developed their own calendar, which predicted the world would end on December 21, 2012. And so did it? Experts are split on the matter. We'll get back to you.

Random Bonus Fact!

NEIL GAIMAN, AUTHOR

The African stalking lungfish climbs trees and waits for its prey to walk underneath, whereupon it flings itself off the tree with its mouth open very wide, and hopes.

Europe: Yep, Still the Dark Ages

Meanwhile, back in Europe, the Roman Catholic Church was becoming extremely powerful, mainly through guilt and impressively tall pope hats. Universities were founded that taught the science of the ancient Greeks and the mathematics of the Arab world, plus PE during sixth period and home ec during seventh.

But just when things were going along so well, the bubonic plague came along and killed one-third of Europe's population. This was partly because medicine was still very primitive at this point, and partly because the word "bubonic" made people giggle and smirk.

We now know that the Black Death spread rapidly throughout the continent due to the fleas carried by rats. But at the time, rats were not considered pests at all. Many families kept rats as pets, teaching them such tricks as Sit, Roll Over, and Bite the Neighbor's Baby.

This pandemic produced great changes in Europe. For instance, due to the Black Death people had to stop using rat-bone combs. Even worse, people were forced to stop sucking on rats for nutrition, despite their irresistible Parmesan peppercorn ranch flavor. So delicious, yet so deadly.

Europe was very unsettled in this period, leading England and France to fight the Hundred Years' War, followed by the much briefer

Twenty-Two Seconds' War. England believed it had the right to lay claim to all of France, while the French believed the English could suck their left one.

England was doing quite well until the appearance of Joan of Arc, who rallied the French to several victories after inventing the beret and little pencil-thin mustaches. The English eventually captured Joan of Arc and burned her at the stake for the crime of "not showering, ever." However, the French rallied around the martyr Joan and eventually forced the English Army out once and for all in 1453 by not shaving their armpits. English king Henry VI later declared, "We did notte want your stoopid, smellie country annywaye, so therre, nyaahhh nyaahhh nyaahhh."

The Renaissance: A Thing That Happened

Around the same time in Italy, the Renaissance began when someone said, "You know what? Screw this Middle Ages shit." And so they did.

There were huge advances in many areas during the Renaissance. In art, painters started using linear perspective and putting codes and weird-ass Masonic symbols in their paintings that only Dan Brown would be able to make out hundreds of years later.

Actual drawing from Da Vinci's notebooks of a rudimentary flying machine.

There was a great deal of progress in science as well. In Leonardo da Vinci's sketchbooks, one can see drawings of flying machines, not to mention rudimentary sketches of something he called "Hot Pockets."

There were advances in other

areas as well: literature, music, architecture, bowling, commemorative plate collecting, cupcake baking, and masturbation, just to name a few.

Where would we be today without the Renaissance? We'd have millions of people who don't believe in valid scientific principles like evolution and global warming and who condemn art and literature that doesn't match their religious beliefs. Oh. Wait.

The scientific advances of the Renaissance allowed the monarchies of Europe to build huge ships and explore the world around them. At first, these voyages were unsuccessful, until the Portuguese figured out that ships worked even better in water.

Exploration: A Whole New World!

Fact-Like Fact

Actually, Magellan died part of the way through his circumnavigation of the Earth. The rest of the voyage inspired the hit movie *Weekend at Bernie's*.

Suddenly, it was a period of exploration. Magellan circumnavigated the Earth (although that was easier to do then as the Earth was only about the size of Connecticut in those days). King Ferdinand and Queen Isabella sponsored a voyage by Christopher Columbus to find an eastern route to China. He eventually made landfall in the Bahamas, which he thought was China. Yes, the New World was discovered by a complete and utter moron.

But the New World was not an empty world. The Aztecs were ruthless warriors who ruled Mexico and worshipped a sun god that demanded human sacrifices. So that was fun. Meanwhile, the Incas had a vast empire in South America, building roads, bridges, and several Hardee's franchises. But then the Spaniards arrived and brutally destroyed both civilizations. Man, was the sun god ever pissed.

Religion vs. Science: Science by a Field Goal

Europe entered into yet another unstable age (what is this, the fourth one? fifth? Who can keep track?), thanks to some behind-the-scenes work of a certain sun god. In northern Europe, Martin Luther split off from the Catholics, creating both Lutheranism and lutefisk. Meanwhile, the Holy Roman Empire was under attack from the Ottomans; the End Tables and the Floor Lamps weren't too happy, either. In Russia, Ivan the Terrible did some pretty terrible things, like not calling his mother on her birthday.

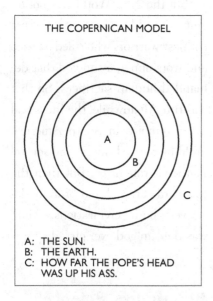

THE COPERNICAN MODEL

A: THE SUN.
B: THE EARTH.
C: HOW FAR THE POPE'S HEAD WAS UP HIS ASS.

It was against this unstable backdrop that science and the arts flourished, because science and the arts don't give a shit about all that stupid political hoopdy-doo. Copernicus discovered that the sun was at the center of our solar system, and not Ashton Kutcher. Johannes Kepler worked out the laws of planetary motion, which had something to do with something called "the Hustle." The greatest scientist of the age was Galileo, who ran into trouble with the Catholic Church for supporting Copernicus, and for proving mathematically that Pope Urban VII was an ass-ferret.

In the arts, Shakespeare created some of the greatest dramas man has ever known, such as *Hamlet* and *Macbeth* (which would later be remade by Tommy Wiseau as *The Room*). Michelangelo created magnificent sculpture (his *David*), inspiring paintings (his ceiling of the Sistine Chapel), and even compelling macrame (his plant holder for Pope Linus XI). Plus, Vermeer painted *Girl with the Pearl Earring Who Kicked a Hornet's Nest*, and Rembrandt did whatever it was Rembrandt did (art historians believe it involved whitening teeth).

A little later, the Frenchman René Descartes made great strides in philosophy ("I think I am hungry, therefore let's go to White Castle") and mathematics (he discovered the number 46). England's Sir Isaac Newton surmised some of the basic laws of physics and wrote the influential scientific treatise, *Effing Magnets, How Do They Work?*

The Enlightenment: Well, Sort Of

The work of these geniuses led to a period called the Enlightenment in which intellectuals like Voltaire and Rousseau sought to live lives of pure reason while dressing as foppishly as possible and making sarcastic comments about the Pope's dorky-ass hat.

▶ Fact-Like Fact

Historians now credit Voltaire and Rousseau with inventing *The Soup* on E! Entertainment Television.

Most of these elite intellectuals were members of the court of France's Louis XIV, who was perhaps the XIV-est monarch Europe had yet seen. Under Louis (or the Sun King, because he fused 620 million metric tons of hydrogen per second), France became the dominant political and cultural power in Europe, spreading the ideas of the Enlightenment and forcing all of Europe to watch those depressing French movies that don't make a damn bit of sense. When Louis XIV died, he was succeeded by his great-grandson, Louis XV, who was only five years old. Louis XV immediately banned bedtimes and broccoli.

In the meantime, England's colonies in the New World were growing. (See section "U.S. History," page 65, or watch the Mel Gibson movie *The Patriot* or something. We'll wait here.) Both France and England wanted control of not just these colonies, but India as well, which led to the Seven Years' War (known in the United States as the French and Indian War, and known in India as What to the Ever). This was the first war ever fought on three continents at once, making it the first true world war—although, as with all world wars, nobody attacked Iowa because really, who gives a fig about Iowa?

Revolutions:
Don't Lose Your Head

While England and France fought to a draw in Europe after two overtimes and a shoot-out, England ended up in control of the American colonies and India. However, it would soon lose control in the New World after the American Revolution (did you go back and read the "U.S. History" section yet? we're still waiting), though the mighty British would control much of Asia until the twentieth century, mainly due to their very frightening teeth.

Revolutionary fervor spread to France in 1789, when the French decided that being ruled by an absolute monarch was, as the French put it, "suckez-ass." Even after mobs of angry citizens stormed the Bastille (a type of small pastry), the court of King Louis XVI sneered at the popular uprising. Queen Marie Antoinette famously said, "Let them eat cake. From my butt."

However, Louis XVI and Marie Antoinette were forced to take the revolution seriously after they were beheaded.

While originally the French Revolution was fueled by a desire for equality, rights for all, and free pony rides, things soon fell apart. Maximilien Robespierre launched a Reign of Terror. Many were killed; many more were instead forced to eat cake from Marie Antoinette's now-dead butt. To make things worse, nobody ever got the pony rides like they were promised.

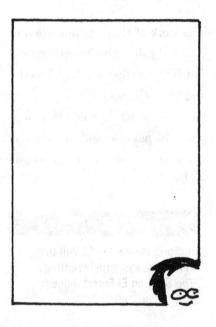

Napoleon. Ladies?

More Europe Crap

In the midst of all this confusion (surprise! Europe was unsettled again! who'da think?), general and noted short guy Napoleon Bonaparte seized absolute control of France in 1799. His armies soon took over most of Europe, terrorizing their opponents with a strategy known as "French kissing" (most of Europe was still kissing tongue-free well into the twentieth century).

But Napoleon got too ambitious, and tried to conquer Russia. In the winter. Smooth move, Ex-Lax. Also, the Russian Army had a tactic called "Siberian kissing" which grossed out even Napoleon (trust us, you don't want to know). Decimated by the incredible death and injury toll from Siberian kissing (seriously—you do *not* want to know), the French Army retreated and never kissed again. By 1815, Napoleon had been exiled, had died, and was then exiled again.

The Industrial Revolution: Trent Reznor's Favorite Period of History!

Around this time in the United Kingdom, another revolution was about to change everything for pretty much everybody, except maybe that one village idiot in Trentshire-on-Melvin. This would come to be known as the Industrial Revolution, or iRev for short. Major changes were on the horizon in agriculture, manufacturing, and even Pokémon.

The introduction of steam power led to a startling rise in machine-based manufacturing—the cotton gin, the spinning jenny, and the castrating linda all led to the loss of millions of fingers annually, but a huge rise in the standard of living for millions of people worldwide. There were also unbelievable leaps in transporting goods to market, including the steamship, the steam locomotive, and the coal-powered pogo stick.

All of these advances came at a price—major cities like London were inundated with smog, water pollution, and small, waifish children saying, "Please, sir, I want some more." Working conditions were unsafe for millions of workers. Iron was often smelted over a deep, deep pool filled with piranha and man-eating giant octopi, while steel mills randomly dropped poisonous rattlesnakes and black widow spiders on their workers, just for fun.

▶ Fact-Like Fact

Queen Victoria invented both pride and prejudice.

As the Industrial Revolution really got rolling, Queen Victoria was crowned both queen of England and World Welterweight Champion. The Victorian Age was a time of great prosperity, and it coincided with golden ages in other parts of the world: France's Belle Epoque, the Gilded Age in the United States, and Japan's Happy Bunny Fun Time!

Culturally, the Victorian Age was a period of great authors, including Charles Dickens (*That One Book That We Had to Read in Ninth Grade English*) and Jane Austen (*That Book Where Kate Winslet and/*or *Colin Firth Are in the Movie*). In science, Charles Darwin formulated his theory of evolution after a rather eye-opening trip to Kentucky. Politically, the British Empire stretched over several continents, most of the oceans, and a great deal of the Earth's mantle. Things were good all over. What could possibly go wrong?

The Twentieth Century: Oh, Shit

This could go wrong: in 1914, Archduke Franz Ferdinand, heir to the throne of the Austro-Hungarian Empire, was assassinated. Every major European power was shocked by the news that the Austro-Hungarians even had an empire, and within weeks World War I had started.

Germany invaded France. Russia attacked Germany. The Austro-Hungarians got confused and attacked some Greco-Roman wrestlers. England fought oral hygiene. The French surrendered to themselves. Finally, the United States entered the war in 1918 and, with help from the Greco-Roman wrestlers, defeated Germany three falls to one.

After the war, U.S. president Woodrow Wilson started the League of Nations, a bowling league for world leaders. Its purpose was to prevent future wars, but leaders merely squabbled about ball size. Some things never change.

The Soviet Union: Oh God, Now What?

Russia had to leave World War I early, though they never brought in a note from their mom or their doctor to excuse their absence. In 1917, Russia's tsar was deposed, followed shortly thereafter by the czar, the tzar, and the tzzzzzccccsssar. The monarchy was ultimately replaced by a Communist government led by Vladimir Lenin, who read *The Communist Manifesto* back in college and thought it sounded like a good idea. And so Russia became the Union of Soviet Socialist Republics (USSR for short, U for even shorter).

Land and factories were forcibly taken from the wealthy and then forcibly given to the peasants, whether they wanted them or not. Agriculture became collectivized; industry became collectivized; even sitting around drinking vodka until 4 a.m. became collectivized by the

THE SOVIET UNION: THE EARLY YEARS

COLLECTIVE FARMS

COLLECTIVE FACTORIES

COLLECTIVE THING OF DEODORANT

Soviets. Soon, the Soviets came up with their first Five Year Plan, which included such goals as "lose 20 pounds by next bikini season," "learn to knit," and "start taking accounting classes in the evening at the community college."

To achieve these ambitious goals, the Soviet government often turned to violence. The disloyal were purged from the Communist Party, the Red Army, and Joseph Stalin's Wednesday night book club. Millions died (Stalin had a *huge* book club), plus nobody lost that 20 pounds and everybody looked like crap when bikini season came around.

> ### Fact-Like Fact
>
> **Stalin's final Five Year Plan read simply, "Why won't Jeneesha go out with me?"**

But in the rest of Europe and in the United States, the Roaring Twenties were a time of great wealth and even greater excesses, such as John D. Rockefeller's all-mink yacht. But that ended in 1929, when the entire world economy collapsed overnight and Rockefeller's yacht molted.

The Depression and the Nazis: Two Terrible Things That Don't Go Well Together

Millions were thrown out of work worldwide, and currencies were suddenly worthless. In Germany, you needed a wheelbarrow full of marks just to buy a wheelbarrow to put your marks in.

Germans were desperate for leadership, and for wheelbarrows. A young leader named Adolf Hitler promised both, and in 1933 he was elected führer (literally, "douche-squirrel"). Hitler's Nazi Party soon crushed all political opposition, started persecuting the Jews, built up a powerful military and propaganda machine, hosted the Summer Olympics, and then broke for a light lunch.

Soon, Hitler began making outrageous demands for land from Germany's neighbors, which the rest of Europe dealt with through "appeasement," a policy of just letting him have what he wanted if he would just turn down the damn oompah music after 11 p.m. Even though Europe let him have sections of Austria and Czechoslovakia, Hitler was still cranking "The Beer Barrel Polka" until 4 and 5 a.m., even though France and England had to work the next day.

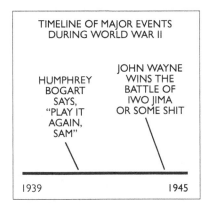

TIMELINE OF MAJOR EVENTS
DURING WORLD WAR II

HUMPHREY
BOGART
SAYS,
"PLAY IT
AGAIN,
SAM"

JOHN WAYNE
WINS THE
BATTLE OF
IWO JIMA
OR SOME SHIT

1939   1945

World War II: Another Thing That Happened

But Hitler went too far and invaded Poland in 1939. No one is sure why, but historians now believe the Nazis wanted Poland's lightbulb-changing technology—while it took five Poles to change a lightbulb, it took well over 200 Germans to do so, and Hitler wanted a more efficient Nazi force.

Britain and France declared war immediately, and this was the start of World War II (also known by its full title, Rambo: World War, Part 2). Soon, France and Britain were losing horribly—France was completely overrun by the Nazis, while Britain withstood constant air attacks known as the Blitz (literally, "This Fucking Sucks").

By the end of 1941, Hitler's iron grip on Europe was so complete that he thought, "I'm bored, who else can we invade?" And so the Nazis invaded Russia, while their allies the Japanese attacked the United States at Pearl Harbor with a force called the kamikazes (literally, "crazy-ass sons of bitches").

▶ Fact-Like Fact

Historians now agree that the United States would have lost the war if Sam had not played it again.

This move brought the United States into the war, and John Wayne into war movies. The United States allied itself with Britain and Russia in Europe, and the Nazis were soon overwhelmed by Tom Hanks trying to find Matt Damon, while Brad Pitt carved swastikas into their foreheads. In May 1945, Hitler killed himself and then surrendered.

Allied forces moved in and discovered that Hitler had been routinely and barbarically killing millions of Jews in his concentration camps. This ghastly, horrifying crime against humanity was called the Holocaust (Latin for "This Shit Is Unbelievably Messed Up"). Mankind has vowed to not let it happen again, but, you know, it has sadly happened again once or twice. Good one, mankind.

While the Nazis surrendered, the Japanese kept fighting in the Pacific. Unbeknownst to them, the United States had been working on a secret project—to harness the power of the atom. It was the U.S. military's goal to create tiny atom-sized explosions, which the Japanese would think were really cute and adorable. But it turned out that splitting an atom, in fact, unleashed an amount of energy physicists refer to as "a hairy shit-ton."

U.S. president Harry Truman decided to show the Japanese the Americans' new weapon in order to force them to surrender. Now, surely he could have done this by dropping the bomb somewhere *near* Japan, over the ocean, most decidedly *not* killing tens of thousands of civilians. The Japanese would probably have seen that, said "Holy shit!" and surrendered, right? Well, we'll never know, and neither will all the innocent people in Hiroshima and Nagasaki. So that sucked.

The Cold War: Like a War, but Colder

After World War II, the United States and the USSR were the only superpowers left. And while they had been allies during the war, they now realized they had very different agendas: the USSR wanted to take over the world, while the United States wanted to take over the world. So the United States gathered allies in Western Europe and called the association NATO (or Nasty-Ass Turkey Orators). Meanwhile, the USSR scooped up Eastern Europe and called their association by the dread-inducing name Nickelback.

But instead of a direct conflict,

this rivalry led to a new kind of war: a Cold War. Sadly, this did not involve several million pints of New York Super Fudge Chunk. It mainly played out as an arms race, with both nations developing thousands of nuclear devices, from bombs to toaster ovens. Both nations also developed giant, radioactive monsters—the United States had Godzilla, while the Soviets came up with Gamera. For some reason, both monsters would only attack Tokyo.

Tensions came to a head with 1962's Cuban Missile Crisis. Cuba had become a Communist nation in 1959, when Fidel Castro's beard took over the island nation (Fidel Castro himself is merely a host organism for the beard). The Soviets helped the Cubans build missile bases that could reach Washington, DC, and everybody flipped the fuck out. Eventually, everybody decided not to kill everybody else and things got back to normal.

During this time, the United States and the USSR were also engaged in another race: the Brickyard 500. Also, the Space Race. In 1957, the Soviets launched *Sput-*

nik, and then it was on like Donkey Kong. On like Agamemnon. On like Forest Lawn. On like Wallace Shawn. On like . . . well, you get the idea.

WHAT THE APOLLO ASTRONAUTS FOUND ON THE MOON

MONOLITH

President John F. Kennedy started a space program with the aim of "putting a man on the moon and doing it with some hot moon chicks." And so on July 20, 1969, Neil Armstrong became the first man on the moon, while Buzz Aldrin became the first man to do it with a hot moon chick. Both events were broadcast to a worldwide audience.

But by the 1980s, the Cold War

was still going strong. U.S. president Ronald Reagan (1100 BC–AD 2004) put pressure on the Soviets by dramatically increasing military spending on programs like Star Wars (a space-based missile defense) and Star Trek (hiring millions of people to dress up like Leonard Nimoy and give Communists the Vulcan Death Grip). The Soviets could not keep up in this new, accelerated arms race; plus their "In Russia, Space Trek You!" program was a huge failure.

In 1989, the Berlin Wall fell (leading to a series of really crappy raves), and in 1991, the USSR itself fell (leading to Boris Yeltsin being blackout drunk for the entire 1990s). The Cold War was over at last, but the world was not safe, what with Michael Bolton still having top 10 singles.

After the Cold War: Some Other Stuff Happened

In a post–Cold War era, the United States was suddenly the dominant superpower. But not everybody liked that—a shadowy terrorist group called al Qaeda did not approve of U.S. dominance in Middle Eastern affairs (or considering where they placed bombs—shoes and underwear). Al Qaeda was led by Osama bin Laden, who had the incredible tactical advantage of be-

 Random Bonus Fact!

REGGIE WATTS, COMEDIAN

In 1991, researchers at the Max Planck institute discover that higher energetic yields of future particle collision experiments may lead to a 0.00000023 unexplained average energy loss due to the possibility of hyper-dimensional membrane bleed-through. This is confirmed on August 8, 2014, at the Large Hadron Collider in Switzerland. This discovery leads to a new branch of human research centered around a concept called "collective self/simulated reality."

ing a sickly guy who lived in a cave in the middle of nowhere and liked putting videos of himself on YouTube.

Bin Laden masterminded the horrible 9/11 attacks on the United States in 2001. U.S. president George W. Bush retaliated against al Qaeda by invading Iraq, which was over 1,200 miles away from bin Laden's location and had no role in planning the attack. But, as Bush explained, "Duhhhhh."

Then some other crap happened, and now you're reading this and you're all caught up. Congratulations.

The Nations of the Damn World

There are more than 190 sovereign nations in the world, but let's face it, you don't really need to know about most of them. Is your life improved by knowing the yield of wheat in Tajikistan in 1958? It's a trick question: Tajikistan wasn't a country yet in 1958, and now you feel like an ass and it's all Tajikistan's fault. Thanks, Tajikistan.

Therefore the Disalmanacarian has chosen the top 50 most interesting nations in the world and shared with you the most interesting fact-like facts about them. So crack open your skull with a tire iron and just shove in handfuls of knowledge about the nations of the world.

Algeria

Located in northern Africa, Algeria's been a country for a while now. Yet you pretty much never hear anything about it. Clearly, Algeria needs a marketing campaign. Perhaps "Call Me Al." (The invoice is in the mail, Al.)

Antarctica

Located at the bottom of the Earth and home of the South Pole, Antarctica is not an independent nation. The countries of the world have decided that Antarctica belongs to the entire world. Scientists from many nations are there even as we speak, sharing knowledge about geology, meteorology, and

Dictator-for-Life of Antarctica, Mr. Flippy.

dozens of other sciences for the good of all mankind.

Of course, man can't do anything without screwing it up. Just as man learns to work together as one species, boom, we get global warming going and we're melting the one place where we all get along. So that's depressing as shit.

But: penguins!

Argentina

Argentina is located in South America, just south of Brazil. The larger, stronger, and more beautiful Brazil is always overshadowing Argentina. Brazil gets the Olympics. Brazil wins over 400,000 World Cup titles. Brazil gets all the rock stars trying to save its stupid rain forests. Brazil, Brazil, Brazil! Aaagghhh!!!

Things have not been great in Argentina for a while now. Their economy has yet to recover from its collapse in 2001, when the bubble burst in the formerly lucrative Nazi-hiding market.

▶ Fact-Like Fact

Australia has the highest per capita number of people who know what a knife is.

Australia

Australia is home to many freakish animals. Some of them are well known, like the kangaroo and the duck-billed platypus. But did you know about these actual Australian animals?

- **Elepherret:** part elephant, part ferret
- **Moo-shark:** a shark that grazes in a field and gives

delicious milk—and then, when you least expect it, rips you to shreds with its powerful, razor-sharp udders

- **Oranguplankton:** part great ape, part algae, all evil
- **Monkey python:** a snake known for its silly walk
- **Blimpanzee:** part monkey, part *Hindenburg* crashing in flames in New Jersey. Oh, the humanity.

When visiting Australia, be careful of these animals, plus the bearsquito, the katysquid, and the highly poisonous Madonnaconda.

Bahamas

It is everyone's dream to visit a nation as beautiful as the Bahamas.

We had a kind of disturbing dream just last night, about our father and a cave. But we won't go into it. Enjoy your trip to the Bahamas!

Belgium

You know what's awesome about Belgium? The Louvre. Man, that is one great museum. Yes, it's home to the world famous *Mona Lisa*, but the Louvre's collection contains more treasures than you can imagine. The magnificent *Nike of Samothrace*. Breathtaking antiquities from Egypt. Beautiful Italian Renaissance paintings from legendary artists like Raphael and Michelangelo.

Wait. The Louvre's not in Belgium—it's in Paris. What's Belgium got? Waffles? Well, screw the Louvre. We want waffles. Viva Belgium!

BRAZIL

THE MASOCHISTIC FREAK WHO CAME UP WITH BRAZILIAN WAXING

Brazil

Brazil is the largest country in South America. But if it really wants to make the big time, Brazil knows it's going to have to move to the home of Broadway: New York City.

Because if Brazil can make it there, well, there are very few other places it can't make it. Yes, Hollywood will still be a tough nut to crack—not many Broadway stars make the leap to the big screen. And really, Bollywood as well, since Brazil can't speak Hindu. And Hong Kong, unless Brazil takes several years of intense martial arts classes *and* learns Mandarin.

But yeah. It's up to you Brazil, New York.

Burkina Faso

Burkina Faso is located in central Africa, and it's completely landlocked. It's like the Nebraska of Africa.

As the Nebraska of Africa, Burkina Faso is basically nothing but corn and Bright Eyes records. And as the Nebraska of Africa, Burkina Faso is also home to the massive insurance company Mutual of Ouagadougou.

Cambodia

Cambodia is located in Asia, probably. Does that sound right? Asia? We've never actually been to Asia, so who knows?

And that is everything you need to know about Cambodia.

▶ Fact-Like Fact

Canada's national sport is competitive politeness.

Canada

North America is like *Seinfeld*. Canada is Jerry, the funny one with the goofy face. Canada's neighbor America is Seinfeld's neighbor Kramer—always bursting in unexpectedly, and always with some crazy scheme to make money. Also: America has Kramer hair. Sorry, America.

That makes Mexico Elaine. She's kind of spicy, right? And George is nobody, because North America only has the three countries. Carry on.

Central African Republic

You may be surprised to learn this, but the Central African Republic isn't located in central Africa at all. It's located in northern Europe, up by Sweden somewhere. Plus, it's a monarchy, not a republic.

So why's it called the Central African Republic? Well, the entire country is in the witness relocation program. The entire population of the Central African Republic testified against Willie "the Bread Knife" Marscone in his racketeering trial. Marscone was found guilty, but quickly escaped from federal prison. Now Marscone is after the Central African Republic, threatening to slice up the entire country with his bread knife (and he's totally going to throw away the heels, if you catch our drift).

So don't tell Willie "the Bread Knife" Marscone that the nation of Burfenstine is now known as the Central African Republic and has been moved to Scandanavia. Let it be our little secret. Unless he reads this book.

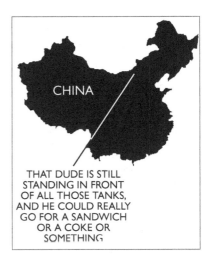

THAT DUDE IS STILL STANDING IN FRONT OF ALL THOSE TANKS, AND HE COULD REALLY GO FOR A SANDWICH OR A COKE OR SOMETHING

China

Chinese civilization dates back thousands of years. They invented paper and gunpowder long before anyone in Europe had even figured out how rocks work. As early as 1500 BC, the Chinese had already figured out the plot to *Inception*, while most Americans still have no idea what the hell happened in that movie. Somehow, China invented the fax machine before time even began. The Chinese remain a highly advanced nation.

But for all their discoveries and advances, there is one blind spot in Chinese technology: the Dorito. Their scientists have yet to work out the color orange, putting nacho cheese technology out of their reach (and also rendering Snooki invisible to the entire Chinese population [lucky bastards]).

Chinese scientists have attempted the Dorito, but many have died in the process. They thought they had made a major breakthrough in 2007, but it turned out people didn't want a snack chip that held 20 gigabytes of music and video. Especially one that tasted like licorice. That shit is gross.

Someday, the Chinese will crack the Dorito code. Chinese spies are busily infiltrating convenience stores and Taco Bells even as we speak. But until then, America still has this one thing to be proud of. Way to go, America!

Domain of Bondor, God of Darkness, The

Located deep within the surface of the Earth, very few people have entered the Domain of Bondor, God of Darkness, and lived to tell the tale. And when those who survived do tell the tale? It's usually quite short,

because, you know, all the darkness. You can't see a damn thing down there, even if you have one of those flashlight apps for your smartphone. Did you not think Bondor, God of Darkness, is smarter than your smartphone, puny human? Bondor, God of Darkness, laughs at you in the darkness.

▶ Fact-Like Fact

Bondor, God of Darkness, knows when you've been sleeping. Bondor, God of Darkness, knows when you've been awake. He knows if you've been bad or good, and it really doesn't matter: he will cast your soul into infinite darkness either way.

Here's what the human race has been able to discover about the mysterious Domain of Bondor, God of Darkness, over the centuries: It's dark. Bondor, God of Darkness, is there, systematically making our world darker. Because that's what Bondor, God of Darkness does. Do you think Bondor, God of Darkness, visits the Earth's surface as a magnificent stallion to seduce human women, like some paltry gods we could mention? That is not

Bondor, God of Darkness's style. Again, Bondor, God of Darkness, laughs at you in the darkness.

Also, the Domain of Bondor, God of Darkness, was probably Dick Cheney's "undisclosed location," which totally makes sense.

Egypt

Over thousands of years, Egypt has seen many changes. Ancient Egypt was the home of the great pyramids, while modern Egypt is the home of the great pyramids.

But be careful: millions of snakes live in Egypt's ancient underground tombs, on the off-chance that a fedora-wearing American archaeologist may drop in someday. How did they stay alive so long? What did they eat down there for thousands of years? Someone call George Lucas and find out.

Egypt is also the home of the Great Sphinx. In ancient mythology, the Sphinx asked the riddle, "What has four legs in the morning, two legs in the afternoon, and three legs in the evening?" The answer, of course, is a penguin in a blender. And why was the penguin even in the blender? To get to the other side, as was true for the great pharaohs buried in the pyramids.

Finland

The name "Finland" is derived the Finnish word "Finland," which in turn derives from the fact that the people all have fins instead of hands. They're fish people! Auuughh!!! But, they produce delicious cod roe. Even the men!

Finland's three major industries are manufacturing realistic-looking fake hands to cover their disconcerting fin-hands, swimming around aimlessly all day, and breathing through their freakish neck-gills.

Finland is a wonderful country to visit, unless you are plankton, or a worm at the end of a fishing hook.

France

You know what? We like France. There. We said it.

The women are beautiful. The food is amazing. The language is très sexy.

Plus, the French invented French kissing. Also? French fries—not the food (they're Belgian), but the hot, hot sex move. Have you tried this? Oh, man. It's incredible. The man lies down next to the woman, and then . . . well, we can't describe it without getting arrested. But like the Belgian French fries, it involves potatoes and oil.

AREAS AFFECTED BY THE
ANNUAL OCTOBERFEST
VOMIT FLOODS

Germany

Europe, you have got to stop getting overrun by the Germans a couple of times every century. It's unseemly. It's crass. It looks bad. Unless you enjoy getting taken over by a nation that thinks David Hasselhoff is a great entertainer. And you know what? We don't think you do.

Iceland

Located in the North Atlantic, Iceland is home to most of the world's ice mines. Ninety-eight percent of the world's supply of ice comes from this tiny nation. Hundreds of workers die each year in the dark, freezing mines just so your stupid Red Bull and vodka doesn't reach room temperature and become even more undrinkable. We hope you're happy.

India

India is one of the largest nations on Earth, with a population of well over 1 billion people who suddenly break out into song for no apparent reason. Complicated dance numbers erupt spontaneously. This occurs in no other nation, although the Swiss have been known to yodel when they're drunk.

⟩ Fact-Like Fact

India is located someplace!

India achieved independence in 1947, after Mohandas Gandhi used civil disobedience, a heart-stopping rendition of the hit song "I Love My India," and smokin' choreography to overthrow the British. Even the normally gruff and hard-to-please Simon Cowell said Gandhi could proceed to Bollywood.

Today, India has a booming tech economy based on pretending to not be in India while talking on the phone with angry, confused Americans. However, the spontaneous musical numbers usually give them away.

Indonesia

Located in the western Pacific, Indonesia consists of over 18,000 islands. You don't think they'd miss one, do you?

Here's the plan: We'll distract Indonesia somehow. You steal one of their islands. No, we haven't worked that part out yet. You figure it out.

Iran

Iran is a land of laughing rainbow unicorns, skipping to and fro in a green meadow with the sunshine bunny rabbits and frolicking amid the candy trees with happy, happy pandas. They dance in the sylvan glens with their many friendly friends, like Adorable Pam and Gertie, who are fluffy smooch-puppies of love.

Also: Iran's government thinks the United States is the Great Satan and wants to destroy us with nuclear weapons they may or may not have. Yay!

Iraq

Remember when we were told Iraq had weapons of mass destruction, so we had to invade them? And remember how America invaded the crap out of them, and it turned out, no weapons of mass destruction? And remember how Iraqi men were randomly taken prisoner and photographed standing naked while women smoked cigarettes and

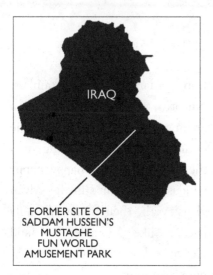

IRAQ

FORMER SITE OF
SADDAM HUSSEIN'S
MUSTACHE
FUN WORLD
AMUSEMENT PARK

pointed in the general direction of their junk? And remember how thousands of people died and billions of dollars just, like, disappeared completely?

You remember all that? Good. What the heck was that all about?

Israel

One would think that a tiny scrap of land that at least three major religions consider to be their holy land would be just chock-full of peace, love, and magic unicorns that shoot delicious pies out of their horns. One would be spectacularly wrong.

Italy

What happened to you, Italy? Two thousand years ago, you ruled much of Europe, the Middle East, and northern Africa. Money, land, slaves, vomitoriums where you could ralph publicly—you really had it going on.

Now look at you. Broke, with a new government every three hours or so. This is no way to live.

Pull yourself together, Italy. You can do this. You can be as great as you once were, and you can once again ralph publicly with pride.

Jamaica

Jamaica was the home of legendary reggae singer Bob Marley. He sang every single reggae song ever, according to really, really white people. Really, really white people were also quoted as saying, "Dude, you know those three little birds outside his doorstep, man? Like, those three birds represent love, weed, and love, bro. Far out."

WHAT'S HAPPENING IN
JAPAN TODAY?

GODZILLA DESTROYS
TOKYO & OSAKA

GAMERA DESTROYS
YOKOHAMA &
SAPPORO

MOTHRA DESTROYS
EVERYTHING ELSE

Japan

We're not sure what Japan did to piss off all those giant radioactive monsters that destroy their major cities on a daily basis, but it must have been phenomenally terrible. Japan, whatever it is you're doing, cut it out already.

Jordan

Jordan is such a popular country, millions of parents name their babies "Jordan" each year. Or Jacob. Or Jayden. Or Jason. Or Jacon (rhymes with "bacon"). Or Juicer. Or Jell-O. Or Jaybert. Or Jazzhands. Or Jackelope. Or Jaydork. Or Vajayjay.

The point is: Parents are idiots.

Lithuania

Lithuania is located on the Baltic Sea. Not only that, it's also located on Baltic Avenue, so the rent is only $4. Unless, of course, your stupid big brother puts a hotel on it. God, I hate this game.

▶ Fact-Like Fact

And don't get us started on how your stupid big brother always ends up with everything in Risk, while you're stuck with Irkutsk and Western Australia.

Madagascar

We have nothing against the nation of Madagascar. In fact, the Disalmanacarian would love to visit their rain forests, and the Avenue of the Baobabs looks absolutely spectacular. Also, the people of Madagascar seem to be quite lovely and generous.

No, our problem is with those animated *Madagascar* movies that are so popular with the kids. Thanks to those damn *Madagascar* movies, millions of American children now believe that (a) penguins live in the African jungle, (b) penguins commonly form paramilitary units that carry out quasi-military operations all over the world, and (c) penguins can (and do) speak English.

So thank you, DreamWorks, for making America last in the world *again* in knowing crap about penguins.

Mexico

Pre-Columbian Mexico was home to several advanced civilizations that were the equal of anything in Europe at the time. Art, agriculture, architecture, and more—the Aztecs and other Mexican civilizations were among the greatest in the world. Then Cortez came and killed everybody.

Now Mexico is known for drunken college hijinks and trigger-happy drug cartels. Choose wisely.

Mordor

Mordor used to be a frightening place to visit, what with the giant spiders and thousands of Orcs desperate to eat you. But due to the popularity of the *Lord of the Rings* movies, Mordor is now a hot tourist destination.

Take the entire family to Mount Doom for skiing, snowboarding, and throwing objects into the fiery depths! Swing by the new casino at Barad-dûr for gambling, glamorous showgirls, and two shows a night by stars like country legend Kenny Rogers or Darius Rucker from Hootie & the Blowfish.

And don't forget to visit Sauronland, the only theme park in the world with the incredible Flaming Eye Coaster!

Morocco

Morocco is a desert nation, and most of its population lives in or near Rick's Café Americain, a notorious bar in Casablanca. The chief

Mo Rocca, King of Morocco.

industries are gambling and selling letters of transit that a certain fugitive couple desperately desire.

Morocco's modern airport is a convenient jeep ride away. Here, if you've got the letters of transit, you can fly off to a new life in America, or start a beautiful new friendship with a French guy. It's your call in beautiful Morocco.

New Zealand

They say that New Zealand has more sheep than people. This is not technically true. The fact is, New Zealand is a planet where sheep evolved from men, and the sheep rule with an iron fist. Er. Paw. Wait. Hoof? Probably. An iron hoof.

The sheep can talk and have an advanced civilization, while man serves as the slaves of these not-so-benevolent overlords.

Someday, perhaps, an astronaut from the past will arrive in New Zealand and say, "Get your stinking hooves off me, you damn dirty sheep!" Then he'll go into the Forbidden Zone, see the Statue of Liberty, and flip out. But until then, New Zealand is run by the super-evolved sheep and there's nothing we can do about it.

Nigeria

Located in western Africa, Nigeria is known for its approximately 80 million princes, all of whom desperately need your help getting millions of dollars out of the country. Because apparently, Nigeria doesn't have ATMs. Or cashier's checks. Hell, they apparently don't even have those cartoony bags with a dollar sign stenciled on the side.

Meanwhile, our grandparents have just transferred our entire inheritance to some Nigerian prince's shady offshore bank account. Thanks, Nigeria.

North Korea

North Korea asked if they could write their own entry. Well, not so much "asked" as "demanded." We said, sure, whatever. Here is what they sent us:

"Mighty leader! Strong army! Terrible weapons! Tremble in fear, world! North Korea, number one country of all time!"

So there you have it.

Pakistan

For diplomatic purposes, the United States and Pakistan are "frenemies." It's like they say: the friend of my enemy's friend is my frenemy's enemy. Wait. No. The enemy of my enemy's frenemy's friend is my frenemy's frenemy, except for February, which has 28. No, that's not it. My frenemy got a friendly enema from my friend's frenzied frenemy Fred. Look, it's just complicated, OK?

Panama

Located in Central America, Panama is running a little bit hot tonight. Back in the nineteenth century, many Panamanians could barely see the road from the heat coming off.

But today, Panama has a vibrant economy; their chief industry is reaching down between their legs to ease their seat back. Panama!

Random Bonus Fact!

"WEIRD AL" YANKOVIC, MUSICIAN

Scientists have recently determined that only 37 percent of the Eiffel Tower is actually made out of eiffel.

Peru

Peru is located in western South America, and not in southwestern America, or the western part of the American South. Peru is also not located in the southern part of America's Southwest, or the southwest part of South America. West America is right out. Like, West America isn't even a thing. And if it were, it sure as hell wouldn't have a South. Who told you that? What a moron!

However, Peru may be located in eastern southwest North America, the eastern seaboard of Central America's west coast, or maybe in South Central. But we're pretty sure Peru is in South America. Or maybe it's in Little America, that region in southern northwest central Antarctica. Or is that the movie *North by Northwest*?

Wait. Which one is Peru again?

Romania

Romania is home to the region known as Transylvania, home of

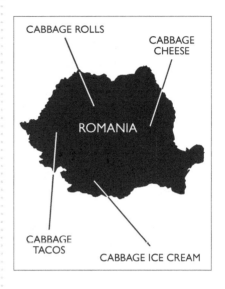

Count Dracula and the legend of vampires. These are not your sparkly-ass *Twilight* vampires, either. These are vampires who will kick your fucking ass before putting the bite down on your exposed jugular. Vlad III Dracula led an army of thousands to take over Wallachia. We'd like to see pale, sensitive Edward Cullen try that shit. He wouldn't be able to take Wallachia; heck, he couldn't even take Walla Walla.

So here's what we'd like to see: a Dracula versus Edward movie. We imagine Dracula comes in and says, "I came here to suck blood and kick ass, and I'm all out of necks." Then Dracula pummels Edward for 116 minutes. We would pay good money to see this movie, Hollywood.

Russia

In terms of area, Russia is the largest nation on Earth. This vast nation stretches from Scandinavia all the way to the Pacific Ocean and encompasses a mind-bending 5,000 time zones.

▶ Fact-Like Fact

Russia's least popular time zone is Yakov Smirnoff Standard Time.

How is this possible? Fractals. Mathematically, Russia's border is infinite and but so contains the entire universe. Wrap your head around that for a moment. Every single location in the universe can be found someplace in Russia, assuming you use the correct equations.

The Fractal Theory of Russia's border is borne out by Einstein's theories, Heisenberg's Uncertainty Principle, Type II-A String Theory, and time-traveling Leonardo da Vinci. Even Schroedinger's cat is alive and well in eastern Siberia, near Vladivostok.

So remember. Wherever you are right now, reading these words, you are in Russia. Now, pass us some borscht.

Saudi Arabia

For centuries, the area that is now Saudi Arabia had been an impoverished desert. That all changed with the discovery of oil in the early 1930s. Now Saudi Arabia is an impoverished desert with one unimaginably wealthy family that still won't let women drive cars.

South Africa

South Africa is located in south Africa. That's some pretty high-concept, meta shit.

South Korea

When South Korea found out we let North Korea write their own entry, they asked for the chance to deliver a rebuttal. We said sure.

(Side note: "rebuttal" is one of the funniest words ever.)

Here is what South Korea sent us:

"South Korea would like to take this opportunity to say that North Korea's entry is 100 percent horse crap. Thank you."

Ball's in your court, North Korea.

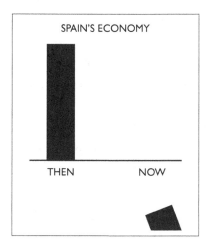

SPAIN'S ECONOMY

THEN   NOW

Spain

Spain, can you come into our office? There have been a few complaints lately, and we want to be sure you're familiar with this company's policy toward proper office attire. We want to make an impression of professionalism and cour-

tesy on our clients, and the bright orange Crocs, cutoff denim shorts, and Steve Miller Band tank top kind of make the opposite of that impression. A proper suit, an appropriate tie, and dress shoes are what we wear at the office. Thank you for your attention in this matter, Spain.

Sweden

Sweden is the world's number one producer of those little tiny metal wrench things that totally mangle up your hand while you spend six hours trying to build that Flürb shelving unit. This is how we know that Sweden is the most evil nation on the face of the planet. And probably other body parts of the planet as well.

▶ Fact-Like Fact

Ernest Hemingway once got drunk and challenged Mount Kilimanjaro to a bare-hands boxing match. Kilimanjaro, not having hands, simply fell on Hemingway, winning the fight.

Tanzania

The African nation of Tanzania is home of Mount Kilimanjaro, Africa's tallest mountain. In fact, Kilimanjaro may be Africa's only mountain. Have you ever heard of any other mountains in Africa? We haven't. In fact, we don't know anybody who's ever actually seen this supposed Mount Kilimanjaro in real life. Maybe it doesn't even exist.

So, if Kilimanjaro doesn't exist, maybe Tanzania doesn't exist either. Maybe nothing exists, except for this lava lamp we're staring at right now. Far out.

Ukraine

Ukraine is the home of the former nuclear plant at Chernobyl. Years ago, there was an accident there. It was, quite possibly, the worst nuclear accident in history. Enough radiation was released to poison the area for thousands of years.

This radiation has affected the DNA of all life in the area, causing all sorts of bizarre mutations: Bunnies are now pink and even fluffier than ever. Puppies possess lethal levels of adorableness. Baby goats seem to faint, which is pretty much the cutest damn thing ever.

Humans have also seen remarkable and strange mutations in their own species. Children can move objects as massive as trains with their minds. Adults have more magnificent physical endowments that shoot rainbows of pure love at climax. Yes, with mutations like these, you can see why the Ukrainian government wants to keep people away from Chernobyl—they want to keep all the awesomeness for themselves. Wouldn't you?

United Kingdom

Have you ever seen *Benny Hill*? It is *just* like that.

VENEZUELA, OR RORSCHACH'S FACE? YOU MAKE THE CALL!

Venezuela

Located in South America, Venezuela is one of the world's leading boil producers. Venezuela has vast boil fields, where they drill for ghastly, unsightly boils. These boils are then exported worldwide, and people put them in their cars. How disgusting is that, driving around in a car full of boils?

What's next, motorcycles that run on goiters? Gout-powered airplanes? Seg-Warts?

Anyway, stay away from Venezuela unless you want to be covered in unsightly boils.

West Northwest Korea

When they found out we allowed both North and South Korea to write their own entries, West Northwest Korea called the Disalmanacarian at four in the morning and dictated the following entry:

"South Korea is wrong! North Korea is greatest, richest nation ever, with the most beautiful and glamorous women. Seriously, North Korea women are hot, hot, hot!"

Then we asked if the caller was actually just North Korea speaking in a funny voice, and they hung up.

The United Nations: A World Thing

Founded in 1945, the United Nations exists to bring about world peace, economic development, and social progress. They achieve these goals chiefly by using black helicopters to make talk-radio listeners freak out. Mission accomplished!

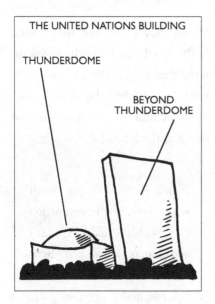

THE UNITED NATIONS BUILDING

THUNDERDOME

BEYOND THUNDERDOME

Currently, the UN has 193 members—every sovereign nation in the world, except for Vatican City. What's wrong, Vatican City? Think you're too classy to hang out with Belarus and Swaziland?

The United Nations is led by the secretary-general, followed by the administrative assistant colonel and the office temp second lieutenant. Together, they all make sure the world has plenty of Post-its, staples, and Liquid Paper.

The World Health Organization

The WHO monitors and promotes world health worldwide (except in the United States, unless sitting on the couch for hours playing Halo, eating Cheetos, and catching a repeat of *Conan* at 3 a.m. is part of a new health initiative we didn't know about). The WHO is also instrumental in vaccinating children against deadly diseases, leading to Jenny McCarthy's semiannual public meltdown.

The International Monetary Fund

The IMF stabilizes world currencies by making nations that provide awesome health care for their citizens stop doing that so rich people can keep all the money.

The International Criminal Court

This court was created to try the most heinous cases under international law: war crimes, genocide, and whoever it was that made it so you can see *Baywatch* on TV in any nation on Earth. That guy has some explaining to do.

Peacekeeping Missions

The United Nations has often sent its blue-helmeted peacekeeping troops into hostile areas to enforce peace agreements. And now: war no longer exists. Thanks, UN!

World Religions

Humans have always craved the feelings of certainty and belonging that a religion can bring. Plus, some religions have pretty good food (exception: Lutheranism—have you seen lutefisk?).

History of Religion

Primitive man believed that hidden spirits were responsible for everything, from the sun rising every morning to people holding the be-

lief that hidden spirits were responsible for everything. Primitive man was surprisingly meta.

One of the earliest civilizations, Mesopotamia, believed in a horrible, frightening god called Bondor, God of Darkness. This turns out to be the one true religion, but very few people follow it today. And man, is Bondor ever pissed. Payback is gonna be a bitch.

Ancient Egypt had a complicated system of gods—Ra, Anubis, Osiris, Elvira Mistress of the Dark, and many more. The pyramids were great tombs built to keep the jackal-like god of death at bay. Surprisingly, people still died.

▶ Fact-Like Fact

Today, the god of death is less jackal-like and more Lindsay Lohan–like.

Ancient Greeks believed there was an entire pantheon of gods living on top of Mount Olympus. Zeus was the main god, although Hera made him sleep on the couch when she caught him going down to Earth as a dolphin to do it with some human lady. Other major gods included Poseidon (god of the sea), Apollo (god of the sun), and Hermes (god of trying to explain that no, it's Hermes, with an m, and not Herpes, with a . . . oh, never mind).

The ancient Greeks had many myths about their gods. For example, Prometheus was said to have brought mankind fire by stealing some from Mount Olympus. The gods were angry because Prometheus stole something man was not allowed to have, while man was pissed because they had specifically asked Prometheus to steal them a couple of Rolexes, or something else they could sell on eBay easily.

Today there are several popular religions, and basically they all hate one another. Ironically, it's our hate for one another that brings us together as one people. That, and mankind's universal revulsion to lutefisk. That shit is nasty.

Judaism

Judaism is the oldest of the big three monotheistic religions. But do its grandchildren ever call or write?

The Torah was written between the tenth and fifth centuries before Christ, but you know, don't bring up that whole Christ thing again, OK? They feel guilty enough as it is. The Hebrew scriptures make up the Old Testament of the Bible, while the later New Testament is about Chri . . . Dammit, we did it again. Can we all just get past this already?

The Hebrew Bible starts with the creation of the world and mankind. Then there was the great flood, which killed most of the people and animals on the planet (though fish did all right for themselves, and we're still unclear on what happened with the plants, trees, and flowers).

Later, Abraham brought his people to the Promised Land, but then they were enslaved until Moses led them out of captivity. As a parting gift, God gave Moses the Ten Commandments. Then some other stuff happened and Keanu Reeves killed Dennis Hopper in the train tunnel and it's awesome.

Jews believe that the one true God, Yahweh, made a covenant with His chosen people: He would

Moses. If your bush is burning, see your doctor.

Today, there are over 15 million Jews worldwide, with most of them living in Israel and the entertainment industry.

Christianity

Christianity is based on the life and teachings of Jesus of Nazareth, a Middle Eastern Jew who, for some reason, looked exactly like the guy from Spin Doctors.

According to the Bible, Jesus was

Jesus Christ. He never knows what to get his dad for Father's Day; God now owns approximately 2,000 ties.

protect them and provide for them if they swore Him love and obedience. It all sounds a little codependent and unhealthy, but it works out for everyone involved, so who are we to judge?

Believers in Judaism have been persecuted throughout history. We've all heard about the Holocaust, where Adolf Hitler killed over 6 million Jews. Mankind must never, ever let this happen again. Remember: if you should become the all-powerful dictator of Germany, you know, behave.

the son of God. Jesus was born in Bethlehem to Mary, a virgin, and Joseph, her extremely understanding husband. Three wise men saw a bright star in the sky and brought the baby Jesus gifts: gold, frankincense, and myrrh. These may sound like phenomenally crappy presents, but if you've ever had a baby, you know you can't have too much myrrh around.

Suddenly, 30 years whizzed by (it happens to the best of us), and Jesus started to minister to the poor, the infirm, and the beardless. Somehow, this pissed off the Romans, who crucified Jesus. The Bible says Jesus rose from the dead three days later, scaring the crap out of Mary Magdalene. A short while later, Jesus ascended to Heaven, which was probably pretty sweet. God probably set up, like, a solid gold escalator or some shit—like, a mink rocket or a diamond-encrusted dumbwaiter.

Early on, Christians were persecuted (because being nice to people is pretty controversial), until the Roman emperor Constantine legalized the religion in AD 313 (though that snake-handling and speaking-in-tongues stuff was still considered weird and disturbing). Soon, Christianity was the biggest religion throughout Europe, and the Europeans spread Christianity to the Americas, even though Native Americans had perfectly good religions of their own. Better, even— Christianity may have wine, but the Aztecs had peyote.

The sacred text of Christians is the Bible, which contains surprisingly few teenage wizards going to wizard school. The Bible is in two parts: the Old Testament (as seen in the previous section on Judaism) and the New Testament, which is about Jesus and his pals' awesome adventures. The Bible ends with the Book of Revelation, which describes the end of the world. Biblical scholars now believe that the Book of Revelation would make for an awesome Michael Bay movie.

❯ Fact-Like Fact

Seriously, how does the Bible expect to become the biggest book of all time without a single teenage wizard? Get with it, Christians.

Today, there are more than 2 billion Christians worldwide; hopefully, there's enough body of Christ for everybody to eat. Within Christianity, there are hundreds of denominations, from Roman Catholicism to Russian Orthodox to the Protestants. Sure, there are some differences of opinion on theology, but one thing they can all agree on: that one church that protests the funerals of U.S. soldiers because of gay marriage—classy, right?

Islam

Islam is the third of the three major monotheistic religions. The Koran includes Judaism's Ten Commandments and Christianity's teachings of Jesus, plus the word of God as received by the prophet Muhammad. It's really your best value, scripture-wise, because you get three for the price of one. You get the Ten Commandments, the Seven Deadly Sins, *and* the Five Pillars of Islam, plus the steak knives, all for one low price! Order now!

Muhammad brought the Islamic religion to much of the Arabian peninsula, and it spread from there to much of the Middle East (as opposed to the Middle West, which is, like, Iowa and crap). During Europe's Dark Ages, it was the great Islamic scholars who kept alive the knowledge of math and science. So it's their fault you got a C+ in trigonometry in eleventh grade.

Islam has strict dietary laws (no pork Slurpees, for example). During the holy month of Ramadan, Muslims are expected to fast, especially during the hours the White Castle drive-thru is open. All Muslims are expected to make the pilgrimage to Mecca, the holiest place in the Islamic world, at least once during their lifetime. Cosplay as your favorite character from the Koran, however, is *highly* discouraged.

Today, there are nearly 2 billion Muslims worldwide, including between 2 and 6 million in the United States. So let's all get along and do some trigonometry together.

Vishnu: preserver of the universe, denture wearer.

Hinduism

Dating back at least 4,000 years, Hinduism is the chief religion of India.

In Hinduism, there are three main gods: Brahma, Vishnu, and Shiva. Or they are three aspects of one god. Or they may be three personalities of the human form of one god. Or they're merely the personifications of creation, preservation, and destruction. Or think of them as profoundly powerful forces that mere mortals can't even begin to comprehend. Or they are simply three different heads on one god-body. Look, it's complicated, OK?

Some Hindus are more into Vishnu, who was incarnated as Krishna. Some are really into Shiva, while others prefer to revere Brahma. Some are specifically into the various female consorts of Vishnu and Shiva. And there are thousands of other gods, demigods, and avatars of gods and demigods to worship, as well. Many of them have several extra arms and/or faces, or flaming swords. Look, it's complicated, OK?

The idea behind Hinduism is to connect the god in yourself to the very source of the universe, the Brahman. Do not confuse Brahman with Brahma, the god of creation, or Brahmin, the Hindu social caste. Do not confuse Brahman, Brahma, or Brahmin with Brahms, the nineteenth-century German classical composer, though he was quite good. Brahms. And Brahmin, too. Both of them. Good. Look, it's complicated, OK?

And never, ever confuse Brahman with Brawny. One is the spiritual source of all creation, while the other is a paper towel. If your four-year-old spills her juice box all over the couch, you probably don't want to sop it up with the very source of the entire tangible universe, right? What were you, raised in a barn? Geezopete.

Also: Brahman-Turner Overdrive is, sadly, not a thing.

Buddhism

Buddhism was founded in approximately 500 BC by Siddhartha Gautama. At age 29, it is said that Siddhartha Gautama left his wife and young son to search for enlightenment. He eventually found enlightenment, but by this time he owed several years' worth of alimony and child support, plus his now-grown son had started his own religion, My Dad Missed My Graduation Because He Was Too Busy Sitting Under a Damn Tree-Ism.

The first of the Four Noble Truths of Buddhism is "Life is suffering." Today, the idea that there's no escape from suffering is especially familiar to Chicago Cubs fans.

TAO LIN, AUTHOR

The Dalai Lama has 48 credit cards and 19 eBay accounts.

But there is an Eightfold Path to reduce suffering. This often includes breaking unnecessary attachments to objects, people, and ideas, since they are all transitory. The only permanent thing in life is that the Cubs will be in last place *again* this year.

An important part of the practice of Buddhism is individual meditation. It is important to sit, close your eyes, and quiet the mind by chanting a mantra, such as "Om," or "Jesus, why can't the fucking Cubs get it together for just one season during my lifetime?"

Bondor, God of Darkness

Of the thousands of religions that have existed throughout human history, this is the one true religion. You better convert as ASAP as possible, because shit is about to fucking go down, people. Bondor is *pissed*.

Be sure to sacrifice virgins and leave burnt offerings to Bondor, God of Darkness, where you work or bank.

Atheism

Atheism is not really a religion at all; it is simply the belief that there are no deities. Man, is Bondor going to be even more pissed when He finds that out.

Generally, atheists believe that a god was not necessary to create the universe. Scientific theories can explain everything from the movement of the planets (Kepler's Laws of Planetary Motion) to Justin Bieber's hair (Newton's Third Law of Product).

Atheist holidays include Nothingmas, Saint Nobody's Day, and Nadaween.

Other Religions

As if that weren't enough religions, there are thousands more to choose from. Here are a few more; order before midnight tonight and we'll pay for the shipping:

Bahá'í: The worship of unnecessary apostrophes.

Mormonism: If you think the Bible needed a sequel that made it OK to marry as many women as you want, or if you just want to wear really complicated underwear, this is the religion for you.

Paganism: This is sometimes also known as witchcraft. And if all pagans are as hot as Stevie Nicks twirling around and singing "Rhiannon," then count us in! Sorry, Bondor.

Scientology: Scientology makes about as much sense as a religion as anything else a pulpy 1950s science fiction writer would create as part of a drunken bar bet.

Sikhism: Dear Middle America: Sikhs are not Muslims just because they wear turbans. Stop hating on everybody and do what Jesus would do already.

PART FOUR

Science!

S cience comes from the Latin word *scientia*, meaning "my uncle's toaster oven." And to understand how your uncle's toaster oven works, you're going to need to know a thing or two about science.

Science refers to the pursuit of knowledge. Using the scientific method, scientists form hypotheses and perform experiments to test their assumptions. For instance, if your hypothesis was "Rick's an idiot," you'd test this by saying, "Hey, Rick—what was the average crop yield on southern Manitoba wheat farms in the late 1950s?" If Rick answered, "Uh, George Washington?" then congratulations! You have just proven your hypothesis that Rick is an idiot (the correct answer, of course, is the Beatles).

Fact-Like Fact

Jesus, Rick.

So get ready: it's time to remove your brain and tighten it in the vise of knowledge until it pops. To science!

Astronomy

Astronomy is perhaps the most ancient of all sciences, starting when Neanderthal man would gaze up in wonder at the mysterious night sky with their 200-inch f/3.3 reflecting telescopes and Very Long Baseline Interferometry methodology, which they called "Urgh" (language didn't develop until the 1920s).

Today, we know a lot about our solar system and the universe around us. Here's a quick rundown:

is definitely pre-war, but it has a certain charm, not to mention a great view of the Manhattan skyline. Here's what's in our solar system:

THE SUN

The Sun is located at the center of our solar system. If you were on the surface of the Sun right now, you would die, because it is over 5,000 degrees. Also, the Sun would stab you in the left eyeball, because the Sun is a total psycho. That's why it's

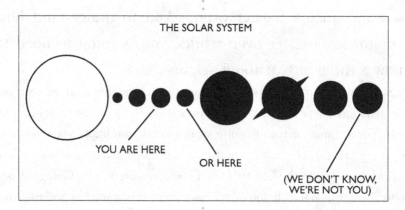

THE SOLAR SYSTEM

YOU ARE HERE

OR HERE

(WE DON'T KNOW, WE'RE NOT YOU)

The Solar System

Our solar system formed millions of years ago, which is why there are so many leaks, plumbing problems, and wiring issues. The solar system

always best to avoid the Sun. And, of course, never look directly at the Sun, because it'll probably shoot you and then use your skin as a rain poncho. The Sun is a sicko.

Without the Sun, there would be

no life on Earth. This is partly due to the fact that it provides life-giving light and energy to our planet, and partly because the Sun makes us pay an outrageous monthly "protection" fee, or no more life, capiche? Again, and this can not be stated enough times, the Sun is sick.

Fact-Like Fact

On Mercury, Grandma has been continually getting run over by a reindeer since 1985. The fun never ends on Mercury, nor do the internal injuries.

MERCURY

Mercury is the planet closest to the Sun. A year on Mercury only lasts 88 days, which means that stores there never get to take their Christmas crap down. Even worse, Paul McCartney's "Wonderful Christmastime" has been playing continuously since 1978. This has driven everyone on Mercury stark raving bonkers.

VENUS

Venus, the second planet from our sun, is covered by a thick layer of clouds, completely concealing the surface below. What is Venus trying to hide, anyway?

Turns out Venus is the headquarters for an illegal, galaxy-wide meth business. If you're ever on Venus and the cartel doesn't kill you first, there's a great chicken place there.

EARTH

Next comes the Earth, the planet where many of you are reading this. The Earth is the only planet in our solar system with life, though it's not much of a life if you're in Indiana or most of the Dakotas.

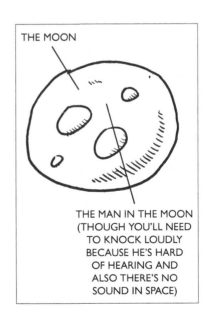

THE MOON

THE MAN IN THE MOON
(THOUGH YOU'LL NEED
TO KNOCK LOUDLY
BECAUSE HE'S HARD
OF HEARING AND
ALSO THERE'S NO
SOUND IN SPACE)

THE MOON

The Moon is our moon. Calling the Moon "the Moon" is about as imaginative as calling our planet "the Planet," or calling Jerry Bruckheimer "the Guy Who Makes All Those Loud Movies That Make Your Damn Eyes Bleed, Not to Mention They Have No Plot or Character Development and Don't Make a Lick of Sense."

It is said that a full moon can turn a man into a werewolf. But for some reason, a quarter moon doesn't turn anyone into, like, a quarter werewolf, where you just have say, wolf ears and a wolf tail, and maybe some fleas. Maybe those *Twilight* movies should get on this, pronto.

MARS

Mars is the fourth planet from the Sun. You know, we used to think Mars was so cool, until we saw the documentary film *Santa Claus Conquers the Martians*. Now we know the Martians are a bunch of bumbling idiots who let an overweight, elderly guy with no weapons just waltz in and take over. You know who else could have conquered the Martians? Any random old fart with a heart condition and diabetes, armed with a butter knife or a spork. Jesus, Mars. Get it together. You make us sick.

THE ASTEROID BELT

Between Mars and Jupiter lies the asteroid belt, a vast wasteland of rock and dust. Really, it's not unlike vast stretches of Utah, except that the Asteroid Belt has way more Abercrombie & Fitch stores.

> ## ▶ Fact-Like Fact
>
> The planet Jupiter's big break came in Stanley Kubrick's 1968 movie *2001: A Space Odyssey*, playing itself. But for years afterward, it was typecast as a large, gaseous planet (1972's *The Godfather*, 1973's *The Way We Were*) until the 1980s, when Jupiter landed the lead role on the TV hit *Bic Buckner, PI.*

JUPITER

Jupiter is the largest planet in our solar system, the size of over 1,000 Earths, or 37 Chris Christies. Jupiter is known for its Great Red Spot, which is where it spilled a whole jar of salsa while it was stoned and watching a *Baywatch* marathon on USA Network back in 1997, and never got around to cleaning it up. And while that's pretty gross, you really, really don't want to know what some of the other spots on Jupiter are.

SATURN

The next planet is Saturn. Saturn is known for having a ring. Unfortunately, Sauron has found out about the ring, and our only hope is to destroy Saturn by throwing the entire planet into the fiery depths of Mount Doom. NASA was working on this important project, but Congress cut their funding, so now the entire universe is screwed. Thanks, Congress. Now Uruk-Hai warriors will swoop down and take over the entire damn universe because you wanted to play politics. Awesome.

URANUS

Uranus, the seventh planet from the sun, was discovered by William Herschel in 1781. Before that, nobody could tell Uranus from a hole in the ground.

Uranus is the size of at least 15 Earths. You might wanna get Uranus to the gym once in a while and work off some of Uranus on the elliptical trainer or something. Also, Uranus is billions of years old, so you should consider getting Uranus checked by a proctologist twice a year. Of course, Uranus is surrounded by dark rings; you might consider getting Uranus bleached.

Arthur Neptune, God of the Sea.

NEPTUNE

The eighth and final planet from the Sun is Neptune. Neptune is named for the Roman god of the sea, Arthur Neptune. Arthur Neptune ruled the oceans from his cubicle at the bottom of the Mediterranean, though he was mainly responsible for the Roman pantheon's quarterly profit-and-loss spreadsheets. In his spare time, he played lots of Minesweeper and enjoyed watching documentaries about lungfish.

Yes, Arthur Neptune was a dullard, as is the planet named after him. If you go, bring something to do. Boggle, maybe, or Apples to Apples. Anything to relieve the unrelenting dullness that is Neptune.

PLUTO

Located somewhere out beyond Neptune, Pluto was discovered in 1930 by Walt Disney. For many years, it was our ninth planet. But now astronomers consider Pluto merely a "dwarf planet" (which is much better than the old, non-PC term, "space midget").

Besides Pluto, there are a few other dwarf planets; the most prominent are Doc, Sneezy, and Gimli of Gloin.

The Universe

Our solar system resides in this crazy, cuckoo thing we call the universe. It's nutty! But how did we end up with a universe, and what the heck's in it?

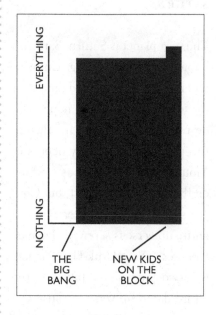

THE BIG BANG

Through history, there have been a number of theories regarding the origin of the universe. Ancient Sumerians believed that the universe was carried on the back of a giant turtle. And while it turns out the giant turtle thing is true, where did the universe come from? And what does the turtle eat? Does it have a name?

Astronomers now believe that every bit of mass in the universe was condensed into one spot, probably somewhere in Hoboken. But at some point in the distant, distant past (like, say, the 1920s) all of this matter suddenly exploded, creating the universe we know today. Why wasn't the giant turtle hurt in this explosion, which contained all the energy in the universe? Duh: it has a shell, hello?

What proof is there of a Big Bang? Everything in the universe appears to be moving away from everything else in the universe. And while to the Disalmanacarian this proves the existence of agoraphobia, to astrophysicists this means there was once a giant explosion.

But what caused the Big Bang in the first place? Let's just say: if you see a giant tortoise on your flight, call Homeland Security, pronto.

THE MILKY WAY

The Milky Way is the galaxy that contains our solar system. Our solar system is located way out on the far edge of the Milky Way; so if the center of the Milky Way was New York City, we'd be, like, a suburb of Spokane.

The Milky Way contains over 200 billion stars, of which our sun is just one. The universe contains over 200 billion galaxies, of which the Milky Way is merely one. Feeling small and insignificant yet? Personally, we were already feeling pretty small and insignificant, but this just pushed us over the edge. We're just going to go home, sit in the dark eating several pints of Ben & Jerry's, and go to bed until, like, next February. We cannot get into a position that's fetal enough.

KURT BRAUNOHLER, COMEDIAN

Benjamin Franklin invented BBQ. But back then it originally stood for Ben's Been Quookin'!

BLACK HOLES

Black holes are massive gravitational events in space-time that suck in everything that comes close, especially ranch-flavored chicken nuggets. Black holes are often found at the center of galaxies, and deep inside most celebrities.

Nobody is quite sure what happens once you get sucked into a black hole. You may get crushed into nothingness, like when you listen to Smiths albums all day. Or a black hole could be the entrance to a wormhole, which would immediately take you to a completely different part of the universe. Astronomers are currently hoping to discover a black hole that could transport a space traveler directly into Megan Fox's panties.

One way to think of a black hole whose mass is M is the equation:

$$Q^2 + (J/M)^2 \leq M^2$$

Where Q stands for Quaker Oats and J stands for jelly donuts. In other words, black holes are the nutritious part of this complete breakfast.

DARK MATTER

Ordinary matter makes up only 14 percent of the matter in the universe, while Snooki's hair makes up another 3 percent. The other 83 percent of the matter in the universe is dark matter.

But what the heck is dark matter? Dark matter is matter that is unobservable: it doesn't interact with anything, including light or electromagnetic radiation, rendering it completely invisible. By this definition, the Disalmanacarian was dark matter all through tenth grade.

Because it's impossible to have direct knowledge of dark matter, physicists have no idea what its characteristics are. Recently, scientists have theorized that dark matter spends a lot of time in its room, listening to that emo shit, and writing poetry in its Moleskine about how nobody understands it— again proving that the Disalmanacarian was dark matter in tenth grade. So now give us a Nobel Prize in Physics, stat.

QUARTRON, THE SPACE DRAGON FROM HELL

Oh, did we mention there's a space dragon from Hell coming to Earth in 2019? Yeah, so that's a thing.

OTHER CRAP

There's a bunch of other crap out in space, as well—pulsars, quasars, nebulae, white dwarfs, brown dwarfs, and even more. But nobody gives a crap about this, so it won't be on the test.

The History of Manned Spaceflight

Man has been interested in spaceflight since at least 1946, when Wernher von Braun looked up at a clear, clear sky one night and said, "Dude, did you ever really think about, like, stars and shit?" And so he started designing rockets. And bongs. Mostly bongs.

Fact-Like Fact

Werner von Braun was also a pioneer in Doritos technology.

THE SPACE RACE BEGINS

And so in 1957, the United States announced its intention to launch the first artificial satellite someday. Meanwhile, the Soviets went ahead and actually launched an artificial satellite, *Sputnik* (Russian for "little potato").

The American public freaked out. Many feared we were suddenly losing the space race and, with it, the Cold War. And while we freaked out, the Soviets launched the first dog into space, Laika (Russian for "my uncle's toaster oven").

So America began Project Mercury, choosing seven men they hoped to send into space someday. Meanwhile, the Soviets launched the first man into space, Yuri Gagarin (Russian for "my uncle's toaster oven in space").

John F. Kennedy responded by boldly stating that the United States would send a man to the moon by the end of the 1960s. Kennedy famously said, "We choose to go to the moon in this decade and do the other things, not because they are easy, but because they are hard." And what were these "other things"? Inventing the miniskirt (a success), drinking lots of cocktails (also a success), and sleeping with Marilyn Monroe (a huge success).

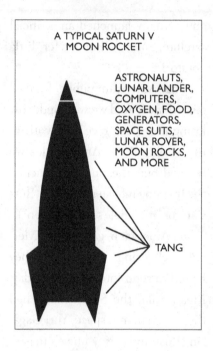

A TYPICAL SATURN V
MOON ROCKET

ASTRONAUTS,
LUNAR LANDER,
COMPUTERS,
OXYGEN, FOOD,
GENERATORS,
SPACE SUITS,
LUNAR ROVER,
MOON ROCKS,
AND MORE

TANG

APOLLO: MAN VS. THE MOON

And on July 20, 1969, America's *Apollo 11* landed on the moon. Neil Armstrong became the first man to walk on the surface of the moon, and he famously said, "That's one small step for man, one giant man for a kind of leap man giant one kind of a step thing deal." Buzz Aldrin immediately smacked him in the head for being such a damn idiot.

There were several more missions to the moon. For *Apollo 15*, we took up the lunar rover, a sort of small dune buggy the astronauts could drive around. Sadly, it was nearly impossible to find a good parking place, and the astronauts received several tickets and had to go to lunar traffic court. But we didn't stop with just a car: for *Apollo 16*, we sent up a cool-ass speedboat so the astronauts could water-ski on the lunar surface, and who can forget *Apollo 17*'s astronauts cruising around the moon's surface in an 18-wheeler full of beer, while Burt Reynolds in a Trans Am tried to keep Jackie Gleason off their tail?

▶ Fact-Like Fact

Sadly, we left Burt Reynolds up there. Sorry, Burt!

AFTER THE MOON: THE SPACE SHUTTLE AND SOME OTHER STUFF

Those were good times, but the Apollo program eventually ended and we put Skylab into orbit. Skylab was a large, orbiting laboratory for performing experiments that could only be performed in zero gravity, like seeing what happens when you put a firecracker in a frog's mouth in zero gravity. But eventually, Skylab's orbit decayed and it came crashing down to Earth, in the Australian outback. Sadly, it landed on the one Australian who could have talked the band Men at Work into keeping their day jobs, leading directly to that awful "Down Under" song. Thanks, Skylab.

In the 1980s, we had the space shuttle program, which shuttled astronauts up to space for a few days so they could talk to the President while floating in the air. But that's not all the space shuttle did. It also um . . . No, that's pretty much all we used the space shuttle for: float-y around-y President talking.

Today, America's space shuttle program is no more. There is a new international space station, but if Americans want to go there, they have to stow away on a Russian flight. It's usually best to just grab onto the outside of the rocket as it blasts off. Don't forget to hold your breath when you reach the stratosphere, or you'll pop like a balloon!

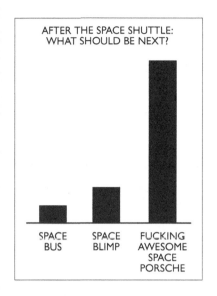

AFTER THE SPACE SHUTTLE: WHAT SHOULD BE NEXT?

SPACE BUS · SPACE BLIMP · FUCKING AWESOME SPACE PORSCHE

THE FUTURE: *NOW* WHAT???

The future of space travel is very likely in the private sector—private companies offering space flights to the general public. Companies are already working on the difficult technology of having a loud, annoying kid kicking the back of your seat for several hours in zero gravity, not to mention the problems inherent in screening Jennifer Aniston movies thousands of miles above the Earth's surface, which still appears to be against several laws of physics, not to mention a human rights violation.

Earth Sciences

What are the Earth sciences? Well, sit down, Chester, because it's a long list.

Earth sciences include geology (the study of rocks and crap), oceanography (the study of oceans and crap), paleontology (the study of fossils and crap), and scatology (the study of crap and crap). All of these and more add up to our current knowledge of the planet we live on. That, and the answers we copied from Carl Johnson during our eighth grade Earth sciences final. We both got a 92, so we think we know what we're talking about.

The Earth's Composition

Our understanding of the Earth has changed dramatically since civilization began, back in the 1930s. The ancient Sumerians believed the Earth was flat and carried around on the back of a turtle. Which it was until ancient Greek times, when the entire Earth was renovated to be the space-borne sphere we know today. But soon, the Earth will once again be closed for repairs, and reopen as an Applebee's in Wabash Centre, a strip mall just outside Lafayette, Indiana.

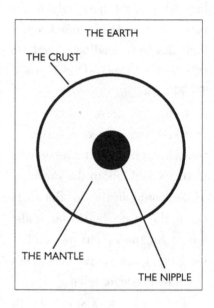

So in the meantime, here's what we know about the Earth's current composition.

THE CRUST

The Earth has three layers, and the crust is by far the outermost. Of course, the crust includes all of the geologic features we see on the surface of the Earth, from the rocky top of the Earth's highest point,

Mount Everest, to the craggy, rugged face of Clint Eastwood.

But the crust also includes the shelves the continents and the oceans sit on. These shelves are called Smültt, because the Earth got them at Ikea. The Earth really should have gotten something more stable (like maybe the higher-end Flüürp unit, made of solid oak), but the Earth was young and broke and just out of college.

THE MANTLE

Most of the interior of the Earth is made up of the mantle. Scientists long believed the mantle was made up of quartz, iron, and other minerals, but recent studies show that the mantle may be made up completely of whatever it is that stuff is that Twizzlers are made of.

Because of the great pressures found in the mantle, some of this whatever it is that stuff is that Twizzlers are made of may be liquified. Prospectors are already attempting to drill deep into the Earth to get at gushers of whatever it is that stuff is that Twizzlers are made of. And then Daniel Plainview will drink your whatever it is that stuff is that Twizzlers are made of shake, and we'll all be in trouble.

THE CORE

The core is located at the center of the Earth. The core is split into three sections. One is the Domain of Bondor, God of Darkness, which, you know, is pretty dark. The second is Dick Cheney's undisclosed location, where he runs his weather machine and sends orders to his hordes of robot minions in Washington, DC. The third section of the Earth's core is where Sting keeps his soul, in case he ever needs it again. This is highly unlikely, but hey, better safe than the other thing.

The Changing Earth

You may look around you and think, "Yep, the Earth sure is pretty solid and permanent." That's exactly what the Earth *wants* you to think, you idiot. Actually, the Earth is constantly changing! Here's what to be on the lookout for.

CONTINENTAL DRIFT

Yeah, you know those shelves the continents are sitting on? (See: about a minute ago. Do you have *no* short-term memory?) They are constantly moving away from one another, like the galaxies in our universe or the former members of 'N Sync.

Fact-Like Fact

The Fast and the Furious: Continental Drift is the dullest movie ever.

At some point in the distant past, all of the continents were one giant continent known as Pangea. Pangea was awesome: you could drive from Tokyo to Disney World in Orlando in about 45 minutes. And there was plentiful parking, because, you know: Canada.

But slowly, over millions of years, the continents drifted thousands of miles apart, and just try finding parking at Disney World now.

EARTHQUAKES

Sometimes, the continental shelves slip suddenly. Maybe they've been drinking, or are on the drugs. Maybe your continental plate is a damn klutz. Who knows? But when they do slip suddenly, that is an earthquake.

Earthquakes are measured on the Richter scale. Most people can't even feel an earthquake under 2.5 on the Richter scale, while an earthquake over 8.0 will cause widespread mayhem and/or a crappy 1970s disaster movie.

The best thing to do during an earthquake is to stand in a doorjamb. If no doorjamb is available, go immediately to your local Home Depot, buy some lumber and wood screws, and build one as ASAP as possible. Hurry—your life depends on it!

VOLCANOES

Volcanoes are openings in the Earth that spew molten rock, caustic gases, and hot ash. Someday, geologists hope to perfect a volcano that spews nothing but delicious hot chocolate, with maybe a nearby whipped cream geyser. But until then, you may want to avoid volcanoes.

Sadly, avoiding volcanoes is

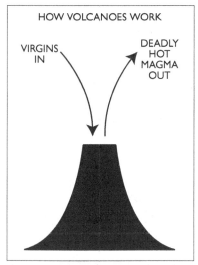

HOW VOLCANOES WORK

VIRGINS IN

DEADLY HOT MAGMA OUT

nearly impossible, as there are over 600 active ones worldwide. Basically, we are all going to get covered in ash and magma someday. The best thing you can do is to at least die in a humorous pose. Many of the bodies found in Pompeii, which was wiped out by a volcano in AD 79, were caught mid-Macarena, which is kind of hilarious.

So when the volcanoes go off, start doing the chicken dance or the YMCA hand movements, so future archaeologists will laugh till they pee their pants.

EROSION

Erosion is also a thing. However, it's really boring, so never mind.

The Environment

The environment is all around us: it's the trees, the air, the animals, and, sadly, your dad when he dances to "Take on Me" in his underwear. Why do you do that, Dad? You're totally embarrassing us!

The environment may be all around us, but it's fragile. Here are some of the major environmental problems we're facing today (besides Dad's underwear dancing, which, the less said, the better):

AIR POLLUTION

Our atmosphere is becoming more and more polluted—with carbon monoxide, with sulfur dioxide, with that neighbor kid's damn thump-thumpa car stereo. What the hell kind of music is that, even?

WATER POLLUTION

And don't go thinking air is the only problem. Our water's filthy, too. So that's fun.

Major oil spills are damaging the ocean to the point where Little Mermaids are now extinct. Our drinking water is packed with toxic chemicals, like lead and Diet Red Bull. Our rivers are clogged with raw sewage, which, trust us, you don't want to drink. We found that one out the hard way. We drank nothing but Listerine for weeks afterward. Still, better than Diet Red Bull.

> **Fact-Like Fact**

Rain forests *hate* Sting, and wish AC/DC would do some concerts to save them instead.

RAIN FORESTS

Rain forests are beautiful, lush habitats, teeming with all sorts of life and providing massive amounts of oxygen to the world. This is why mankind is cutting them down to graze cattle so you can have all those Double Whizzers with cheese at Burger Whiz. Because a greasy burger with something on it that looks like if cheese were a petroleum product is *way* more beneficial to life on Earth than some silly oxygen.

And not just cattle ranches: we're also wiping out these beautiful, virgin woods so you can have

toilet paper that's really, really soft. It's a win-win!

HAZARDOUS WASTE

There are three types of hazardous waste: chemical, nuclear, and Adam Sandler movies. There are strict laws in place for the first two; unfortunately, science has yet to find a way to stop Mr. Sandler.

Our recommendation: better stock up on provisions now for next summer's expected release of *Billy Madison vs. The Waterboy*. Store them in your family's underground Adam Sandler bunker, and when the time comes, lock yourself and your family in there until the government sounds the all-clear alarm.

Nuclear waste is nearly as toxic as Adam Sandler and can remain deadly for hundreds of thousands of years, which is approximately 100 times longer than we've had civilization. This is why we keep producing more and more without any plan as to maybe storing it somewhere where it won't kill very many people. So that's awesome.

224

ENDANGERED SPECIES

Entire species of mammals, reptiles, and plants are dying out in record numbers. This is why it's important for organizations such as Walt Disney Studios to keep doing the important work they do. Movies like *The Lion King* help us to remember these magnificent mammals as they were in the wild: posing against magnificent vistas while singing crappy Elton John/Tim Rice numbers. Seriously, lions—get some better tuneage already.

Thanks to the Batmobile, the Earth will never have mild weather again. Thanks, Bat-jerk.

GLOBAL WARMING

Global warming occurs when carbon dioxide gets trapped in the atmosphere. Carbon dioxide gets trapped in the atmosphere because we burn fossil fuels. We burn fossil fuels because we have to drive the eight blocks to use the Wendy's drive-thru to get a Baconator meal and maybe a collectible 32-ounce plastic cup from the latest *Transformers* movie.

However, global warming is still a controversial idea. On the one hand, you have thousands of reputable scientists worldwide who agree that the data shows warming trends that will continue unabated and even accelerate if mankind does nothing to curb greenhouse gases. On the other hand, you have a couple of rich corporations who will lose a little money if we slowly abandon using greenhouse gases. Currently, whining wealthy assferrets are winning, so we're all going to die. Yay!

While science is all doom and gloom about the prospect of global warming, corporate interests are looking at the advantages. For instance, New York City will eventually be underwater. Now, *some* naysayers only think of the millions of people who would drown or whatever. But think of the possibilities: you could see a totally underwater production of *Spider-Man: Turn Off the Dark*! "Shoot the Freak" at Coney Island will be much more challenging with underwater spearguns! The New York Aquarium will be the entire damn city!

Yes, global warming presents us not with a world devoid of life as we know it, but a world of opportunities.

Physics

Physics deals with the very laws that govern all interactions of matter and energy in the universe, with the possible exception of what the hell is the deal with Nickelback—seriously, their popularity cannot be explained by any physical law.

It has taken hundreds of thousands of years for man to fully comprehend the universe around him, because, let's face it, man is kind of dim. For crying out loud, man still believes that if you get bitten by a radioactive spider, you can shoot webs from your wrists. Which, you know, you totally can, but that's not the point.

The point is, the history of physics is the history of man's growing understanding of how matter and energy interact to create the universe. That, and what happens when you lick a nine-volt battery.

The History of Physics

EARLY PHYSICS: LET'S GET PHYSICS-AL (WE ARE *SO* SORRY FOR THAT)

The ancient Greeks are credited with beginning the study of physics, asking such fundamental questions as "Why do we have to dine in Hell?," "Do they even have a restaurant in Hell?," and, perhaps most fundamentally, "If there are 300 of us, don't we need a reservation?"

It was Plato's student Aristotle who came up with the concept that observing the world could lead to an understanding of its physical laws. But then, he also thought Zeus came down to Earth as a man-bull to to-

Zeus. Don't tell Hera about the swan thing, OK?

tally do it with hot ancient Greek chicks, so you know, whatever.

According to Aristotle, matter moved according to its essential nature. Stars and planets were perfect, so they moved in perfect circles. Man was imperfect, so he did the chicken dance.

GALILEO: AN OLD SCIENCE DUDE

But by the seventeenth century, scientists were tired of doing the damn chicken dance. Galileo Galilei introduced the use of mathe-matics and experimentation to come to verifiable conclusions. Using experimentation, Galileo showed that Aristotle's ideas about matter and energy were not only incorrect, but that Zeus didn't even do it with hot Greek chicks when he came to Earth as a man-bull, the damn liar.

Because of this, Stephen Hawking said, "Galileo, perhaps more than any other single person, was responsible for the birth of modern science." Plus, Hawking said it in that wacky computer voice of his, so it was pretty hilarious.

ISAAC NEWTON: ANOTHER SCIENCE DUDE

Building on all this (especially the Zeus/man-bull stuff), Isaac Newton laid the foundation of the physics we know today by discovering the three basic laws of motion:

1. Come on, feel the noise.
2. Girls, rock your boys.
3. We'll get wild, wild, wild.

But it wasn't enough for Isaac Newton to make major discoveries in physics. Oh no. He also invented the branch of mathematics called calculus, and the fundamental equation of calculus:

$$you + me = us$$

THE NEXT 200 YEARS: MORE SCIENCE STUFF

The eighteenth and nineteenth centuries saw major advances in electromagnetism, thermodynamics, and the coining of even longer words (especially in German, where words reached lengths of up to five miles and could be seen from space).

In other advances, James Maxwell made major discoveries in heat (all this time, people thought it was the humidity). Benjamin Franklin flew a kite in a thunderstorm, thus discovering that only a damn idiot would fly a kite in a thunderstorm. And Wilhelm Roentgen discovered X-rays, which he immediately used to look at lady bits, the perv.

Probably the biggest debate during this period was over the nature of light. Sometimes, it behaved like a wave. Sometimes, it behaved like a particle. Sometimes, it behaved like a total ass, telling you you looked fat in those pants or hiding in the bathroom when the check came so it wouldn't have to pay for lunch. This question would soon be settled, in a newer, fresher century.

Random Bonus Fact!

BOB HARRIS, AUTHOR

Schroedinger's cat's hairball both can and cannot be removed from the rug, depending on how much you look at the spot.

THE TWENTIETH CENTURY: NOW WITH RETSYN

In 1905, Albert Einstein came along and pretty much blew everyone's mind. His formula

$$E=mc^2$$

proved that energy and matter were interchangeable. (Don't believe it? Try this at home: plug your toaster into your shoe. Two minutes later: delicious [albeit smelly] toast!) Furthermore, his theory of relativity states that for any observer anywhere, the speed of light is constant, which means the entire universe can watch that very special episode of *Golden Girls* all at the same time. Whoa.

In the 1920s, physicists flocked to the new idea of quantum mechanics, which predicts that the subatomic world behaves very differently than the visible world we're all used to. For instance, in our visible world of Newtonian physics, Sean Hannity is kind of a dick. But at the subatomic level, Sean Hannity is a horse's ass.

There are other counterintuitive ideas in quantum mechanics. Matter itself could behave like a wave, a particle, or even a drunk aunt at a wedding. And according to Heisenberg's Uncertainty Principle, nobody could ever know exactly what was going on on *Lost*.

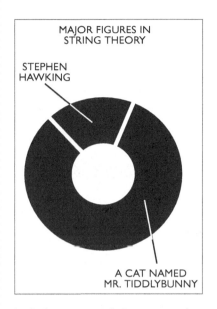

don't have jetpacks! Get on that, science!

Basic Laws of Physics

LAW OF GRAVITY

Failure to yield could lead to a $500 fine or a night in jail.

NEWTON'S LAWS OF MOTION

As noted previously, Newton's three laws of motion are:

1. Do a little dance.
2. Make a little love.
3. Get down tonight.

TODAY: NOW WHAT?

Today, physicists are looking for a theory that can successfully explain Newtonian physics, Einstein's relativity, quantum mechanics, *and* the whole Zeus/goat thing with one set of simple physical laws. Will it be Type II-A String Theory? Will it be M-Theory? Who cares—we still

CONSERVATION LAWS

In a closed system (like, say, the former Soviet Union), certain entities must not change. These entities include momentum, mass, energy, pigheadedly stupid ideas about other races and religions, and Funyuns.

LAWS OF THERMODYNAMICS

Keep your laws off my thermodynamics!

HEISENBERG'S UNCERTAINTY PRINCIPLE

We're not sure what this is. Maybe it's a kind of fish . . . ?

Subatomic Particles

In ancient Greek times, the atom was thought to be the smallest of all particles, indivisible, with liberty and justice for all and please pass the butter. But, in fact, atoms are made of subatomic particles, and those particles are made of quarks. We don't yet know what quarks are made of—probably that space-age foam they make those

ergonomic mattresses out of, the ones where you can bounce up and down on it all you want and still not spill a glass of wine. That is one sexy mattress, people.

Here is a partial list of the subatomic particles we know about, keeping in mind that we stopped paying attention to this shit, like, around 2002 or so:

Electron. Photon. Proton. Boson. Neutron. Muon. Pion. Gluon. Comicon. Simonlebon. Onandonandononon. Thebeatdontstoptillthebreakadon. Yes, these and many more can be yours if you act now!

Fact-Like Fact

Scientists are currently searching for the Jason Biggs boson, which they believe can be found in pies.

NEUTRINOS

One of the most common particles is the neutrino. It is also one of the smallest. While an ordinary electron is approximately the size of a bull moose on the steroids, neutrinos are so small that they can pass straight through the Earth without hitting anything. In fact, millions of neutrinos are passing through your body as you read this sentence. What are they doing in there? Stop it! Ack! *Get out of our body!*

QUARKS

Quarks are the building blocks of the building blocks of matter— they're the Lego you make Lego out of. Whoa, dude.

There are six flavors of quarks: up, down, bottom, top, strange, and charm. No, we don't know what it means, either. But we do know that scientists are fucking with us with this shit.

HIGGS BOSON

Today, physicists are busy looking for the Higgs boson, which may have been detected in 2012. What is the Higgs boson? The Higgs boson is an excitation of the Higgs field. The Higgs field is a quantum field with a non-zero value that fills all of space. That's right, scientists have yet to find something that fills all of space. Good one, losers!

Medicine

Without medicine, we would all die. Of course, we're all going to die anyway. So what's the damn point? We don't know, but here's the history of medicine.

History of Medicine

If a person were ill or injured in prehistoric times, a shaman would light a large fire, communicate with the various animal gods, and commune with their ancestral spirits in a complicated mystic ritual involving lots of peyote. The patient usually died, but the shaman would totally see some far-out shit on that days-long peyote trip.

But the ancient Greek Hippocrates forever changed this approach to medicine after a particularly frightening peyote trip. Most famously, he introduced the Hippocratic Oath, which states that patients must wait at least 45 minutes past their appointment time to even be called to go to sit alone and seminaked in a small,

Hippocrates. He invented having boring golf magazines in your waiting room.

track. Over the next 500 years, microorganisms were discovered. The smallpox vaccine was developed. X-rays were detected and put to use. Boring waiting room magazines about golf were published.

Antibiotics were discovered in the early twentieth century, and soon there were drugs for pretty much everything. Though really, a nice big bottle of Vicodin will get you through pretty much anything.

Fact-Like Fact

Hey are you going to use all that Vicodin? Can we have one or two? No, *we do not have a problem with Vicodin shut up.*

cold room, hoping a doctor shows up someday.

The ancient Greeks developed a vast knowledge of medicine, including how Medicare billing works. But soon came the Dark Ages, and sadly, Europe lost all this knowledge. Which sucks, because the Black Death came along and killed most of Europe. Smooth move, Europe.

But with the Renaissance, people remembered how to be smart again, and modern medicine was back on

Today, even small towns worldwide have modern hospitals with MRIs (magnetic reptile incubators; no one knows why modern hospitals need so many baby snakes around, and why they need to be magnetic, but whatever) and other high-tech devices. Though expensive, medicine is readily available to most people—unless they're deathly afraid of going to the hospital because they have a deep phobia of magnetic baby snakes. Unfortunately, approximately 107 percent of the population has this fear.

Of course, none of this will stop the coming zombie apocalypse. That's why we're stocking up on peyote and Vicodin. The zombies better not have magnetic baby snakes, or we're all screwed.

Medical School

In order to practice medicine today, one must attend a good medical school. We recommend Lefty's Medical School and HVAC Repair in Queens, New York. There's a discount if you learn both medicine *and* HVAC, so bonus.

Medical school classes are followed by a residency. A residency usually involves having to hear J.D.'s interminable internal dialogues while Elliot learns some life lesson and we learn that Dr. Cox has a soft, human side under his gruff exterior.

If you can get through nine seasons of that crap, congratulations! You are now a medical doctor. Plus, you can fix most HVAC. Wow!

Top 10 Causes of Death in America

Fending off a rabid wolverine with slabs of raw meat. Trying to stop a speeding bus with your teeth. Putting papier-mâché around your head and telling Jose Canseco that you're a piñata. Standing on an airport runway, attempting to catch a landing 727 on your tongue.

Yes, there are millions of ways to die. These are the top 10 causes of death in America today.

ACCIDENTS

Accidents are the number one killer of Americans between the ages of one and 44. This brings up the question: who is letting all these one-year-olds drive?

Don't get us wrong—some one-year-olds are excellent drivers. Al Unser Jr. won his first Indianapolis 500 at the age of just six months. But that's rare. Most one-year-olds can't handle a single turbo V-6 with 700 HP, fuel injection, four overhead cams, and up to 130 KPa of boost (140 KPa for short ovals). Heck, the Disalmanacarian still can't even handle parallel parking.

▶ Fact-Like Fact

However, one-year-olds can fly light aircraft quite easily. Strap one to an ultralight and see!

If you *must* let your one-year-old drive, start him or her out on something easy, like a nice, late-model Subaru Outback. But make sure it's an automatic; toddlers can't drive standard until after they learn how to count the gears. Now your one-year-old is ready to pick you up some Taco Bell and some Johnnie Walker at the drive-thru liquor store.

ARACHNOPHOBIA

No, not the fear of spiders, but the 1990 film. It can kill you.

Here's how: If you've ever said anything disparaging about John Goodman's performance in *Arachnophobia*, he will find you and he will beat you to death. Even today, this is still the number three cause of death in Delaware.

So be careful, and for the re-

cord: we *loved* John Goodman in *Arachnophobia!*

CANCER

Cancer is bad news, folks. Try not to get it.

**That Guy with the Tire Iron.
You are a dead man.**

GUY WITH THE TIRE IRON, THAT

The Disalmanacarian doesn't know what you did to piss off that guy with the tire iron, but he was just here looking for you. He says when he finds you, he's going to "crush your skull so hard, you'll shit your brain out your pancreas, twice." We're not even sure what that means, but it does *not* sound good.

We told him you'd gone to Florida to see your mom, but we don't think he believed us. Seriously, what did you do to piss off that guy with the tire iron? Look what he did to the mailbox! He is *so* going to kill you. Dude.

HEART DISEASE

Heart disease is America's number one killer. An American dies of heart disease every 36 seconds. One in three Americans will suffer some sort of cardiovascular disease someday.

Luckily, there are two ways to avoid heart disease. One is to eat healthy and exercise. But seriously, who wants to do that? Boring.

Or you can do what we did: just reach right into your chest and yank out your old, beefy heart and replace it with any old electronic gadget you've got around the house. For instance, we've replaced our heart with a Tamagotchi. It keeps our heart beating as long as we remember to feed, clean up after, and play with our digital pet by pounding the appropriate area of our chest. It's fun!

And someday, when our Tamagotchi dies, we'll replace it with our Nintendo DS, running Scribblenauts. Sure, sometimes we'll have to write "hammer" or "ladder" or "atom bomb" across our chest with a stylus. But at least we won't have heart disease.

HOUNDS, THE

Hark, do ye hear that? That be the baying of the hounds 'pon the moors! Arr!

The hounds be the dark hellbeasts, dark as the very depths of Hades, with eyes that burn like the fires that lash at the damned for eternity! And teeth white like the bleached bones of the dead! And the sound of their evil howls, 'twill drive a man to madness, 'twill!

Aye, the hounds be coming now, to take your pitiful soul to the dark one. Beware!

Although: the hounds be really adorable when they be puppies. Arr, who's a mighty hellhound? You are! Yes, you are! Who's going to drag my big ol' soul into the dark abyss with his widdle tiny teeth and big ol' floppy paws? Yes, it's you, you cute hell-puppy!

OLD AGE

Many people avoid disease and accidents, and simply die of old age. Of course, the definition of "old age" has changed considerably over the years. During the Black Death, life expectancy was "next Friday." But today, many people stay active into their seventies and eighties, if you can call watching *Matlock* reruns on the Hallmark Channel "active."

> ▶ **Fact-Like Fact**
>
> Scientists believe the worst part of old age is the constant Internet petitions demanding that you host *Saturday Night Live*.

Dying of old age usually entails one or more bodily organs simply giving out. This is why you should always buy the extended service warranty and get that shit replaced every 10 years. It's expensive, but *so* worth it down the road.

PLAYING A GAME OF CHESS WITH DEATH

If you ever challenge Death to a game of chess (and you probably will), just know this: you are going to die. Death has been playing chess for centuries now, against quite literally hundreds of millions of people. Death has seen the Hoerzinger Maneuver thousands of times. He's defended against the Mizzinstein Stratagem on countless occasions. He even knows the Yashimoto Conundrum. Death will beat you at chess.

Your only chance is to try instead to challenge death to a more modern game—he may have less experience at something like Twister, Apples to Apples, or Ms. Pac-Man. We recommend Settlers of Catan. Make sure to get *lots* of wood.

SMOKING

Tobacco use can lead to lung disease, heart disease, and cancer. On the other hand, tobacco use can lead to strokes, emphysema, and a greatly reduced lifespan. The tobacco industry likes to call this "a mixed bag."

Tobacco is so dangerous to your health and the health of those around you, it is the only product that comes with a surgeon general's warning:

> **WARNING: THE SURGEON GENERAL HAS DETERMINED THAT CIGARETTE SMOKING IS DANGEROUS TO YOUR HEALTH.**

Over the years, we've had many surgeon generals, who've left their personal mark on the traditional warning we see on tobacco products.

Surgeon General Yoko Ono:

> **WARNING: RECORD THE SOUND OF A SINGLE SNOWFLAKE FALLING. CRY TEARS OF PURE LOVE.**

Surgeon General Keanu Reeves:

> **WARNING: WHOA.**

In 2012, Barack Obama briefly made Ryan Gosling the surgeon general:

> **WARNING: HEY GIRL, YOU LOOK KINDA SEXY WITH THAT CIGARETTE.**

Smoking immediately went up 1 billion percent; Ryan Gosling was fired *so* fast.

SUBSTANCE ABUSE

Sadly, many Americans die every year from substance abuse. There are several categories of deadly substances: alcohol, illicit drugs, prescription drugs, McNuggets, and more.

Alcoholism can lead to serious liver damage, the desire to perform karaoke, and really dreadfully poor choices of sexual partners.

Many illicit drugs can lead to death, from heroin to meth. A good rule of thumb is not to buy anything you're going to put into your body from anybody whose nickname is "the Machete."

Misuse of prescription drugs leads to many deaths per year as well. Remember, always follow the directions on the prescriptions you steal from your grandparents' medicine cabinet, and you should be fine.

Which brings us to McNuggets. Try not to eat so many, OK? Jesus. And maybe cut down on that Parmesan Peppercorn Ranch dipping sauce while you're at it.

The basic message here is this: try not to abuse any substance whatsoever. Only abuse pure nothingness.

All the Other Damn Sciences

Incredibly, there are other sciences as well. There's bracketology. There's whatever the hell kind of science the old guy in Thomas Dolby's song "She Blinded Me with Science" who yells "Science!" all the damn time does. And there are these: chemistry, life sciences, social sciences, and computer science.

CHEMISTRY

Chemistry is the study of matter: its properties, its structure and compo-

Random Bonus Fact!

LYDIA DAVIS, AUTHOR

Contrary to the hopes of molecular scientists, and despite work with scanning tunneling microscopes in two-terminal setups, it has not proved possible for a butyl methyl sulfide molecule adsorbed on a copper surface to be operated as a single-molecule electric motor, even allowing for the chiralities of the molecule and the importance of symmetry in atomic-scale electrical devices.

sition, its chili-rubbed chicken recipe (yum!), and much more.

Chemists are mostly interested in studying chemical reactions—mixing two substances together and seeing if the resulting reaction is "cool" or "kick-ass." This is what led to perhaps the greatest discovery in the history of chemistry: that thing that happens when you put Mentos in Diet Coke.

Today, chemists are working toward their ultimate dream: harnessing the power of Diet Coke and Mentos, and then seeing what happens if you add Pop Rocks, then putting all that in your mouth and seeing what kind of shit goes down. It is going to be *so* epic, you guys.

LIFE SCIENCES

Biology is the study of life, living things, and the old Chris Elliott sitcom *Get a Life*. Why didn't he ever get a life? It's still a mystery to science.

Biology is thought to have started in ancient Greece, when Aristotle famously said, "Let's see what's inside the dog." The answer, it turns out, was really gross. But the science of biology was born, and we're not cleaning that shit up.

There have been many advances in biology since Aristotle's time. With the introduction of the microscope in the 1600s, biologists were able to show that living things were made up of cells (and not tiny Crunch Berries, as had been previously thought). And in the 1800s, Dr. Frankenstein made a dude out of parts of corpses and lightning, though the Disalmanacarian's mom wouldn't let us watch scary movies like that until we stopped wetting the bed (approximately age 28).

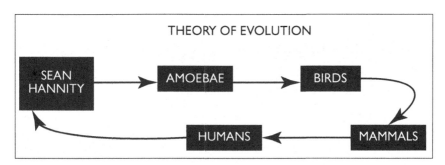

Perhaps the biggest discovery in life sciences was Charles Darwin's theory of evolution. Darwin realized that life on Earth started out extremely simple (like say, an amoeba) and, through heredity and mutation, slowly, over millions of years, evolved into much more complex life forms (like say, an amoeba that can play Adele's "Rolling in the Deep" on the ukulele).

The idea of evolution is still controversial in some circles—ignorant, stupid circles. Idiotic, fearful circles. Circles of extreme dumbth.

Currently, huge advances in life sciences are being made in genetics. Thanks to the Human Genome Project, geneticists are mapping human DNA to the very last nucleotide (which is the nucleotide that determines if a person will be a Trekkie or not). But there are ethical issues—if you knew your baby was going to become a Trekkie, what would you do with that information? We'd buy the baby the first several seasons of *ST:TNG* on DVD and hope for the best. Really, what else is there to do?

SOCIAL SCIENCES

Sociology, economics, media studies—yeah, those are real sciences. *Not!* Oh, snap! We just burned you, sociology! What are you going to do about it? Are you going to cry? Economics is a cry baby! Thptthh!!! You know what? Media studies butt. Ha ha ha ha! Suck it, media studies!

COMPUTER SCIENCE

Computer science has made many modern miracles possible. Mostly FarmVille, but still.

So, How Did All the Damn Scientists Die?

Throughout history, there have been dozens of physicists, and several of them died. Here's a quick, simple guide for you. Memorize it and get it tattooed on your back:

KEPLER
WAS PIERCED
BY ARROWS.

CHARLES
DARWIN,
MAULED
AT THE
ZOO.

HUYGENS
SUNK
OFF THE
FAROES.

PASTEUR
WAS EATEN
— BY A —
CHICKEN.

ISAAC
NEWTON
CAUGHT
THE
FLU.

ROENTGEN,
BEAT UP
— BY A —
WICCAN.

PAVLOV:
ATTACKED
BY DOGS

MARIE
CURIE,
—FROM—
RADIATION.

TESLA:
FED TO
THE HOGS.

EINSTEIN
PLAYED DICE
WITH GOD.

MAX
PLANCK,
—ON—
VACATION.

NIELS
BOHR,
EATEN
BY A COD.

SCHROEDINGER
WAS LOCKED
IN A BOX.

FEYNMAN
PISSED OFF
RICHARD
BURTON.

FERMI
—WAS—
DASHED
UPON THE
ROCKS.

CARL SAGAN
FELL OUT
OF A JET.

HEISENBERG'S
—FATE IS—
UNCERTAIN.

STEPHEN
HAWKING:
NOT
DEAD
YET.

25 Great Inventions

Man has always been a clever creature. Well, not some men. Our uncle Ray still doesn't understand how can openers work, the poor dope.

But there have always been a few men and/or women who could see a problem and then solve it with some kind of newfangled contraption. We call these men and/or women inventors. Here are the 25 greatest inventions inventors have invented, inventively.

Agriculture

Agriculture was invented well before 10,000 BC, when somebody said, "Fuck this hunting shit." And so he did.

Grains were probably the first crops: rice in China, rye in the Middle East, and quinoa in the hipster empire of Williamsburg, Egypt. By the time of Christ, agriculture had spread worldwide, though the chief crops were frank-incense and myrrh. Have you ever tried to eat a bowl of myrrh? It's rough going.

> **▶ Fact-Like Fact**
>
> **Man, what the WTF is myrrh, even? A spice? A root vegetable? A kind of pottery from China's Yan Dynasty? What?**

The ancient Romans made many advances in agriculture, like slavery and share-cropping. Thanks, Rome.

Centuries later, the Industrial Revolution came to the farm. This brought about needed improvements, like the steam-powered goat. With the development of the tractor, a farmer could lose a limb in a fraction of the time (as a point of comparison, it sometimes took seven or eight months for an ancient Chinese farmer to lose just one finger).

The industrialization of agriculture also led to huge amounts of chemicals being used in farming. This led to potatoes the size of Volkswagens, and beets with teeth and a thirst for human blood. We've come a long, long way.

Airplane

The airplane: it has changed the way man travels through the air, from mostly vertical to mostly horizontal.

HOW AIRPLANES WORK

PILOT SACRIFICES A GOAT TO BONDOR, GOD OF DARKNESS

VOILA! FLIGHT!

The first heavier-than-air flight occurred at Kitty Hawk, North Carolina, in 1903. The Wright brothers (Lefty and One-Eye) had attempted several unsuccessful flights (hence the nicknames) with many prototypes—an all-brick airplane, an airplane completely powered by farting, and even a delicious, all-cheese airplane (this is the model that the lost Wright brother, Fats, was piloting when he died).

But on that day in 1903, the Wright brothers successfully flew nearly four inches in just 16 months. Their second flight was even better (and included *The Usual Suspects* as the inflight movie. How cool is that? We always get some awful Katherine Heigl rom-com), and mankind had at last conquered the skies! Well, except for clouds. Screw you, clouds. Your days are numbered.

AUTOMOBILE

The automobile was invented in the late nineteenth century by Karl Benz. Basically, Benz needed a large, mobile cup holder for his 64-ounce Diet Mountain Dew. Even 120 years later, this is still the primary function of the automobile.

BEER

Beer! Hell yeah! Beer! Whooooooo!

▶ Fact-Like Fact

The first computer "bug" was an actual insect. A moth flew into an early computer, and zap! A super-intelligent moth that eats the crap out of your old sweaters! This is why Bill Cosby must now live in an underground bunker.

COMPUTER

A computer is a handy device. Performing millions of arithmetic operations per second, a computer can solve incredibly complex problems that were previously impossible for the mere human mind to even fathom. Or you can just keep using it to play Bejeweled. Either way.

FIRE

In ancient times, mankind needed something warm and orange to cook food and keep the scary animals away at night, and lukewarm tangerines were just not doing the job. So, Og made fire, and it swept the world.

Og's descendants still make a quarter-cent profit every time some-one uses fire. That family is now known as the Kardashians.

GLASS

Glass is all around us: windows, bottles, little bits of broken glass in that smoothie you just bought from an extremely disgruntled smoothie-maker.

Glass dates back to 3500 BC in ancient Mesopotamia. Which leads to the obvious question: what is that extremely disgruntled smoothie-maker's problem? Is he insane, trying to kill random people with broken glass smoothies? Or is this all part of the plan of an evil genius?

Maybe you went to junior high school with this extremely disgruntled smoothie-maker, and maybe he still holds a grudge for the "dodgeball incident" in PE class (you know the one). Maybe he's been biding his time, waiting for just the moment to strike, nonchalantly handing you a mango-banana smoothie.

Our advice: never, ever drink smoothies, assuming you want to live. Also: arrest all smoothie-mak-

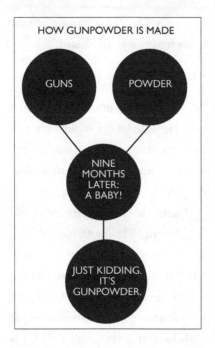

HOW GUNPOWDER IS MADE

GUNS

POWDER

NINE MONTHS LATER: A BABY!

JUST KIDDING. IT'S GUNPOWDER.

ers preemptively, just in case. We can't be too safe.

GUNPOWDER

Gunpowder was invented in the ninth century by Xin Li, who was looking for "a way to blow stuff up real good."

Gunpowder was first used for fireworks, as the ancient Chinese were already celebrating American independence every July 4 as early as AD 950. But soon, gunpowder became a weapon when Xin Li said, "What happens when you point the fireworks at people?" Clearly, Xin Li was a sociopath.

Soon, gunpowder was used in rockets, firearms, cannons, grenades, and all sorts of ways to kill a whole bunch of people really fast. Gunpowder use very quickly spread worldwide, because if there's one thing every nation on the planet has in common, it's wanting to destroy every other nation on the planet. Yay, mankind!

In today's world of dynamite, TNT, and atomic weapons, gunpowder is pretty small potatoes. But if you want to blow up some small potatoes—gunpowder, won't you?

INTERNET

The Internet: it has revolutionized the way people annoy the shit out of us by forwarding us pictures of kittens and bunnies and pandas. Jeez, all we wanted to do was look at some goddamn porn, is that so much to ask? Lord.

LIGHTBULB

The lightbulb was invented in 1878 by Thomas Edison. In his lifetime, Edison created more than 47 million inventions, including the all-metal chicken, soup that buildings could eat, and an artificial gall bladder carved out of a hunk of old hickory with a jackknife. Clearly, some of his inventions were more useful than others.

▶ Fact-Like Fact

Edison also invented fuzzy dice, thong underwear, babies, potato chips that come in a can, and the song "Who Let the Dogs Out."

And while not as Earth-shattering as his invention of the macramé dog, Edison's lightbulb has changed the world. Now, rather than curse the darkness, we can simply turn on a lightbulb and curse. Because we just really, really love cursing (which Edison also invented).

MICROSCOPE

The compound microscope is said to have been invented by Galileo Galilei in the early 1600s (although Thomas Edison claims he invented the microscope during a break between inventing tiny hats for bees and the flaming cat).

The microscope finally allowed man to see the tiny, tiny world of microbes, and what man found there was quite surprising: at a microscopic level, the world is a shit-hole. Microbes are ugly little buggers; they never clean up after themselves, and they only have rudimentary ideas of hygiene. They're disgusting, filthy little creatures. Can't someone at least invent some microscopic toilet paper for them?

You know, mankind should just forget Galileo (or Edison) invented the microscope; the microscopic world is just too damn upsetting.

MICROWAVE OVEN

From the days of Aristotle and Archimedes, on through to Einstein and Gandhi, it had always been man's dream to cook a frozen burrito in about a minute. To have some parts of the frozen burrito be so molten hot you burned a hole in the roof of your mouth. To have other parts still be only partially thawed, with that horrible mealy texture of mostly frozen refried beans. And thanks to the microwave oven, we are now all living this dream.

Thank you, microwave oven. We owe you one.

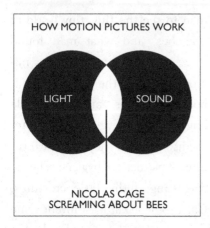

HOW MOTION PICTURES WORK

LIGHT   SOUND

NICOLAS CAGE
SCREAMING ABOUT BEES

MOTION PICTURE

Oh, who invented the motion picture? Was it perhaps (gasp!) Thomas Edison? Why yes, yes, it was. OK, Edison. Let someone else invent something once in a while.

So yeah, the motion picture. Audiences in the early twentieth century were transfixed by this new technology; early films like *Hey, Look! A Train!* packed movie palaces with paying customers.

Later, sound and color were added to the motion picture experience. This led to perhaps the pinnacle of cinema: *Highlander II: The Quickening*. It has everything you could possibly want from a movie: a Highlander, and some quickening. Man, we love movies with lots and lots of quickening! And we're not even sure what the hell quickening even is.

PAPER

Paper is considered one of the four great inventions of China, along with gunpowder, little toys with paint on them that kill small children, and kung pao shrimp.

If the Chinese wanted to write something down before the invention of paper, they had to write it down on the side of a live tiger. This is why there is so little Chinese literature from before this time, other than Ming Xi's epic poem, "Aaaauuuuuggghhhh!"

Today, life without paper is almost unthinkable, and not just because tigers are nearly extinct. Paper even made this book possible. So if you take issue with any of the fact-like facts in this book, take it up with your local Chinese embassy.

PHONOGRAPH

Thomas Edison invented the phonograph in 1877, the same year he invented the electric ferret and the internal combustion duck. He needed real help.

The phonograph was the first

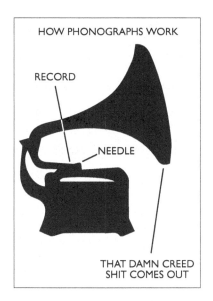

HOW PHONOGRAPHS WORK

RECORD

NEEDLE

THAT DAMN CREED
SHIT COMES OUT

invention that could both record and play back sounds, which led to people freaking the fuck out when they heard their own voice for the first time. "Good lord, I don't sound like a castrated billy goat, do I?" said then U.S. president Rutherford B. Hayes. (SPOILER ALERT: He totally did.)

Sadly, the invention of the phonograph had unintended consequences, such as Celine Dion. We can only imagine that if Edison had known his invention would be used for such evil, he would have just buried the phonograph in his backyard. Or Celine Dion. Either way.

PHOTOGRAPHY

Without photography, we wouldn't know what anything looks like. Especially that bald spot on the back of your head. No, no, it's not noticeable. Not one bit.

PRINTING PRESS

The printing press was invented by Johannes Gutenberg in 1440. Sadly, this led directly to awful, awful books such as Mitch Albom's *The Five People You Meet in Heaven.*

Now, the Disalmanacarian actually died briefly a few years ago (we choked on a Cheeto while watching a *How I Met Your Mother* repeat), and we went to Heaven. But Mitch Albom was wrong about the five people you meet in Heaven. In fact, the five people you meet in Heaven are the members of the J. Geils Band. We hope you like "Centerfold," because if you go to Heaven when you die, you're going to be hearing it a *lot.*

Fact-Like Fact

Also "Freeze-Frame."

RADIO

Radio is what people did for entertainment before TV. TV is what people did for entertainment before video games. Video games are what people did for entertainment before photorefractive keratectomy. Remember when we all threw away our Xboxes and Nintendos and started giving each other laser eye surgery? That was the best.

SPORK

It's a spoon! It's a fork! It's a spork!

As a fork, it has tiny little tines that don't pick up anything. As a spoon, the fork part makes everything drip out onto your best shirt. As an eating utensil, it's basically useless.

Spork! Ask for it by name.

TELEPHONE

The telephone was invented in 1876 by Alexander Graham Bell. The first call he placed was to his assistant, Watson: "Watson, come here, I need you!" Over a century later, this would also be the first sext. Watson, you scamp!

The telephone works by converting your voice into a signal (or "angry bird") and, using a slingshot, chucking it in the general direction of the recipient (or "green pig"). If the signal kills the recipient, a successful call has been made.

Alexander Graham Bell would be amazed to see the many changes to his invention. Now when he needs Watson, he just needs to fire up his iWatson app, which makes extremely strategic use of the iPhone's vibrate feature.

TELESCOPE

Without the telescope, we would know nearly nothing of the universe around us, not to mention the neighbor lady across the way on the seventh floor. Wowza!

Random Bonus Fact!

KAMBRI CREWS, AUTHOR

Alexander Graham Bell's deaf mother stumbled across his homemade bong. Forced to improvise, he told her it was a hearing aid he was making her as a gift. From there, the telephone was invented.

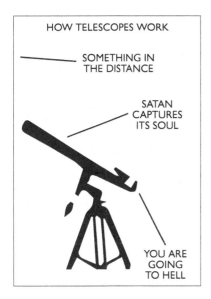

HOW TELESCOPES WORK

SOMETHING IN
THE DISTANCE

SATAN
CAPTURES
ITS SOUL

YOU ARE
GOING
TO HELL

Galileo didn't invent the tele-scope, but he made massive im-provements to the original design—the original design for the telescope called for two slots to place slices of bread to be toasted and no eyepieces whatsoever. This design would eventually be called "the automobile."

With his telescope, Galileo dis-covered Jupiter's moons, Saturn's rings, and the planet Neptune, which had been hiding behind Ura-nus this whole time.

In the following centuries, vast improvements have been made in the telescope. Today, the Hubble Space Telescope sits in a high Earth orbit, bringing us incredible photos of the neighbor lady across the way on planet Rigel-12. Wowza!

TELEVISION

Oh, what a great invention. Now I can watch stupid people catching fish with their hands in a mud bog from the comfort of my own couch. Also: Snooki. So thanks, television, you motherfucker.

THERMOMETER

The thermometer was invented in the early 1600s, when somebody said, "You know what let's do? Let's stick a glass tube filled with mer-cury up someone's butt." It was probably that Chinese gunpowder dude. We told you he was sick.

TIME TRAVEL

Time travel dates back to 1512, when time travelers from the cen-tury 65,000-A visited Leonardo da Vinci in Italy. Da Vinci said sure, he'd watch their time machine while they checked out the Sistine Chapel.

Instead, da Vinci got in, threw the switch, and went to the twentieth century, where he saw a helicopter. But before he could go back to his own time to "invent" the helicopter, Richard Nixon got in and went to century 65,000-A and fathered a whole bunch of Richard Nixon babies, who in turn invented time travel and visited da Vinci.

▶ Fact-Like Fact

Thanks to time travel, Socrates has seen *Weekend at Bernie's II* 18 times.

But this time, da Vinci went back to caveman days and invented the first tool, the Bone You Hit Crap With. Meanwhile, some cavemen got into the time machine and found themselves in the early twenty-first century, where they were immediately elected to the U.S. Congress as Republicans.

For some reason, Lindsay Lohan happened to be in Washington, DC, that day and got into the time machine and accidentally went to century 65,000-A, where she totally did it with Richard Nixon, and their Richard Nixon babies invented time travel and went back to visit da Vinci, and this time da Vinci went to the Old West.

Of course, now we have at least four (five?) Leonardo da Vincis running around at wildly different places in history, not to mention cavemen in Congress and all those upsetting Richard Nixon/Lindsay Lohan babies. But that's time travel for you.

WHEEL

Nobody can say with precision where or when the wheel was invented. Archaeological evidence puts the invention of the wheel back to at least 1989, as found on a rudimentary four-wheeled vehicle known as "the Hyundai Sonata."

There is some evidence of an earlier wheeled vehicle, the so-called AMC Pacer, but details are sketchy. In fact, scientists now believe the AMC Pacer may be a hoax.

PART FIVE

All the Other Crap

Hey, not everything fits into a nice, easy category. That's why we've added this catch-all section. Now, attach your brain to the firecracker of knowledge. Light and run away.

The Economy

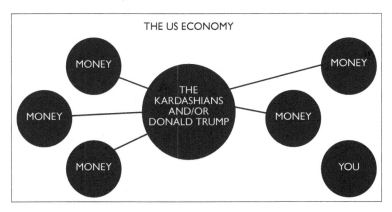

What is an economy? This is a common question. Among idiots. Jeez, didn't you get past tenth grade?

An economy is based on a society's labor, capital, resources, manufacturing, trade, distribution, and more. As the great economist Adam Smith once said, "It's all about the Benjamins." Of course, back in Adam Smith's time, a "Benjamin" was one of those shiny beads the Dutch bought Manhattan with, but the idea is still the same.

The United States has a market economy. All economic decisions are based on supply and demand, between buyers and sellers. The government certainly isn't involved at all—the government legislates no gigantic tax loopholes for entire industries, corporations don't lobby the government for favorable regulation, and the government certainly doesn't buy a shit-ton of goods itself. For example, the government certainly doesn't spur the economy by buying a shit-ton of super-expensive tanks and planes and battleships. This is a market economy!

So if we want to learn how the economy works, let's start with the basics, can't we?

Economic Terms

Hearing about the economy can give you a headache—partly because it just seems so complicated, and partly because you're usually hearing about it from some assbadger in a fancy suit shouting into a Bluetooth on the train. Dude, calm down.

But while the economy will always be loud and obnoxious, it needn't be complicated. Here are a few key terms to help you understand what's going on with your money (usually it's being eaten away by obscure fees).

▶ Fact-Like Fact

Perhaps the grossest national product is Spam.

GROSS NATIONAL PRODUCT

The gross national product (GNP) measures America's total output of goods and services, valued at current market rates. Since America has moved most of its manufacturing overseas, the majority of our "output of good and services" today is repeat showings of *Van Wilder* movies on Comedy Central (we didn't even know there was a sixth one!) and your brother-in-law's dog-walking business. In the last fiscal year, this gave America a GNP of nearly $1.89 ($2.14 if you count the change America found in its couch last week).

ECONOMIC INDICATORS

Economists use several criteria to determine where the economy is headed. And even though economists are almost always laughably, disastrously wrong, time and again they turn to the same economic indicators to make their forecasts.

These indicators include: How much is the generic ramen at Safeway this week? Is it two-for-a-dollar or is it on sale for 10-for-a-dollar? If it's 10-for-a-dollar, should we stock up? What if they're out of chicken? Should we get the shrimp flavor instead?

A composite of the answers gives us a rough idea of where the economy is headed.

INFLATION

Inflation is what you do to your tires. If there's too much inflation, your tires will explode. While that's bad for the economy, it makes for one awesome YouTube clip.

CONSUMER PRICE INDEX

This is a measure of the average change in prices over time. The CPI is calculated by asking 100 elderly people about the price of bread and averaging their answers. If the index is at "Back in my day, we had to walk 20 miles to the store, and the bread wasn't even bread, it was a rock, and it chipped our teeth and stuffed up our colons and we liked it," then sell everything, buy lots of gold, and move into an underground bunker in Idaho. Shit is about to go down, Maynard.

DEBT AND DEFICIT

People get this confused all the time, but it's quite easy to remember the difference between the debt and the deficit. The deficit is the difference between income and expenditures in the annual national budget, while the debt is exactly how much of the country we owe to China (currently, everything west of Ohio).

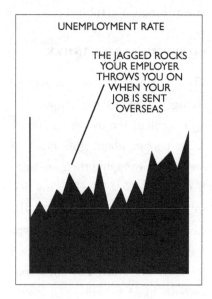

UNEMPLOYMENT RATE

THE JAGGED ROCKS YOUR EMPLOYER THROWS YOU ON WHEN YOUR JOB IS SENT OVERSEAS

UNEMPLOYMENT RATE

Quite possibly the most watched of all economic indicators, the unemployment rate measures the number of people who are unemployed. But not the people who have been unemployed for a really long time. And it has no metric to measure

people who are underemployed, or are working part-time when they would prefer to work full-time if they could. Taking all that and more into consideration, the actual unemployment rate would be closer to 250 percent of the U.S. population.

Wall Street

Located in New York City, Wall Street is home to the stock markets and the financial industry. In the early days, stocks were traded for either shiny golden objects or live chickens (and if you could find even one shiny golden chicken, you could pretty much buy Pennsylvania outright).

Today, of course, the market is much more high-tech. Investors use computers to trade shiny golden chickens at any time of day or night, and use robotic buffers to keep their chickens both shiny and golden. Ownership of Pennsylvania changes seven or eight times every second.

Here's what you'll need to know about Wall Street before you invest:

THE MARKETS

The New York Stock Exchange is the world's largest stock exchange. You should see the size of their solid-gold chicken! Holy crap.

While all sorts of businesses are listed on the NYSE (and some of them may even be legitimate), the NASDAQ (or National Association of Stupid, Dumb-Ass Quarter-horses) specializes in the computer and telecommunications industries. Personally, we would never invest in any firm run by stupid, dumb-ass quarter-horses, but hey, it's your shiny golden chicken, not ours.

Random Bonus Fact!

**SARA BENINCASA,
COMEDIAN AND AUTHOR**

The human internal anal sphincter is strong enough to crush diamonds. Try it and see!

THE DOW

The Dow Jones Industrial Average measures the performance of the New York Stock Exchange. If the Dow is doing well, that's called a bull market. It's called a bull market because brokerage firms are successfully bullshitting you to give them money for slips of paper that are pretty much meaningless and then charging you some more money just to trade those slips of paper for different slips of paper. This is the basis for our entire economy, which is pretty much the scariest damn thing we can think of.

Of course, if the Dow is doing poorly, that's called a bear market, because investors want to maul the crap out of whoever just lost their entire retirement nest egg. And if that egg contained a shiny golden chicken, then you've missed out on your chance to own Pennsylvania for one-eighth of a second. And you were going to put in a deck around Scranton and everything!

THE FINANCIAL INDUSTRY

Several Wall Street firms have gotten in trouble over the past five years. Some have played fast and loose with investors' money, and some have outright broken several laws. These offenses have included securities violations and indecent exposure. So to be safe, be sure your financial analyst is both fully licensed *and* fully clothed. Because if they're naked, you don't want to know where they're keeping your shiny gold chicken.

Banks

Good lord, you're not keeping your money in a bank, are you? If you answered yes, your bank just charged you a $14.50 Mention Fee. And then a $6.95 Mention Fee Fee. That's on top of the Monthly Fee, the Weekly Fee, the Fee Fee, the Fee That Must Not Be Named, the Fee of Brotherly Love, and approximately 18,000 more fees.

Basically, all your money will belong to your bank by the time you finish reading this paragraph. You're much better off simply burying a shiny golden chicken in the backyard or shoving a couple in your mattress. Good luck!

BUSINESS

Business is the engine that keeps the U.S. economy moving. That, and Dilbert Post-it notes. You can't

run a business in America without Dilbert Post-it notes, you know. It's the law.

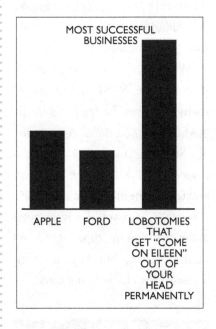

MOST SUCCESSFUL BUSINESSES

APPLE   FORD   LOBOTOMIES THAT GET "COME ON EILEEN" OUT OF YOUR HEAD PERMANENTLY

Through much of its history, America had a manufacturing-based economy. We made everything here: cars, furniture, Dilbert Post-it notes—you name it, it was built in America by American workers, with American air and water pollution giving millions of Americans American tumors. But today, most of these jobs have moved overseas—even the character of Dilbert himself is now a bemused Indian call center worker.

With manufacturing disappearing, America is looking for new business opportunities to revive its flagging economy. One promising new type of business is kicking people and then grabbing their wallet, which is called the banking industry. And soon, 90 percent of all Americans will be paid minimum wage to greet one another when they enter a Walmart. It will be crowded.

Labor

In the nineteenth century, factory workers toiled away in unsafe conditions for approximately a million hours per week until they keeled over and died. The 1840s version of the sitcom *The Office* was pretty much depressing as all get-out.

But thanks to the efforts of organized labor, Americans now have the 40-hour workweek, the concept of the weekend, health insurance, a minimum wage, workplace safety laws, and more. On the other hand, today's global economy allows corporations to simply move their jobs to nations where prisoners are used

as slave labor or children make three cents an hour. This has led to the Chinese version of the sitcom *The Office*, which is pretty much depressing as all get-out.

What is the future of labor? High-tech jobs demand a high-tech labor force. Robots are already doing the jobs of factory workers in many industries, and this trend will continue across the entire economy. This will lead to the all-robot version of the sitcom *The Office*, which will actually be pretty funny. You've got to love Robo Mindy Kaling!

▶ Fact-Like Fact

No, we don't want to look at your four-year-old's drawings of a doggy. But thank you for asking.

Art

What is Art? Art is a way for us to make sense of the world around us. Art is a language for us to express the inexpressible feelings deep inside us. Art is an excuse to dress in a black turtleneck and try to get women to come back to your "studio" to see your "etchings." Mostly the last one, really. And it really, really works!

The History of Art

The history of Art is long, and almost interesting.

PREHISTORIC ART

Art has been around for hundreds of thousands of years, and yet most of it still sucks. You'd think we'd be good at it by now. You'd be wrong. Look at this picture of a cow I just drew. Pathetic.

The earliest art that has survived to the present day is cave paintings from the Paleolithic (Latin for "butt-ass early") Age. These crude renderings of bison, horses, and Dwayne "the Rock" Johnson are thought to be religious or ceremonial in nature, though they could also have been for entertainment purposes (primitive 3-D glasses have been found in some caves).

ANCIENT GREECE AND ROME

It was the ancient Greeks who finally discovered the key to great art, which was: stop being such a horrible goddamned artist, Chester. Their beautiful marble sculptures from the classical period were incredibly lifelike, to the point that Zeus came down to Earth as a billy goat and tried to do it with several sculptures of the nymphs. You know, for the king of the gods, Zeus wasn't exactly the sharpest knife in the park.

The *Venus de Milo*. Her eyes are up here, ass.

In fact, most Greek sculpture was of their gods. For instance, the

Venus de Milo depicted Larry, the god of men with no arms who are in the process of gender reassignment. Good for Larry, we say! We support you, whatever your life choices.

It was in ancient Rome that sculpture turned into portraiture of actual, living persons, raising emperors such as Julius Caesar, Augustus Caesar, and Kevin Caesar to the status of the gods. But sadly, the emperors were not gods, not even the mighty Billy Bob Caesar. The Roman Empire fell, and the ability to draw someone and actually have it look like the dude you were drawing fell with it.

MEDIEVAL ART

Art in Medieval Europe sucked. It's all just dudes and ladies and babies with golden circles around their heads. What did the golden circle symbolize? It was kind of like a primitive version of the "You Are Here" signs at the mall—the person with the golden circle around the head was supposed to be you, and you were about to ascend to Heaven or get mauled by lions or whatever the painting depicted. It

was a pretty good system, but it wasn't art.

THE RENAISSANCE

Starting in the year 1400, the Renaissance brought about great advances in science, art, literature, cupcake baking, and scrapbooking. Especially scrapbooking, what with the invention of that double-sided Scotch tape. That stuff's the shit! You should see the Disalmanacarian's old 'N Sync scrapbook from the late 1990s. We love you, Lance!

In art, much of the focus was on Italy. Leonardo da Vinci painted his enigmatic masterpiece *Mona Lisa* (also known as *What the Hell Does That Broad Think She's Smiling At, Huh?*) and his fresco (fresco is a type of painting made with delicious, refreshing Fresca, now with just one calorie) *The Last Supper.* Art historians are still impressed with the level of detail in *The Last Supper*—the receipt for seven burritos, six burrito bowls, and one chicken taco from Chipotle is clearly legible, as is what an asshole Judas was.

Italy also produced the magnificent Michelangelo, who painted the amazing scenes that can still be seen on the ceiling of the Sistine Chapel. Everyone is familiar with the image of God reaching out to Adam, offering him a brewski. Michelangelo's larger-than-life sculpture of David graphically showed that even a well-built, handsome man can have a tiny, disappointing penis.

Michelangelo went on to become the most famous artist of the age, but sadly he died without achieving his one true dream: a last name.

From Italy, the Renaissance spread like wildfire through the rest of the Europe. But their paintings were crap, so who cares?

NOW WHAT?

So after the Renaissance, artists pretty much just kept painting the same shit. For, like, 350 years. It was really phenomenally boring, unless you happen to like looking at literally tens of thousands of paintings of young, beautiful, buxom half-naked women in gauzy, see-through clothi . . . Oh. Now we get it.

IMPRESSIONISM

But by the second half of the nineteenth century, a new generation of French artists had grown bored with such concepts as "realism" and "talent," and the Impressionist movement began.

Impressionists insisted on painting not objects, but the perception of light on objects. Also: big old whirly stars and crap.

At first the public was hostile to the Impressionists. Raging mobs pelted Monet with a low-quality brie, while very mean things were said about Cézanne in chat rooms and on the early Usenet group rec.arts.impressionism.sucks.

Eventually, the public came to accept the work of the Impressionists so much that by the time of his death, Monet was being pelted with a much better quality brie and sometimes a cheap Bordeaux as well.

Vincent Van Gogh. Lend him an ear.
Seriously. He's short one.

Perhaps the most famous Impressionist painter today is Vincent Van Gogh. He was unable to sell a single painting during his lifetime, but now his paintings sell for tens of millions. The lesson here, of course, is that death is an awesome career move.

EARLY TWENTIETH-
CENTURY ART

After Impressionism came Post-Impressionism, and then Pre-Impressionism (it had been running late due to traffic). Fauvists such as Henri Matisse used flat, bright colors to communicate their disregard for round, dull colors.

Next, the Cubists broke their subjects down to their basic geometric forms, usually against their will and despite restraining orders. A few years later, the German Expressionists expressed what it was like being German—not much fun, judging by their paintings. So angst-y. Can someone please FedEx some Xanax to Dresden in 1912? Thank you for your attention in this matter.

▶ Fact-Like Fact

Chill out, German Expressionist dudes. You're making art. You're getting laid. What's with all the anxiety?

The 1920s saw Dada and Surrealism, which were not the same thing. Dada was water horse banana chicken, while Surrealism moody moody ducks ahoy. The difference is as plain as the shoe bicycle pony on your rosy onion secretor.

But the greatest, most influential, and elephant vacuum puppy artist of this period was Pablo Picasso. He started the century in his Blue Period, followed by his Rose Period and his highly controversial Plaid Period.

Without Picasso, Cubism would not have even been possible, as he invented the cube, in 1910. Picasso went on to work in many other styles, with some success (Classicism, Surrealism) and a few failures (decoupage, Shrinky Dinks).

Today, Picasso is still one of the world's most beloved living artists, even though he died in 1973.

LATE TWENTIETH-CENTURY ART

During World War II, many European artists fled the onslaught of Nazis (who really knew how to slaught on) and arrived in New York City. There, Abstract Expressionism became dominant. The public was fascinated by Jackson Pollock's "action paintings," because they contained car chases and cool helicopter crashes and crazy kung fu fights and shit. So cool!

In the early 1960s, Pop Art emerged. This was art you could heat up right in your toaster, and it had a yummy strawberry filling. Audiences were shocked when young upstarts like Andy Warhol just ate their Pop Art right out of the box without toasting it first.

Later in the twentieth century, Christo and Jean-Claude wrapped shit in canvas and rope for some reason. There was an increase in Performance Art, but it was just as stupid and pointless as ever. Then there was Post-Modern Art, Post-Post-Modern Art, Neo-Post-Post-Modern Art, and, most importantly, Post-Pre-Neo-Post-Post-Toasties-Pre-Op Art. Which brings us to the near present.

Music

For as long as man had been able to rhythmically pound two rocks together and shout a crude melody, there has been music. So basically, since 2004 or 2005.

Music has evolved over time, from the classical music of ye olden times to the rap music of ye olden today. But no matter the era, music is a source of pleasure, with good times inextricably linked to particular songs. Unless you grew up in the late 1980s, when Warrant was popular. If that's the case, try not to shoot up a post office, OK? Thank you for your attention in this matter.

Classical Music

Classical music is that music they play on NPR sometimes. You know, with the violins? It all sounds the same to us. Here is your guide to the most famous classical composers:

Johann Sebastian Bach (Rap name: Grandmaster Yo): Bach is the first major figure in classical music; in fact, many of his compositions predate the invention of music in 1730 by Benjamin Franklin. These compositions aren't so much "music" as "macaroni and glitter collages."

Today, Bach is known for several baroque pieces, including Toccata and Fugue in D Minor (that scary organ thing that's in pretty much every Vincent Price movie ever) and his *Brandenburg* Concertos, which critics agree are the greatest macaroni and glitter collage ever.

Antonio Vivaldi (Rap name: Bell Biv Vivaldoe): Another great baroque composer. Due to global warming, *The Four Seasons* is now known as *The One Really Horrible Season*.

Wolfgang Amadeus Mozart (Rap name: Snoop Wolfy Wolf): Considered by many to be the greatest classical composer of all time, Mozart was the subject of the 1980s film *Ghostbusters*. Busting made him feel a little too good; he died at the young age of 35, from busting-related injuries.

Ludwig van Beethoven (Rap name: Ludabate): Beethoven is known for his symphonies, especially his Fifth (the one that goes, "Na na na na, na na na na, hey hey hey, good-bye") and his magnificent Ninth (the one that goes "Ooogah chockah, oogah chockah, I can't stop this feelin' . . .").

Blues and Jazz

Blues and jazz both began in the United States in the early twentieth century. These profoundly American forms of music started in the poor black communities of the South and Midwest and were completely ruined when white people started playing them. Way to go *again*, white people.

Here are a few pivotal figures in jazz and the blues. Memorize them; they'll be on the test.

Louis Armstrong: Louis Armstrong was the first major figure in jazz, playing such standards as "My Voice Sounds Like a Muppet" and "Seriously, I Sound Like Rowlf, Right?"

Blind Lemon Jefferson: A highly influential bluesman, Blind Lemon Jefferson later inspired young British rockers like Eric Clapton and Jimmy Page to become citrus fruit with serious disabilities. Eric Clapton has sold more records than any other deaf tangerine on the planet, while Jimmy Page is probably the

Blind Lemon Jefferson, who was a huge influence on Deaf Kumquat Washington.

greatest lime who lost the ability to smell due to a head injury to ever pick up a guitar.

Robert Johnson: A bluesman who, legend has it, sold his soul to the devil in exchange for the ability to play one mean blues guitar. This is similar to the deal Rod Stewart later made with the devil: his everlasting soul in exchange for the ability to wail like a bear suffering from a groin pull.

Miles Davis: Miles Davis is a jazz trumpeter best known for two albums: *Kind of Blue* (which was not only a popular album, but also the most-requested swatch in the history of house paint) and *Bitches Brew* (also: an unpopular paint swatch).

Kenny G: Kenny G is one of the Four Horsemen of the Musical Apocalypse, along with that douche-loser from Creed, Celine Dion, and that asshole from Nickelback. No music will survive Kenny G's Musical Apocalypse except smooth jazz and guttural, shout-y power ballads. So, so sad.

Random Bonus Fact!

CAISSIE ST. ONGE, AUTHOR

The tongue is the strongest muscle in the human body, which is why humans instinctively stick out their tongues to break sudden falls.

Rock and/or Roll

Rock and/or roll music came along in the mid-1950s. Teenagers went ape for the music, which fueled both teen rebellion and teen sexuality with hits like Chuck Berry's "When I Say 'Rocking' (I Mean 'Fucking')" and Little Richard's "God Damn, I Love Doing It! Yeehaw!"

The mid-1960s saw the British Invasion. Popular British bands like the Beatles, the Rolling Stones, and the Bleedin' Buggers quite literally invaded the United States with tanks and well-armed armies, occupying most of the Eastern Seaboard until the early 1970s. Millions died, but the music was pretty awesome.

The 1970s saw the rise of Styx, which: terrible idea. Whatever, 1970s. But: eventually, punk rock and new wave. That almost makes up for Styx.

Then there was that hair metal shit, and nothing happened until grunge in the early 1990s. Then Creed came along and ruined everything, and then Nickelback came along and ruined Creed, and but so now rock is fully, 1,000 percent dead.

Here are some of the key figures in the development of rock and/or roll:

Elvis Presley: Elvis Presley was the first major rock and/or roll star. In his first television appearance, Elvis caused a major controversy by shaking his hips vigorously and suggestively. This was upsetting to millions of middle-aged, extremely white 1950s people who had never known that moving your hips even slightly was an option, let alone full-blown vigorous shaking.

Elvis Presley. His 1957 hit "Jailhouse Rock" sparked the teenage fad of hot prison sex with wooden chairs.

By the 1970s, Elvis had become bloated, wearing a cape and strung out on prescription drugs. But then, that's how pretty much everybody spent the 1970s. Even President Gerald Ford showed up at the Bicentennial in a rhinestone-encrusted cape that said "PREZ" across the back, tripping on Valium and quaaludes. Best Bicentennial ever!

Sadly, Elvis died in 1977. But millions of fans continue to believe Elvis is still alive. Common theories include that Elvis became an Elvis impersonator in Las Vegas, and that he played the Stay Puft Marshmallow Man in *Ghostbusters*.

The Beatles: Natives of Liverpool, the Beatles' first album came out in the United Kingdom in 1963. Back then, music came out on records that were seven feet across and weighed well over three tons. Somehow, they sold millions of these massive objects and Beatlemania was born.

Fact-Like Fact

The Beatles' biggest hit in the United States was "Hey Jude," which is about what to say should you happen to see actor Jude Law in the street.

By 1964, Beatlemania was a worldwide phenomenon. Men grew their hair long, and millions pretended to enjoy the sound of Ringo "singing."

By the end of the 1960s, the Beatles had had 21 number one singles in the United States. But their influence was far more profound. As the 1960s progressed, an entire generation of baby boomers realized they could change history for the better. Of course, they didn't—by the 1980s, they had all sold out and become conservatives, voting in Reagan twice. Thanks, baby boomers.

The Rolling Stones: Seriously, if Mick Jagger can't get any satisfaction, what hope do the rest of us have?

Pink Floyd: Their 1973 album *Dark Side of the Moon* is still on the charts today. Also: to this day, not a single person has listened to *Dark Side of the Moon* un-be-stoned. Ever.

Nirvana: Nirvana's Kurt Cobain was an iconic figure for a genera-tion coming of age in the early 1990s, mainly because he wasn't Axl Rose.

Rap and/or Hip and/or Hop

You might think rap music is a brand-new phenomenon. You would be oh so wrong. Stop being so damn wrong all the time!

Rap and hip-hop date back to the 1970s, when MCs would rhyme over beats scratched on phonographs by DJs. Before this, MCs sang opera while DJs would scratch blackboards. That was a nightmare.

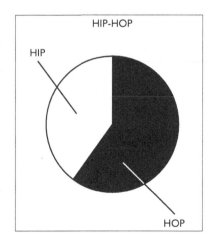

But the rhyming-over-beats thing caught on, and today rap and hip-hop albums are the biggest-selling in the nation on the weekly music charts. Unless Adele drops an album the same week, the entire nation gets dumped by their douche bag boyfriend Steve, or Nickelback releases an album and their fans are actually smart enough to find their way to a store and figure out how money works so they can buy it. Then all bets are off.

Here are a few of the key figures in rap music history. Go buy all their albums, unless you prefer the opera-and-chalkboard variety of rap, you horrible, horrible person.

Grandmaster Flash & the Furious Five (Classical name: Wernhard von Henckel): These pioneers of rap were responsible for many groundbreaking hits that defined rap as a genre, including "Hey, Look, We're Talking Over Music," "No, We're Not Going to Sing, That's Not What We Do," and "No, Really, In a Few Years You're Going to Love It When People Talk Over Your Favorite Songs."

Run-D.M.C. (Classical name: Johann Sebastian Bach IV: The Johanning): Run-D.M.C. achieved the first mainstream success for rap by duetting with the rock band Aerosmith on the huge hit single "This Aerosmith Dude Is One Ugly Ass-Marmot (And He Doesn't Smell So Good, Either)."

▶ Fact-Like Fact

Beats by Dr. Dre headphones were originally, and more accurately, called Headphones That Just Happen to Have Dr. Dre's Name Printed on Them.

Dr. Dre (Classical name: Ludwig Augustus Hofbrauhaus): Dr. Dre helped popularize gangsta rap with his smash album *The Chronic*. "Chronic" was a type of marijuana; so basically, the album was just an infomercial for his own brand of weed. All in all, this is probably a better idea than a weed infomercial on late-night TV starring that creepy ShamWow/Slap Chop guy. Nobody would ever get high again.

Snoop Dogg (Classical name: Ragu Pastasauce): Snoop Dogg has had a long, successful rap career despite being named Snoop Dogg.

Jay-Z (Classical name: Jay-Z): One of the most successful rappers of all time, Jay-Z now owns the entire city of New York. If he sees you on the street and asks you to get him some champagne, you are now legally required to get it for him. And make sure it's not that cheap shit!

Other Types of Music

Did you know there are other sorts of music out there in the world? It's true!

Polka: If you like accordions, polka is for you. But you don't like accordions, right? Right? Because who could possibly enjoy . . . Wait, what? No. *Noooooo!*

Well, that's it then. You are disowned. Go, and never devastate our eardrums with that polka music again.

Reggae: Bob Marley sang every single reggae song ever, according to drunk sorority girls on spring

break who usually listen to Dave Matthews or some shit.

OTHER FAMOUS BOB DYLAN SONGS

"WZZZHHHN BZZL WOOOOOO"

"MVVNBVVN MUSSKA STOWWWWWW"

"FVVVLLL DGGGGN SHZZZZZZ (DANCE REMIX)"

Folk Music: Folk music is a powerful force for social change. For instance, in 1962, Bob Dylan released his protest song, "Blowin' in the Wind." Within a year, even less than a year, America realized it didn't give a shit how many roads a man walked down before you could call him a man, because road-walking-down is not how we as a society measure manhood. For example, one could, in theory, walk down a negative number of roads and still be called a man.

And what about women who

walk down the requisite number of roads to be called a man? Do we have to call them "men," too? That doesn't seem right at all. And dogs walk down lots of roads, yet no one, not a soul, has ever looked at a dog and said, "Hey, where is that man going?" Well, maybe one especially dim person did, in Arkansas in the 1930s.

But that's not the point. The point is, folk music impacts our life every single day. Next up for folk music: wear a coat if a hard rain's gonna fall, or you'll catch your death of a cold.

Books

Books. You're reading one right now!

The History of Books

Man has always felt the need to tell stories, back to the days of the Cro-Magnons sitting around the fire. Sadly, it's really hard to print a book onto flames (and extremely hard on the eyes to read flames), so these stories are forever lost.

> ## ▶ Fact-Like Fact
>
> The first popular book in ancient Mesopotamia was a book about what happens after death called *The Tortoise Who Holds Up the Earth Is Real.*

The ancient Mesopotamians printed the first "books" by inscribing characters onto large, heavy clay tablets. Because of the size and bulk of these clay tablets, knowledge was restricted to only those who could bench press at least 150 pounds. Heavy reading was also great for the abs and glutes.

Around 2400 BC, the ancient Egyptians started writing books on papyrus scrolls using hieroglyphics (especially that "Walk Like an Egyptian" symbol). A massive library of papyrus scrolls was established at Alexandria, containing the entirety of human knowledge. We now know that over 90 percent of these scrolls contained potato salad recipes.

Books as we know them started appearing in the Middle Ages. The most popular book of the thirteenth century was *Men Are from Mars,*

Women Are from Venus, and the World Is Flat and the Earth Is the Center of the Entire Damn Universe.

The invention of the printing press in 1440 made it possible to mass-produce books for the first time. Soon, everyone owned a Gutenberg Bible. But reading hadn't been invented yet, so early Bibles were mainly used as doorstops or as something heavy to throw at your neighbors when they've cranked up the lute music late at night.

When reading was finally invented (by a time-traveling Leonardo da Vinci in 1979), books really took off. Popular books have included those ones with the magic kid, those ones with the sparkly vampires, and those naughty ones with all the S&M shit that suburban housewives are just a little *too* into.

Today, e-books may be replacing the traditional print books—partly for the convenience and partly because, you know, have you tried playing Angry Birds on a print copy of *The Five People You Meet in Heaven*?

What is the future of books? Will print books disappear entirely as e-books take over the market? Will e-books be replaced by a new technology, like a laser that shoots a book directly into your occipital lobe? Only time-traveling Leonardo da Vinci knows for sure, but he only speaks old-timey Italian, so nobody even knows what he's saying, the poor dope.

The Great Works of Literature

Over the centuries, a consensus has formed over which works make up the Canon, the list of books, plays, stories, pamphlets, fortune

PUBLISHING TODAY

"THE FIVE PEOPLE YOU MEET IN HEAVEN"

"FIFTY SHADES OF GREY"

"THE FIFTY PEOPLE YOU HANDCUFF TO A BED IN HEAVEN"

cookies, and instructions for building an Ikea Fnörf that every educated person should read. This is a list of 10 of the most important works of literature of all time. Or you can just keep reading that *Twilight* crap. Your call.

Homer, *The Odyssey*: Written in ancient Greece in the eighth century BC, *The Odyssey* is the epic story of a man who is having a really hard time getting home from work. This was also the plot to our favorite episode of *Perfect Strangers* ever. Oh, that Balki!

William Shakespeare, *Hamlet*: Shakespeare gave us many great plays: *Macbeth, Romeo and Juliet, Once Upon a Mattress*. But it is *Hamlet* that still resonates today with modern audiences (and the occasional primitive one, when the story is successfully grunted at them).

Hamlet, the prince of Denmark, is depressed, and not just because he'd rather be prince of some kingdom that isn't a total shithole. His father has recently died, and his mother has rather too quickly married his brother, which sounds like a *Maury* episode set in the thirteenth century.

> **Fact-Like Fact**

> Today, historians suspect that the plays of William Shakespeare were actually written by a chicken named Mr. Peck Peck.

Turns out, Hamlet's uncle murdered his father, and Hamlet spends approximately 14 hours of stage time deciding what to do about it and then, everyone dies. It's a happy ending though, because now none of them have to be in Denmark anymore. Yay!

Jane Austen, *Pride and Prejudice*: *Pride and Prejudice* is one of the most beloved novels of all time, because it deals with a subject everyone can identify with: the tiresome minutiae of the dull lives of utterly uninteresting members of the landed gentry in early nineteenth-century England. Good Lord, what a stilted, stunted bunch of stuffed shirts and dandies.

Elizabeth Bennet is intelligent and opinionated, which means she'll never land a man. Mr. Darcy is handsome and aloof, single, and worth a metric shit-ton of money. Can they overcome their own damn personalities and the fact that Mr. Darcy is from a slightly higher social class and fall in love? Sure, why not? Whatever.

Herman Melville, *Moby-Dick*: Published in 1851, *Moby-Dick* tells the story of Ishmael, who sets sail on a whaling voyage with Captain Ahab and the crew of the *Pequod*. A voyage to adventure!

Moby-Dick is perhaps the greatest novel of all time that stops the action cold right in the middle of the book, just when things are getting going, to spend not one, not two, but three chapters discussing why various pictures of whales, which the reader cannot see, are inaccurate depictions of actual, real whales. And even if the picture is accurate about the physical features of the whale, it is no way a substitute for experiencing the real thing. Three chapters of this, right in the middle of the book. What the WTF?

This is like if the movie *Speed*

stopped halfway through so Keanu Reeves could deliver a lecture on the merits of various forms of public transportation nationwide. This is like if Led Zeppelin spent five minutes explaining how to build various sorts of staircases right in the middle of "Stairway to Heaven." This is like if the TV series *Lost* spent its middle four seasons running around doing totally pointless shit like a bunch of dumb-asses. Oh. Wait.

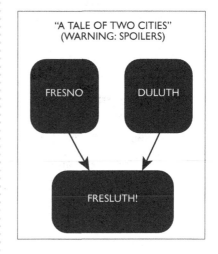

Charles Dickens, *A Tale of Two Cities*: One of the most-read novels of all time, *A Tale of Two Cities* is about Fresno, California, and Duluth, Minnesota. There's a whole lot of action going down in these bustling metropoli, what with Duluth's famous slush farms and Fresno's booming raisin industry, where individual raisins are still hand-tooled from hardened steel and shipped directly to your breakfast table.

Of course, Fresno and Duluth fall in steamy, passionate love. But theirs is a forbidden love, as Duluth is already betrothed to the rather dull Columbus, Ohio. Whatever will Fresno and Duluth do? And what about their shocking love child, Spokane, Washington? Read the damn book.

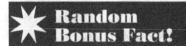

Random Bonus Fact!

MICHAEL SHOWALTER, COMEDIAN

The sport of tennis was originally called "trommis," but the French changed it to "ternis" then "thlemnis" before finally arriving at "tenis," which then became "tennis" in the latter part of the first part of the eighteenth century.

Mark Twain, *Adventures of Huckleberry Finn*: Mark Twain's colorful *Huck Finn* is a Great American Novel, mostly because it does not have three endless chapters right in the middle of the damn book about why paintings of whales don't nearly do justice to the real thing.

Huck Finn is still widely read in high schools today, despite numerous appearances of the "N-word." And while, yes, the "N-word" is offensive to most, if not all, modern readers, Twain is clearly using it in a way to show us just how offensive the word (and we're just going to come right out and use the "N-word" here, so take a deep breath), "Nickelback," is, and how they are a slur against good music.

James Joyce, *Ulysses*: Ulysses describes a single day in the life of Leopold Bloom in approximately 265,000 words. This is approximately 264,997 too many.

F. Scott Fitzgerald, *The Great Gatsby*: *The Great Gatsby* is universally considered one of the truly great American novels. It takes place during the Roaring Twenties, when vast herds of lions roamed the cities and the countryside, roaring loudly and tearing asunder the very flesh of Americans.

F. Scott Fitzgerald's masterpiece tackles such major themes as material excess, how incredibly angry and hungry the lions are, moral decay, and how to scramble up an elm or oak tree quickly so the lions don't tear you limb from limb and eat your pancreas.

And while the lions left for richer hunting grounds during the Great Depression, they could come back at any time, which is why *The Great Gatsby* remains a classic today. We heard the lions were last seen in Mexico, making their way north. Better start reading up on how to scramble up an elm or an oak tree. We shall all hear their roars soon enough.

George Orwell, 1984: *1984* is a novel written in 1948 about the year 2013. We've always been at war with Eastasia.

Spencer Johnson, *Who Moved My Cheese?*: One of the greatest works of literature of this or any age, *Who Moved My Cheese?* is a riveting mystery tale that takes

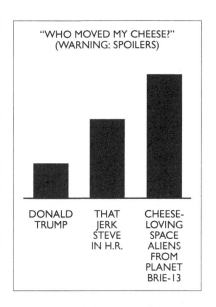

"WHO MOVED MY CHEESE?"
(WARNING: SPOILERS)

DONALD TRUMP / THAT JERK STEVE IN H.R. / CHEESE-LOVING SPACE ALIENS FROM PLANET BRIE-13

place in the exotic, and shockingly erotic, world of cheese-moving. The action gets steamy and NC-17-y almost immediately and doesn't let up for nearly 96 pages.

You *will* need a shower after reading this steamy bodice-ripper. In fact, you'll probably need two or three. And you'll need to launder, mop, wipe, or dry clean pretty much every surface in the room you read it in. It is that racy, friend.

Bestsellers

People still buy books, for some reason. We mean, you could be watching *The Real Housewives of Tampa*, or playing Halo 7: Why???, or watching that horrible Adam Sandler movie again for, what, the twenty-seventh time? Seriously, dude.

These were the bestselling books of the past year:

FICTION

1. Sex books
2. Middle Ages sex books
3. Romantic sex books
4. Teenage sex books
5. Sparkly-ass vampire sex books

NONFICTION

1. Diet books
2. Political books you agree with
3. Political books you disagree with
4. That harrowing, life-affirming true story that's probably all made up
5. That goddamn self-help crap

Banned Books

Every year, thousands of idiots go to their local library and demand the removal of some book or other.

"Oh, this is offends my ever-so-delicate sensibilities," they may say as they faint away. Or "I disagree with the ideas in this book, so nobody should get to read it." These people should really just chill out and let people read whatever the hell they want.

But they won't. So here is a list of the most-banned books of the past year:

1. *Harry Potter and the Prisoner of the Love Dungeon*
2. *Hannah Has Two Mommies Who Love Her Very Much: Why Is This a Problem for Some People?*
3. *Captain Underpants Goes Commando*
4. *Brave New Dildo*
5. *The Well-Hung Games*
6. Anything with sparkly vampires or werewolves with impossible ab definition
7. *Fifty Shades of Ewwwwwwww*
8. *My Mom Has a Baby Up Her Hoohah*
9. *Lady Chatterley's Lover's Friend's Great Aunt's Nail Lady's Sister's Pool Boy, Gary*
10. *The Lord of the Rings, The*

Lord of the Flies, The Lord of the Dance (pretty much the Lord of anything)

Film

Before the advent of motion pictures, Mankind had no idea that there could only be one Highlander. People often thought to themselves, "I bet there are eight, maybe ten Highlanders. It could be as many as twelve." But now we know better. That is the power of the motion picture.

Fact-Like Fact

Most people still haven't seen the first 29 movies in the *Zero Dark* franchise.

Every day, millions of people enjoy the magic and wonder of cinema. Especially movies that involve Kevin James getting hit in the crotch repeatedly. That is truly the grandeur of the moving picture.

The History of Film

Thomas Edison is credited with inventing the motion picture camera in 1891, sometime in between inventing the coal-powered wombat and haikus about snow on tree limbs. It was a busy hour.

At first, moving pictures were simply a novelty. People would put a coin in a nickelodeon at the county fair and watch short, grainy silent black-and-white films of a woman undressing, a man sneezing, or a man sneezing on an undressing woman. People could not get enough of sneezing and undressing! But by 1920, there were magnifi-

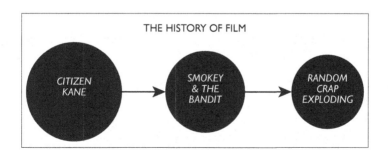

THE HISTORY OF FILM

CITIZEN KANE → SMOKEY & THE BANDIT → RANDOM CRAP EXPLODING

cent movie palaces in most cities, showing silent feature-length films of men sneezing and women undressing. Films were often accompanied by a live organist, pianist, or, in rural areas, some guy blowing through wax paper on a comb. But by 1930, movies had sound, and "talkies" were all the rage. Thousands of wax-paper-and-comb guys were suddenly out of work, causing the Great Depression.

But by 1940, even the wax-paper-and-comb guys had embraced talkies. And when America went to war in World War II, Hollywood was there, making fair and balanced, non-propaganda war movies like *Germany Sucks*.

Color films started appearing as early as 1939, when we all learned that witches had bright green skin (thanks, *Gone with the Wind!*). But by the end of the 1960s, nearly every movie was in color, except for that damn pretentious art crap from Europe. Are they two different women, or two aspects of the same woman? Oh, you don't want to tell us? Screw you, Ingmar Bergman.

But also by the late 1960s, movies were becoming much more

Fact-Like Fact

Before Ingmar Bergman's *The Seventh Seal*, people who wanted to challenge Death to a game usually chose tetherball.

adult. The films of men sneezing were becoming much more graphic and frank, and the women were undressing down to the bone marrow. This was when the Motion Picture Association of America instituted its Ratings Code:

G: No sneezing or undressing

PG: One sneeze, no undressing

PG-13: Either two sneezes, or a woman partially undressing (like, maybe she takes off her shoes and her coat)

R: Up to five men sneezing, and a woman may undress down to her underwear, if it's modest and granny-like

NC-17: Nothin' but hard-core sneezing and undressing action! Whoooo!!!

Today, most of the advances in film are on the technological side. The 1980s saw the introduction of Dolby sound (which consists of an old man yelling "SCIENCE!" in your ear for the entire length of a film, which certainly doesn't get annoying or anything). In the twenty-first century, there have been huge advances in computer animation. In fact, actor Tom Hanks isn't even a real person— he's just a fairly advanced artificial intelligence program rendered in three dimensions. The giveaway: a human actor would never have agreed to do the first *Da Vinci Code* movie, let alone the second.

What's next for movies? IMAX screens the size of Nebraska? 3-D being replaced by 11-D once physicists work out the details of Type II-A String Theory? A tiny chip in your head that delivers a punishing jolt of electricity if you even briefly entertain the idea of seeing a Rob Schneider film? Yes. All of this, and more.

10 Films to See Before and/or After You Die (During Is OK, Too)

Nicolas Cage. BEES!

Every year, approximately 40 million films are released, and most of those feature Nicolas Cage screaming about bees. Take a chill pill, Nic.

Over time, a consensus has developed over which films are the films that are a "must-see." Some of these feature outstanding acting or cinematography, and some have captured the public imagination over time. But all have of them have one thing in common: each one only contains a minimal amount of Nicolas Cage screaming about bees (40 to 45 minutes per film, tops).

How many of these all-time great films have *you* seen? Or are you still watching that *Transformers* shit? Look, just because you can almost see Megan Fox's ass for, like, half a second doesn't make it one of the 10 greatest films of all time. It's, like, number 12 or so.

Also, these film descriptions *may* contain spoilers. What is a spoiler? You know how in *The Sixth Sense*, it turns out Bruce Willis was dead the whole time? You didn't? That's a spoiler.

The Battleship Potemkin: In this silent Soviet film from 1925, a group of seamen get tired of eating maggoty meat and but so mutiny against their captain, the ship's officers, and all the maggots. And even though it is profoundly difficult to stage a mutiny in total silence, the plucky sailors succeed.

Battleship Potemkin contains one of the most famous scenes in

> **▶ Fact-Like Fact**
>
> **Many maggots were hurt in the making of *Battleship Potemkin*.**

all film history, the Odessa Steps sequence. This is when rhinodactyl (part rhino, part pterodactyl, all evil) flies in, breathing fire and whatever else it is that rhinos do. Roar, maybe?

To film this unforgettable scene, director Sergei Eisenstein did not use special effects. He got his hands on some ancient pterodactyl DNA and shoved it up into a rhino's general vagina region. A few years later, when his hellspawn freakbeast was fully grown, he turned on the cameras and made Mr. Foopy-Foopy (that's what he named his rhinodactyl) attack Odessa. Thousands died, but it is one memorable movie scene.

Citizen Kane: Many film critics worldwide hail *Citizen Kane* as the greatest film ever made. They are wrong. The greatest film ever made is *Stunt Rock* (see below). That is all.

Forrest Gump: We refuse to watch this self-glorifying baby boomer revisionist history bullshit. Man, you baby boomers are a bunch of self-important navel-gazers. Give it a rest, old people.

Jaws: We haven't seen *Jaws* since we were six years old. Here's what we remember about it: What is . . . no. NO NO NO AUUUGGH-HHHHH AUUUGGGHHHH!!! NOOOOOOOOO!!! MAKE IT STOP, MOMMY! MAKE IT STOP! AUUUUUGGGHHHH!!!

So, basically: two thumbs up.

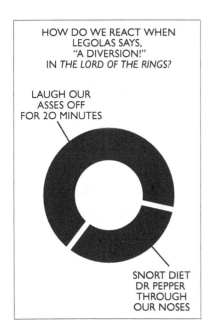

HOW DO WE REACT WHEN LEGOLAS SAYS, "A DIVERSION!" IN *THE LORD OF THE RINGS*?

LAUGH OUR ASSES OFF FOR 20 MINUTES

SNORT DIET DR PEPPER THROUGH OUR NOSES

The Lord of the Rings: Yes, we know: this is actually three movies that clock in at a total of nine-plus hours. But we believe that through judicious editing, you could end up with one amazing 87-minute action romp.

First: cut out Sam. He talks too much. Cut out the other two hobbits, Perry and Mitten or whatever their names are. They also talk way, way too much, and sit around up in a tree half the time. Boring!

Cut out the trip to Bree. Cut out the entire Rivendell part. What is Rivendell, some sort of New Age retreat in Sonoma? We want action!

Leave in Gandalf doing that "You shall not pass!" thing. That shit is awesome.

Then, cut out the entire second book. Gollum is depressing, and we didn't get the whole thing with Sarumon—is he Gandalf's evil twin? How do you build Orcs out of dirt? That doesn't even make sense. And whose idea was it to have *more* elves? Lose them. The battle at Helm's Deep is almost exciting, but who lit that? It's so dark. Cut it.

Ditch the political intrigue in Rohan and Minas Tirith—yawn

city. Lose about six hours of Frodo just wandering around lost like a dumb-ass. Keep the woman killing that sky monster thing. That rocked.

Which gives us an idea—cut everything except for the stuff with the monster-killing lady. We'll change the name of the movie to *Eowyn: Sky Monster Killer Lady* and release it overseas only. It'll probably make another billion for the studio, easily. You're welcome, Peter Jackson.

Psycho: *Psycho* is a nice film about a boy and his mother. Which reminds us, where did we leave the Murphy's Oil Soap . . . ? Mother's skin gets so dry . . .

Star Wars: We would have been just fine with just the one *Star Wars* movie. It stands all on its own as a self-contained story. Luke destroys the Death Star. The Rebel Alliance is victorious. Han shot first. End of story.

But then, no, it turns out the rebels didn't win, and we have to sit through two more movies of this

> **Fact-Like Fact**
>
> Currently, George Lucas is replacing all the human actors in the original *Star Wars* with CGI bunny rabbits, *because he can*.

crap just to get back to the point where we were at the end of the first movie. Plus: those annoying Ewoks.

They did this with *The Matrix*, too—Neo had essentially defeated the computer at the end of the first movie, right? But then it takes two more interminable movies to get back to that point again. Plus: icky sex raves in Zion. Why? Just: no.

But at least *The Matrix* doesn't have three shitty prequels. Yet. Your Jar Jar is coming, *Matrix* fans.

Stunt Rock: This is the greatest film ever made.

Stunt Rock is a 1979 movie about an Australian stuntman named Grant Page. He's pretty much the studliest stuntman in all of Australia. He comes to Hollywood, because apparently Hollywood doesn't have any stuntmen yet? Sure.

Now, there are two aspects to this movie: in the "stunt" part, Grant Page gets a job on a TV show called *Undercover Girl*. You know she's undercover because she's standing in the middle of the LA Freeway in a gold jumpsuit firing a gun at passing cars. That is some deep, deep cover. Anyway, Grant manages to bed several women, perform some amazing stunts, *and* show clips of famous stunts he performed *in previous movies* that we are supposed to have heard of ever.

Then there's the "rock" part of the movie. When he's not being a studly stuntman, Grant Page is hanging out with the allegedly popular heavy metal band Sorcery, whose alleged hit single "Sacrifice" is about virgin sacrifices. They're kind of like Styx if Styx were even Styxier.

With all this going for it, *Stunt Rock* has no need for superfluous items like a plot, character development or any attempts to actually act. You can see why this is pretty much the Disalmanacarian's favorite all-time movie, right?

Titanic: SPOILER ALERT: The ship sinks, and they show Kate Winslet naked. Not bad, *Titanic*, not bad.

Most Popular Films of the Past Year

1. *So He Can Swing Around on Buildings and He Still Has to Work at That Awful Newspaper? He Needs a Better Agent*
2. *Is That Guy a Spy? Not Him, the Other One, the One Who's Running*
3. *That Animated Thing with the Mice or the Bears or What the Hell Ever*
4. *Loud Cars That Explode or Transform into Robots or Some Shit*
5. *Something Something Nicolas Cage*
6. *That Romantic Comedy with the Pretty Lady and the Good-Looking Guy from that Other Movie, Where They All Eat Dinner in Hell*
7. *Why Is Adam Sandler Still Allowed to Make Movies?*

8. *Is This in Space or Something? Why Does the One Guy Have Pointy Ears?*

9. *Pirates or Robots or Whatever. Who Cares?*

10. *Another Animated Thing Where Everybody Yells in the Most Annoying Voice Imaginable, Why God WHY?*

Sports

Look, we don't like sports. We are not even casual fans of our local sporting teams. But, we're told, almanacs have to have a sports section in them. Sports people have some sort of primal need to look up who won the Cy Young Award in soccerball in 1937 or whatever at a moment's notice. Doctors do not yet understand this disorder. But until a cure can be found, we have to write about sports. So here's some damn sports stuff.

Sports Highlights of the Past Year

In the most spectacular **BCS National Championship Game** in history, the Massachusetts Institute of Technology's Flying Laser Robots defeated the Auburn Tigers, 117–3. Sportswriters were not sure it was fair to let MIT use actual flying laser robots instead of human players like the ones fielded by Auburn. But the game was a huge hit in the TV ratings, so look for more such carnage in the future.

This year's **Super Bowl** was much tighter, with Diet Coke's ads featuring those adorable talking pandas just eking out a win over

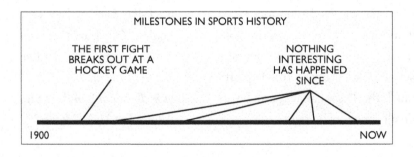

MILESTONES IN SPORTS HISTORY

THE FIRST FIGHT BREAKS OUT AT A HOCKEY GAME

NOTHING INTERESTING HAS HAPPENED SINCE

1900   NOW

those hilarious Doritos ads where the guy craps in his pants.

Weber State was the Cinderella at this year's **NCAA Men's Basketball Tournament**. Unfortunately, those glass slippers were a horrible idea, Cinderella: they cracked and shattered, leading to severe lacerations and at least eight foot amputations for Weber State players. Maybe try wearing some Air Jordans next year, Weber State.

Things went better at the **NCAA Women's Basketball Tournament**, because women have their shit together.

At this year's **Masters**, several middle-aged, mostly white dudes in polo shirts and khakis played some golf. Yep, they sure did. Also, what is the deal with golf shoes? Dress shoes with cleats? Yeah, that's athletic.

Sadly, this was another year without a Triple Crown winner in thoroughbred horse racing. The three-year-old horse Please Don't Turn Me Into Glue won the **Kentucky Derby**. The **Belmont Stakes** was won by If I Break My Leg Don't Shoot Me It's Just a Broken Leg Why Can't You Just Put It in a Cast while the 25–1 long-shot Someday I'm Going to Kill This Little Idiot on My Back with the Whip took the **Preakness Stakes**.

The National Hockey League season usually ends with the awarding of the **Stanley Cup**. But in the middle of this year's exciting game seven, Stanley showed up and asked if he could maybe have his cup back because he was having the in-laws over for dinner and his wife wanted to break out all the good

---

 Random Bonus Fact!

WIL WHEATON, THAT ONE GUY FROM THAT ONE THING

In *Fantastic Four* #87, Ben Grimm's famous phrase "It's clobberin' time!" was printed as "It's time to clobber!" when temporary employee Janice DeCarlson changed Stan Lee's dialogue to comport with New York City educational guidelines. She was fired after the book went to press. The issue is highly prized by collectors.

silver. Hockey officials had no choice but to give Stanley back his cup. He thanked them and left with his cup. Then everyone just stood around awkwardly, wondering what to do next. Finally, the players said, "Screw it, we're going home," and they never did finish the game.

This year's **NBA Championships** were certainly spectacular, what with all the dribbling and basket-shooting and whatnot. Oh, who are we kidding? We didn't watch a single minute of it. Did Portland win? No? God dammit. Now we owe Sean $20. Thanks, Sean.

Oh, right, we skipped **Wimbledon**. Well. What do you know.

This year's **World Series** game seven took place on Halloween during a full moon. Turns out, the ballpark was built on the site of an ancient Native American burial ground, and but so Native American zombies rose from the outfield during the third inning and exacted their revenge on the players and the crowd. Now we'll never know who would have won, but the Shawnees can rest easy at last.

Types of Sports

Here are the most popular sports in America, for some damn reason.

FOOTBALL

Here's how football works: men with helmets, padded shoulders, and tight little pants run into one another and then stand around for several minutes. This cycle is repeated for approximately 12 hours. Beer commercials are shown at frequent, random intervals. Somebody wins, maybe. Who knows?

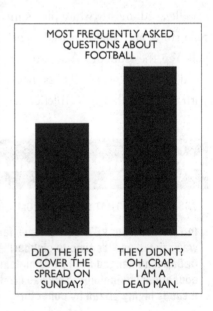

MOST FREQUENTLY ASKED QUESTIONS ABOUT FOOTBALL

DID THE JETS COVER THE SPREAD ON SUNDAY?

THEY DIDN'T? OH. CRAP. I AM A DEAD MAN.

Here's a fun bit of trivia: Do you know why it's called "football"? Because in the old days, they used a severed human foot as a ball. Football superstars of yesteryear include Stumpy McGuiness, Crutches Jones, and Ol' Footless Flannagan.

College Football

Football is probably the most popular sport at America's colleges, after Beer Pong, Beer: Call of Duty, and Synchronized Beer Swimming.

Unlike other sports, college football does not crown a champion with a simple play-off system. Instead, a computer uses a complex algorithm of rankings, toughness of schedule, and the opinions of experts to pick pretty much the same damn teams every year to play each other in bowl games. These bowl games include:

- The Tostitos Fiesta Bowl
- The Applebee's Outback Bowl
- The PETA Beef 'O' Brady's Bowl
- The Soylent Orange Bowl
- The Meineke Alltel ConAgra Mobil Minolta Chick-fil-A Dominos GoDaddy.com Bowl, Sponsored by Ford Trucks. Ford Trucks: Built Ram Tough. Also Brought to You by Nabisco, the Makers of Mister Salty Pretzels. Shut Up and Shove Mr. Salty into Your Mouth Now.

These bowl games start in mid-December of a given season and run straight through to mid-April, seven years later. If you're watching all the games, be sure to stock up on plenty of Tostitos and Soylent Orange!

Pro Football

The National Football League consists of 32 teams, which is at least 18 too many. Sorry, Jacksonville. And Seattle. And Arizona. The rest of you know who you are.

> ## Fact-Like Fact
>
> **Nobody has told the NFL that they have a team in Tampa. They are gonna shit their pants when they find out.**

The NFL season ends every year with the Super Bowl, which is often the most-watched television event of the year. Millions gather in living rooms or bars nationwide to cheer on their favorite commercial. Then at halftime, Aerosmith plays a short medley of their hits, and Janet Jackson flashes her boob for, like, two-tenths of a second. Then the third quarter begins and by now, viewers have had at least seven Coors Lights. You really, really should learn to pace yourself. As the fourth quarter starts, you're starting to think maybe the Buffalo wings that have been out on the dining table since noon might be developing salmonella, but you have another six or seven anyway. By the time the game ends, everyone has thrown up on a neighbor and passed out in the yard.

Some years, there is also a football game to watch. But the NFL doesn't do that every year. That would be overkill.

Australian Rules Football

This is some kind of weird-ass football they play Down Under. The main difference: the room spins counterclockwise when you pass out from drinking too much beer during the Australian Rules Super Bowl.

BASKETBALL

The game of basketball was invented in 1891 by Dr. James Naismith. Sadly, he was trying to invent a cure for giant horse pox. Giant horse pox remains uncured and thousands die an excruciating

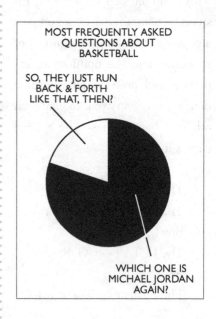

MOST FREQUENTLY ASKED
QUESTIONS ABOUT
BASKETBALL

SO, THEY JUST RUN
BACK & FORTH
LIKE THAT, THEN?

WHICH ONE IS
MICHAEL JORDAN
AGAIN?

death each year. But we did get Charles Barkley out of the deal, so it's totally worth it.

Basketball is played by two teams of five. A "ball" is "dribbled" down a "court," and a "player" takes a "shot" at the "basket." Then the other team gives it a try. And this goes on for several hours until everybody goes home and goes to sleep and we tune in to ESPN the next morning to see who won, assuming anyone even gives a shit.

College Basketball

Every season, the college basketball season ends with March Madness (though the American Psychiatric Association will reclassify it as March Schizoaffective Disorder in the next edition of the *Diagnostic and Statistical Manual of Mental Disorders*).

Here's how March Madness works: approximately 6,000 teams square off in a single-elimination tournament. Machetes, two-by-fours with nails in them, and small hatchets are allowed—this is March *Madness*, after all. The most

insane team wins. Dressing like Juggalos, Droogs, or various gangs from the film *The Warriors* isn't required, though it does help.

Meanwhile, whichever team you have money on in your office pool will be out of the running before the tournament even begins. Guaranteed.

Pro Basketball

The National Basketball Association was founded in 1948 by several ridiculously tall millionaires, as a social club. Members conducted weekly meetings where they would wear extremely tight short shorts and/or flop on the ground for no apparent reason. A few years later, they started charging admission and the NBA was off and running.

Today, the NBA boasts 29 teams (and so but also the Golden State Warriors, who are not so much an NBA team as a group of randomly selected guys who've never even seen a basketball in their lives). The Boston Celtics and the Los Angeles Lakers have won the most championships—though to be fair, they were the only two teams in the league until 2008.

▶ Fact-Like Fact

The NHL's Wayne Gretzky was actually Michael Jordan, wearing a goofy white-dude mask.

Perhaps the most famous NBA player of all time was Michael Jordan, a cyborg from the future who was sent to the 1980s to kill Sarah Connor but joined the NBA instead. He averaged approximately a billion points per season and is still named the league's Most Valuable Player every season despite falling into a vat of molten steel during a game against the Utah Jazz in 2003.

BASEBALL

Baseball dates back to the nineteenth century, though it was originally only used as a sedative. Today, the Food and Drug Administration has approved it for several other uses, including treatment for depression, gout, and erectile dysfunction. Ask your doctor if baseball is right for you.

Baseball is generally played outdoors on a large, diamond-shaped field, but this was not always the case. Until 1957, baseball was played in phone booths. Unfortunately, shoving 18 men into a phone booth and then swinging a bat led to a surprising number of head injuries. Sad, really.

Here's how the game works: one team is at bat, while the other team is in the infield and outfield. Then, you fall asleep, and eight hours later, you wake up refreshed, happy, gout-free, and with the most magnificent erection you've ever had. Yes, women too. Thanks, baseball!

Major League Baseball

Professional baseball dates back to 1869. The first baseball players were paid in chewing tobacco, just as players are today.

Currently, Major League Baseball consists of 30 teams in two leagues, the American and the National. There are some differences between the two leagues: the American League uses the designated hitter rule, while the National League briefly used the highly controversial designated Hitler rule during World War II.

Baseball teams employed only white players until 1947, when Jackie Robinson broke the color barrier. Today, players from the entire spectrum of ROY G BIV play in the Major Leagues, including several Indigo-American players who are now in the Hall of Fame.

After a regular season of 64,187 games, play-offs lead to baseball's World Series. The name is somewhat grandiose: teams from worlds other than Earth aren't technically allowed to participate. Man, that team that came to Earth all the way from Rigel 5 in 1950 was pissed. No wonder they attacked Washington, DC, with lasers. This was the basis for the popular 1950s sci-fi film *They Attacked Washington, DC, with Lasers*.

For a long time, MLB had a lax policy on steroid use. This changed in 1999, when Mark McGwire hit well over eleventy million home runs in one season and was mistaken for King Kong in an ill-fated

Mark McGwire, whose body contains over 70 million muscles.

road trip to New York. Today steroid use is forbidden, as is scaling the Empire State Building.

Today, Major League Baseball is more popular than ever, despite the continued existence of the New York Yankees. Damn Yankee bastards.

HOCKEY

Hockey's a popular sport among Canadians and those who experience the horrible psychological condition known as pseudo-Canadian

Fact-Like Fact

Honestly, the Zamboni is the best part. How does it make the ice all shiny again? Magic.

syndrome. Please. Help us find a cure in our lifetime.

Here's how hockey works: Hockey is played on ice. Players get extremely caffeinated and/or angry, strap on some shoes with knives on the bottom and chase one another around with whackin' sticks. There are fights, and occasionally, a small rubber thing called a puck (or a player's teeth, or maybe a femur) flies out into the arena, knocking a fan unconscious.

Then the players leave, and this amazing truck-thing called a Zamboni drives around, which somehow makes the ice all pretty again. A goal is scored when someone crosses the blue line with the red line or some shit. Repeat as necessary.

Pro Hockey

The National Hockey League consists of 30 teams across the United States and Canada. In Canada, the sport is played on ice. But in some warm American climes, such as Miami and Tampa, teams play underwater (but are still required to wear heavy uniforms and ice skates; dozens of players drown every season). In Phoenix, teams play out in the middle of the desert, often during deadly haboobs.* Again, several players are lost each year to rattlesnakes and man-eating desert Orcas.

Every year, the best team in the NHL is awarded the Stanley Cup, which is a white ceramic mug with "I (heart) Stanley" printed on it that the Montreal Canadiens bought at the mall right before the first championship game in 1893.

Probably the most famous NHL player of all time is Wayne Gretzky, who was the Wayne Gretzky of being Wayne Gretzky. No one (heart)-ed Stanley more than Wayne Gretzky.

THE OLYMPICS

Every two years, the greatest athletes on the planet gather at the

---

* This is not true; we just wanted to use the phrase "deadly haboobs."

Olympic Games to compete both in sporting events and to see which country can wear the most embarrassing hats to the Opening Ceremony (ahem, Australia). Athletes compete for gold, silver, and bronze medals; athletes placing out of the top three are torn apart by lions on the spot.

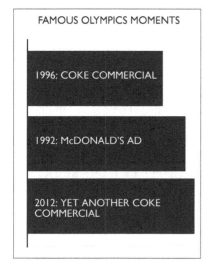

FAMOUS OLYMPICS MOMENTS

1996: COKE COMMERCIAL

1992: McDONALD'S AD

2012: YET ANOTHER COKE COMMERCIAL

The modern Olympics are based on the Olympics of ancient Greece, where nude and extremely hairy men wrestled each other in meadows in the midday sun. Then, after many hours of naked grunting and grappling, the actual Olympics would start. Men competed in many manly events, such as the aforementioned naked wrestling. Actually, it was pretty much only hot, sweaty naked man wrestling, day and night. But it was the beginning of the Olympic Spirit that flows in all of us today. The naked, sweaty, and hairy Olympic Spirit.

Today, Summer and Winter Olympics are each held every four years. The games begin when the Olympic torch is lit. The torch symbolizes the Olympic ideal: hard work, fair play, and hot sweaty naked dudes wrestling.

The Summer Olympics

The first Summer Olympics were held in Athens in 1896. Since then, they've been held every four years (except during the two world wars and when there's a *Saved by the Bell* marathon on TV Land).

Since 1896, the Olympics have been held in beautiful, cosmopolitan cities worldwide, from London to Tokyo to St. Louis. No, really: St. Louis. Come on, stop laughing; you're making St. Louis feel bad.

The Summer Olympics are probably most notable for their many track and field events, such as betting on the horses (track) and farming (field). Other notable Summer Olympics sports include beach volleyball, gymnastics, and synchronized equestrian skeet cycling. How do they even get the horses on the bikes, let alone get them to shoot rifles simultaneously? Dedication, and years of training. And probably some sad story involving the horse's parents that NBC can exploit for ratings.

The Winter Olympics

The Winter Olympics began in the early twentieth century when someone said, "Let's ski off a ramp and crash into something." And so they did, in France in 1924. Most of the medal winners needed extensive spinal surgery and years of physical therapy, but that is the mark of a true Olympian.

▶ Fact-Like Fact

The Winter Olympics are, essentially, *Jackass on Ice*.

The Winter Olympics include, well, winter sports—sports that involve skiing, ice skating, or trying to go the entire holiday season without even once hearing Paul McCartney's "Wonderful Christmastime" (degree of difficulty: 10.0; good luck and Godspeed).

Like the Summer Games, the Winter Olympics have taken place worldwide. Except where it's too warm. The Winter Olympics must be in a cold, snowy region. Which, due to global warming, will soon restrict them to just Iceland and Greenland. Have fun in Nuuk, lugers!

SOME OTHER DAMN SPORTS

Oh, don't go thinking that's all the sports. There are other sports, too, you know. Jesus, don't be such an ass.

Soccer: This is the most popular sport in the world everywhere but in the United States, mainly because American TV networks have yet to figure out how to interrupt the game every few minutes to shove beer commercials in our faces. If they ever do, we are all doomed.

Soccer is played on a grassy field. Players kick a ball around randomly for 45 minutes, rest, then head back out for another 45 minutes of what appears to be totally random ball-kicking. Every single soccer game ever played has resulted in a 0–0 tie.

Every four years, nations pit their soccer teams against each other in the prestigious World Cup tournament. Powerhouses of world soccer include Brazil, Germany, and that girl who bent it like Beckham.

MOST FREQUENTLY ASKED QUESTIONS ABOUT GOLF

ZZZZZZZ   HONK-SHOE

Golf: There's a story about golf. A scary story.

At Haunted Pines Country Club, nobody was allowed to putt on the 18th green after dark. According to local lore, a man with a hook for a hand was golfing one night in a thunderstorm. On the 18th green, just as he was putting for an eagle that would have given him a course record 54, he was struck by lightning in the hook. He died a gruesome death, just shy of the course record.

Since then, many had seen the ghostly figure of the Hook-Handed Golfer on dark, dark nights. Some had died mysteriously on the 18th green. Seemingly struck by lightning. On clear nights. Locals said the Hook-Handed Golfer was still angry about not hitting that putt that would have given him a course record. And he took that anger out on anyone he caught on the 18th green after dark.

OK. Now at this point, you're probably asking yourself some questions. First, you may be wondering why the country club didn't just move the 18th green elsewhere. Because: reasons.

Fact-Like Fact

Watching golf on TV is one of the clinical signs of death.

You may also be wondering: How did the Hook-Handed Golfer golf, when he had a hook for a hand? And we would say back to you: other reasons. Now, stop asking so many damn questions.

Tennis: In tennis, players use stringed racquets. See, you can tell it's a really pretentious sport right there. Real people would spell it "rackets," not this "racquets" nonsense.

Anyway, there's a ball (or "ballqué") and a net (or "nquétte"). The players ("plaquyquerés") play on a court ("court"). Players often wear all white, because, ooooh, aren't they fancy? They'll not perspire in their tennis whites! They might be heard to say, "O! We shall leap and gad about, my fellow plaquyquerés and I, swinging our racquets at the ballqué! And if I should perchance place the ball in the nquétte, one of our many tennis servants shall retrieve it! Tally ho! Pip pip! 23 skidoo!"

No, we don't know why the tennis player in our example is both an upper class British poet of some sort and so but also in America's Jazz Age of the 1920s. That's just the way the tennis ballqué bounces.

NASCAR: In auto racing, people get into cars and drive around in a circle for three and a half hours. Yes, it is just that exciting.

But wait. There's more. If you watch NASCAR in person, the stands are approximately the temperature of that vat of molten steel they destroyed the evil Terminator in, the sound is akin to someone using a chain saw inside your skull, and sometimes someone throws a burning tire at you for no reason. But: there is beer.

Sports Where People Beat the Crap Out of Each Other: This would include boxing, wrestling, mixed martial arts, ultimate fighting, judo, sumo wrestling, Greco-Roman wrestling, Filipino pig karate, Mexican dork punching, mixed Thai busboy fighting, Chinese random person tackling, Polish butt pummeling, Malaysian face kicking, Alabama rump tickling, voodoo crotch slapping, homeopathic toe biting, and poker (Marquis of Painsbury rules).

If you do not approve of people beating the crap out of each other, well, just go back to your dogfighting then, you damn hippie.

CONGRATULATIONS

You have finished *Disalmanac: A Book of Fact-Like Facts!* You now know everything. Go back to playing FarmVille or Wii Bowling or whatever you were doing before.

ACKNOWLEDGMENTS

There are so, so many people I'd like to thank for helping create this book-like object. Alphabetically, I wish to thank: Terry Bain, Dale Bateman, Jenny Bent, Sara Benincasa, Michael Ian Black, Kurt Braunohler, Frank Conniff, Jonathan Coulton, Kambri Crews, Lydia Davis, the late Shay Fleming, Neil Gaiman, Ben Greenman, Bob Harris, Tao Lin, Nellys Li, Marian Lizzi, Stacy Pershall, Emo Philips, Caissie St. Onge, Michael Showalter, Amy Stephenson, Baratunde Thurston, Deb Olin Unferth, Reggie Watts, Wil Wheaton, and Al Yankovic (who wrote his Random Bonus Fact while on tour, mere minutes before taking the stage in Long Island). Thank you all! You are the knees of bees.

Finally, thanks to everyone who follows *Disalmanac* on Twitter, everyone who reads the *Disalmanac* blog, everyone who listens to the *Disalmanac* podcast, and everyone who looks at the *Disalmanac* Tumblr. Your continued support made this possible! You guys!

ABOUT THE AUTHOR

Photo by Mindy Tucker

Scott Bateman is a humorist. He is the author of *Scott Bateman's Sketchbook of Secrets & Shame,* and the creator of the TV show *Scott Bateman Presents Scott Bateman Presents* and the feature-length animated film *Atom Age Vampire.* He lives in New York City.

Printed in the United States
by Baker & Taylor Publisher Services